Guilt-free Gourmet

Vicki B. Griffin, PhD, MACN

Gina M. Griffin

Printed by
Remnant Publications

The Guilt-free Gourmet

Copyright©1999 By
Vicki B. Griffin, and Gina M. Griffin

Printed by
Remnant Publications

ISBN 1-891041-25-8

Foreword

$\mathcal{I}$ was pleased and honored when Dane and Dr. Vicki Griffin asked me to write the foreword to their wonderful cookbook. For the past five years I have been lecturing and writing about the dangers of excitotoxin additives in processed foods and excitotoxin concentrates, such as hydrolyzed plant proteins and amino acid extracts.

One of the most frequent questions I am asked is, "Well, if all these processed foods are harmful, what should I eat ?" Until the publication of this wonderful, information-packed cookbook, I could only give them vague examples and patch-work suggestions.

What is found within the pages of *The Guilt-Free Gourmet* is accurate, well researched health information and recipes that are almost totally free of harmful excitotoxins and other adulterating additives. But these delicious recipes are even more than that. They group together foods that give one a balance of nutrients that not only prevent disease but promote health and longevity. God created foods for man that contain a wondrous army of vitamins, minerals and assorted phytochemicals that have defied man's attempts to duplicate.

Modern research has shown that the constituents of assorted foods act together in ways that can never be duplicated by individual supplements. Degenerative diseases, such as arthritis, diabetes, Alzheimer's disease, Parkinson's disease, and even aging itself, are increasingly being shown to be related to harmful dietary choices. Likewise, prevention of these disorders is being shown also to depend on one's diet.

The recipes in this cookbook are not entirely free of excitatory amino acids since several foods do contain such natural components. But, except for those at a high risk developing one of the neurodegenerative disesases such a Parkinson's disease, Lou Gerhig disease, or Alzheimer's dementia, these foods should be safe. This is because the glutamate or aspartate is released slowly into the system and is cleared from the system before elevated blood leves can occur. The most dangerous excitotoxins are those intentionally added to foods by processors.

Finally, only recently, has our science confirmed what has been suspected by some all along—that early nutrition determines our susceptibility to diseases later in life. This cookbook allows parents to provide their children with nutritious, tasty recipes that will greatly improve their chances of a healthy, disease-free life.

The Griffin's daughter, Gina, has also provided a nutrient breakdown chart that proves a very useful assessment of the various components, so that one can evaluate actual individual nutrient intakes.

The Griffin's cookbook is a unique addition in our search of food free of harmful additives and nutrient-debased processing.

Russell L. Blaylock, M.D.
Neurosurgeon and author of numerous scientific
papers and the book: Excitotoxins: The Taste That Kills

Ministry Of Healing

The Ministry of **Healing**

Direction for Healthful Living
E.G. White

Have you checked out a newsstand lately? New magazines on health, fitness, diet, and exercise seem to be taking over more shelf space every month.

Maybe your old enough to remember a time not that long ago when nobody ever talked about aerobics, jogging, cholesterol, and workouts. But today it's obvious that the pursuit of health and fitness is more than a quick fad. It's here to stay. Looking and feeling good isn't optional for most people these days—it's a high lifestyle priority.

So millions of us are shedding pounds, running marathons, joining health clubs, reading food labels, pumping iron, chucking tobacco and alcohol, and getting back to the basics. That's wonderful! But is that all there is? Is there something more to embracing a healthy lifestyle than merely trying to prolong life or prevent disease?

The Ministry of Healing is a book that crusades for total fitness, not just physical fitness, because we humans are more than just bodies. So these pages speak to the needs of the whole person: body, mind, and spirit.

For a lot less than the cost of one visit to the doctor; this classic on health will tell you how to manage stress, renew your health, prevent disease, and live a vibrant life.

Special Note

As you read through this recipe collection, you will see certain ingredients marked with a footnote number, like Millet[9], for example. These are items that may be unfamiliar to most readers, or may have to be purchased at a health food store or food co-op. The items are listed below.

1. **Bulghur wheat** - A par-boiled, cracked wheat that is available at health food stores. You can use cracked wheat as a replacement.
2. **Butter Flavor** - This can be found at your local grocery store with the spices and extracts, such as maple, vanilla, etc.
3. **Carob Powder** - This chocolate substitute is available at health food stores.
4. **Chick-it Seasoning** - An excitotoxin-free chicken-like seasoning (see Misc.)
5. **Date Sugar** - Can be purchased at most health food stores.
6. **Emes Gelatin** - A vegetable gelatin powder with no animal products. Use the unflavored variety for cheeses. It is available at most health food stores, or from Weimar Institute (1-800-525-9192.)
7. **ENER-G** - A calcium carbonate-based baking powder available at many health food stores. (Don't get the one marked "soda")
8. **Fine's Herbs** - Available at most grocery stores.
9. **Millet** - A grain that is available at health food stores. To cook millet, use 1 part millet to 4 parts BOILING water. Simmer covered for 45 minutes, or until millet is soft. 1/2 cup raw millet will yield 2 cups of cooked millet; 1 cup raw will yield 4 cups cooked.
10. **Nutritional Yeast Flakes** - Available at health food stores. DO NOT buy the powder, it is too strong.
11. **Oat Bran/Wheat Germ** - Can be purchased at most grocery stores in the cereal section. Also available at health food stores.
12. **Postum/Roma** - Coffee substitutes that can be found at most grocery stores in the coffee section, or at health food stores.
13. **Raw cashews** - Can be purchased at most health food stores.
14. **Raw sunflower seeds** (hulled) - Can be found at health food stores. DO NOT use roasted seeds. They give recipes a different taste.
15. **Sesame tahini** - Can be found at most health food stores. It is a chalky beige color, not dark brown like Sesame butter. DO NOT substitute!
16. **Soy beans** - Available at health food stores. To soak, cover 2 cups of beans with 3 inches of water and let sit overnight. Drain the water and freeze in plastic bags for future use. Always have some soaked beans in the freezer.
17. **Summer savory** - Available in the spice section of most grocery stores.
18. **Tofu** - Available in many grocery stores in the produce section or at health food stores. Tofu is soy bean curd.
19. **Unsweetened Coconut** - Can be purchased at most health food stores.
20. **Vegetable Salt** - We suggest either *Herbamare* (available at health food stores) or make the recipe for *Seasoned Eatings!* in Miscellaneous section.

Table of Contents

Breakfast Bonanza

Regal Rice Pudding

Makes 16   2/3 C Servings

- ❑ 5 C .... Cooked rice
- ❑ 3 .... Bananas, medium, ripe
- ❑ 1 .... 20-oz. can, crushed pineapple
- ❑ 1/3 C .... Milk powder (soy, rice, or tofu)
- ❑ 1/3 C .... Cashews[13], raw
- ❑ 1/3 C .... Shredded, unsweetened coconut[19]
- ❑ 1 1/2 C .... Raisins
- ❑ 1 tsp .... Salt
- ❑ 1/3 C .... Honey
- ❑ 2 Tb .... Orange juice concentrate

- • Place raisins, rice, coconut in large bowl.
- • Blend bananas and crushed pineapple (1/2 at a time if your blender is small).
- • Pour over rice, raisins, and coconut.
- • Blend soy milk powder, cashews, salt, and honey with just enough water to make a smooth cream.
- • Add to rice mixture and stir thoroughly.
- • Bake in sprayed, covered casserole at 350° for 50 to 60 minutes.

SERVING SUGGESTIONS

- • This pudding is lovely topped with a little granola and/or fresh fruit.
- • This pudding is good hot or cold.
- • Try it for a great light supper with some fresh fruit!

Pineapple Cream Pudding

Makes 12   2/3 C Servings

- ☐ 1 C .... Millet
- ☐ 4 C .... Pineapple juice
- ☐ 1/2 C .... Water
- ☐ 2/3C .... Raw cashews[13]
- ☐ 1/2 tsp .... Lemon extract
- ☐ 1 tsp .... Salt
- ☐ 4 Tb .... Lemon juice
- ☐ 1/3 C .... Honey
- ☐ 1 .... 20 oz. can, crushed or chunk pineapple
- ☐ 1 Tb .... Vanilla

- • Simmer millet, water, pineapple in covered sauce pan on low heat until well cooked, usually 1 hour.
- • Stir occasionally.
- • When cooked, add remaining ingredients, stirring well.
- • Blend, 2 cups at a time, until thoroughly creamy.
- • Pour into pre-baked pie shells (see Desserts).
- • Top with coconut, ground granola, or carob chips.
- • Chill until set, at least several hours.

SERVING SUGGESTIONS

- • This recipe will quickly become one of your favorites! I like to make it in a big casserole dish with Crunchy Granola Pie Crust (see Desserts) for a delicious, nutritious breakfast treat.
- • Try it layered with granola and sliced bananas (chill overnight).
- • Try it as a meal with popcorn, toast, and fruit. Yum!
- • Pour it into a casserole dish and top with granola, then, after it sets up, add thickened blueberries for a real sweet-tart start to your day! (See Blueberry Buckle Topping recipe in this section.)
- • Chill it in individual serving cups with a sprinkle of coconut and a strawberry on top for a great light dessert. (Add the strawberry after it sets up.)

Appl'oat Delight

Makes 12   2/3 C Servings

- ❑ 2 C .... Oats (rolled or quick)
- ❑ 1 C .... Raisins
- ❑ 1/2 C .... Shredded, unsweetened coconut[19]
- ❑ 1/2 C .... Pecans, chopped
- ❑ 2 .... Apples, shredded
- ❑ 3 C .... Soy or tofu milk
- ❑ 1/2 tsp .... Salt
- ❑ 1 Tb .... Vanilla

- •Spray an 8" X 8" or round baking dish.
- •Sprinkle 2/3 C of the oats on the bottom of the dish.
- •Next, layer 1/2 of the raisins, 1/2 of the coconut and pecans, and 2/3 C more oats.
- •Sprinkle all of the shredded apples on top.
- •Add the remainder of the raisins, oats, and coconut / pecan mixture.
- •Whiz the salt, vanilla and milk in the blender; pour over the layered mixture.
- •You may need to add more milk until liquid comes to the top of the mixture.
- •Cover and bake 45-60 minutes at 350°.
- •Uncover to crisp and brown on top.

SERVING SUGGESTIONS

- •This is a wonderful recipe for a quick, hot breakfast. Just mix it all up the night before, and pop it in the oven an hour or so before you hear "What's for breakfast, Mom?" Then, whip it out of the oven and onto the table for a delightful, tasty, nourishing tummy warmer! Serve with fresh peaches or blueberries, or with hot applesauce. You'll be the hero of the day!
- •For a real treat, make up some fruit smoothies or banana ice cream, and pile it on top of the casserole for a nutritious summer treat or birthday "cake"!

Wheat Treat Hot Cereal

Makes 5   1/2 C Servings

- ❑ 1/2 C .... Dextrinized (see directions below) bulghur wheat[1]
- ❑ 2 C .... Water
- ❑ 8 .... Chopped, pitted dates
- ❑ 2 Tb .... Shredded, unsweetened coconut[19]
- ❑ 1/2 tsp .... Salt

> • To dextrinize wheat, place it in a saucepan (without water or oil) over medium heat and allow to heat, stirring constantly to prevent burning. Wheat will turn a light golden brown. Takes about 5 minutes.
> • When wheat is browned, add ALL ingredients and bring to a boil.
> • Turn down and simmer, covered, for 35 minutes. No need to stir during simmering.
> • Serve!

SERVING SUGGESTIONS

- • This delicious cereal is even better when you top it with a bit of Better Butter (see Dressings), a drizzle of honey, and a good milk replacement (see Breakfasts).
- • It is also wonderful topped with applesauce.

Blueberry Buckle

Serves 12

- ❏ 3 C .... Oat flour (blend 3 C of oats into flour)
- ❏ 3 C .... Whole wheat flour (OR half whole wheat and half unbleached white flour)
- ❏ 2 tsp .... Salt
- ❏ 1 Tb .... Coriander
- ❏ 1/2 C .... Oil
- ❏ 2 C .... Warm water with 2 Tb honey
- ❏ 2 Tb .... Yeast
- ❏ 2 Tb .... Vanilla
- ❏ 3/4 C .... Honey
- ❏ 1 C .... Chopped apples

- •Dissolve yeast in the honey/water solution.
- •Mix dry ingredients in large bowl and add apples.
- •Combine oil and remaining honey in another bowl, then pour ALL LIQUID ingredients into dry ingredients.
- •Preheat oven to 375°.
- •Pour batter into sprayed 13x9 inch pan and allow to rise for 5 minutes.
- •Bake at 375° for 15 minutes.
- •Let cool, then lower heat to 350° and bake an additional 30 minutes.
- •Top with Blue Blaze Sauce and Streusel Topping (recipes in this section) when ready to serve.

Blue Blaze Topping

Makes 10   1/2 C Servings

- ❏4 C .... Blueberries
- ❏6 oz. .... Raspberry/white grape juice concentrate OR apple juice concentrate
- ❏4 Tb .... Cornstarch
- ❏1 tsp .... Orange peel

- •Put concentrate into saucepan.
- •Add cornstarch and stir until dissolved.
- •Thicken, stirring constantly; add blueberries.
- •Turn off flame and let cool.
- •Pour over cake when cake is COOLED.
- •Sprinkle with Streusel Topping (recipe below.)

Streusel Topping

Makes 20   1/4 C Servings

- ❏2 C .... Quick oats
- ❏1 C .... Shredded or flaked unsweetened coconut[19]
- ❏1 pinch............... Salt
- ❏1/2 C .... Slivered almonds
- ❏2 Tb .... Vanilla
- ❏1 tsp .... Coriander
- ❏1/2 C .... Dates, blended with 1 banana (add just enough water to make it blend).

- •Stir mixture thoroughly together in a bowl.
- •Place on sprayed cookie sheet.
- •Bake at 250° for 15-25 minutes.
- •Mixture will be lightly browned, but still have some moisture.

Applause Apple Crisp

Makes 16   2/3 C Servings

Place in large pan:

- ☐ 1 .... 12 oz. can, 100% apple juice (concentrate)
- ☐ 2 Tb .... Lemon juice
- ☐ 1/2 tsp .... Coriander
- ☐ 1/4 tsp .... Cardamom powder

Stir in well:

- ☐ 1/4 C .... Cornstarch: mix with 1/4 C cold water

Cook until thickened, then add:

- ☐ 8 C .... Sliced, cored apples (golden delicious are best)
- ☐ 1/2 C .... Raisins

> • Cook for about 5 minutes, stirring constantly.
> • Place in sprayed pan or casserole dish.
> • Top with Crunchy Crumb Topping (see Breakfasts).
> • Bake at 350° for 45 minutes.

Very Berry Crisp

Makes 15   2/3 C Servings

- ☐ 1 .... 12 oz. can, raspberry/white grape juice concentrate (100% juice)

Stir in well:

- ☐ 1/4 C .... Cornstarch: mix with 1/4 C cold water

Cook until thickened, then add:

- ☐ 8 C .... Blueberries (or blackberry, cherry, etc.)

> • Cook for about 2-3 minutes, stirring constantly.
> • Place in sprayed pan or casserole dish.
> • Top with Crunchy Crumb Topping (see Breakfasts).
> • Bake at 350° for 45 minutes.

Peachy Keen Crisp

Makes 15   2/3 C Servings

Place in large pan:

- ❏ 1 .... 12 oz. can, peach/white grapejuice concentrate (100% natural)
- ❏ 2 Tb .... Lemon juice

Stir in well:

- ❏ 1/4 C .... Cornstarch: mix with 1/4 C cold water

Cook until thickened, then add:

- ❏ 8 C .... Peeled, sliced peaches

> • Cook for 2-3 minutes, stirring constantly.
> • Place in sprayed pan or casserole dish.
> • Top with Crunchy Crumb Topping (see Breakfasts).
> • Bake at 350° for 45 minutes.

Crunchy Crumb Topping

- ❏ 1 1/2 C .... Whole wheat pastry flour
- ❏ 1 1/2 C .... Quick rolled oats
- ❏ 1/2 C .... Wheat germ
- ❏ 2/3 C .... Date sugar
- ❏ 2/3 C .... Chopped nuts
- ❏ 2/3 C .... Unsweetened coconut[19]
- ❏ 1/2 tsp .... Salt
- ❏ 1/2 C .... Oil (optional)

> • Mix all ingredients together in a bowl.
> • Sprinkle liberally over crisp of choice.
> • Can store in refrigerator or freezer until needed.

Good Earth Cereal

Makes 26   1/2 C Servings

(adapted from 100% Vegetarian From Your Kitchen)

Combine the following in a large bowl and mix well:

- ☐ 8 C .... Quick oats
- ☐ 2 C .... Oat or wheat bran
- ☐ 1 C .... Cornmeal
- ☐ 1 C .... Wheat germ
- ☐ 2 tsp .... Salt
- ☐ 1 C .... Chopped nuts (almonds, walnuts, etc.)

Mix in:

- ☐ 1/4 C .... Oil (optional)

In a separate container mix together:

- ☐ 1 .... 12 oz. can unsweetened frozen apple juice concentrate
- ☐ 2 Tb .... Molasses
- ☐ 2 tsp .... Vanilla

- • Stir liquids into dry ingredients, mixing well and breaking up all lumps.
- • Spread out evenly in 2 sprayed cookie sheets or casserole dishes.
- • Bake at 250° for 75-90 minutes, stirring every 15-20 minutes to insure even drying.
- • If cereal starts browning too quickly, reduce oven temperature and finish cooking as normal.
- • Turn off heat and allow cereal to REMAIN IN THE OVEN UNTIL COOL to complete the drying process.
- • Store in airtight container in a cool, dry place.

SERVING SUGGESTIONS

- • This cereal is light and crunchy. It is wonderful layered with pineapple cream pudding and fresh fruit topped with a fruit smoothie in the summertime!
- • Of course, this cereal is perfect in an old fashioned cereal bowl with soy milk on top—a perfect "Good Morning" breakfast!

Almonds Ahoy! Granola

Makes 25   1/2 C Servings

☐ 8 C .... Quick oats
☐ 1C .... Shredded, unsweetened coconut[19]
☐ 1/2 C .... Raw sunflower seeds[14]
☐ 1 1/2 C .... Slivered almonds
☐ 2 .... Ripe bananas
☐ 1 1/4 C .... Pitted dates or date pieces
☐ 1/2 C .... Water
☐ 1/2 C .... Walnuts
☐ 1 1/2 tsp .... Salt
☐ 1 Tb .... Vanilla

- Mix oats, coconut, sunflower seeds and almonds together in a bowl.
- Whiz remaining ingredients in blender. You may need more or less water depending on size of bananas.
- Bake on sprayed cookie sheets or casseroles at 250° until light brown and crispy; about 2-3 hours.
- Leave in cold oven overnight.

SERVING SUGGESTIONS

- See Nutty Crunch Granola for serving suggestions.

Nutty Crunch Granola

Makes 23   1/2 C Servings

- ☐ 12 C .... Regular rolled oats (*NOT* quick)
- ☐ 2 C .... Shredded, unsweetened coconut[19]
- ☐ 2 C .... Chopped nuts
- ☐ 1 tsp .... Salt
- ☐ 3 C .... Dried fruit (raisins, diced pineapple, pears, etc.)
- ☐ 2 C .... Oat bran or wheat germ[11]
- ☐ 1/2 C .... Honey, dissolved in
- ☐ 1 12-oz. can .... Apple juice concentrate, warmed
- ☐ 4 Tb .... Vanilla **OR** 3 Tb maple extract (optional)

> - Combine liquid ingredients & add to dry (except fruit); mix very thoroughly with your hands.
> - Put granola on a sprayed cookie sheet or a sprayed turkey pan.
> - Bake at 250°, stirring occasionally, until golden brown and crispy (several hours). Stir more often as granola nears completion.
> - Turn oven off; leave granola in oven overnight.
> - Add dried fruit when granola if FULLY dry.

SERVING SUGGESTIONS

- This granola is great with fruit sauce, juice, or a milk substitute on top.
- Try layering it with your favorite lemon or carob pie filling recipe and sliced bananas.
- I love to use this granola for crisp topping, or for a great pie crust (see Desserts).

Holiday Granola

Makes 21   1/2 C Servings

- ☐ 8 C .... Regular rolled oats (NOT quick)
- ☐ 1C .... Shredded, unsweetened coconut[19]
- ☐ 1/2 C .... Nuts, your choice
- ☐ 1 C .... Pumpkin seeds
- ☐ 1/2 tsp .... Salt
- ☐ 1/2 C .... Honey
- ☐ 2 Tb .... Vanilla
- ☐ 1 Tb .... Maple extract

- •Mix dry ingredients together in a bowl.
- •Mix wet ingredients separately and add to dry.
- •Bake on sprayed cookie sheets or casseroles at 250°
  until light brown and crispy; about 2-3 hours.
- •Leave in cold oven overnight.

SERVING SUGGESTIONS

- •For a nice change, try lightly roasting the nuts and seeds for 15 minutes separately at 250°. Add nuts, seeds, and coconut AFTER the granola is cooked.
- •You can also add RAW nuts and seeds after the granola is cooked.
- •See serving suggestions for Nutty Crunch Granola.

Morning Millet Milk

Makes 8 Cups

- ❏ 1 C .... Hot, cooked millet
- ❏ 1 C .... Raw cashews[13] OR almonds
- ❏ 6 C .... Water
- ❏ 1 tsp .... Salt
- ❏ 1-2 tsp .... Vanilla
- ❏ 1 Tb .... Honey

- • Simmer 1/4 C millet in 1 C water for about 45 minutes, or until soft.
- • Put millet and ALL other ingredients in a bowl and mix well.
- • Blend 2-3 cups at a time until very creamy and smooth.
- • Chill and serve.

SERVING SUGGESTIONS

- • This is a very mild and pleasant tasting milk. It is especially good for those with wheat or soy allergies.
- • I like to blend a cup of crushed pineapple with it for a tropical flair.

Creamy Cashew Milk

Makes 5   1 C Servings

- ❏ 1 C .... Well cooked brown rice
- ❏ 2/3 C .... Raw cashews[13]
- ❏ 1/3 C .... Unsweetened coconut[19]
- ❏ 1 Tb .... Vanilla
- ❏ 1 tsp .... Salt
- ❏ 2 Tb .... Honey

- •Grind cashews and coconut in a blender.
- •Add ALL ingredients and blend until very frothy and creamy in about 3 cups of water.
- •Pour into 1/2 gallon container, add water to fill, and chill in refrigerator.
- •Shake well before each use.
- •For richer, sweeter milk, add less water. Makes a great thick cream over pies.

SERVING SUGGESTIONS

- •MOOOOve this one right in where you've used the *udder* milk in the past.
- •Leave out the honey and vanilla to use this recipe to make GRRReat mashed potatoes.

E-Z Almond Milk

Makes 8   1 C Servings

☐1 C .... Almonds, raw

- Boil 1 pint of water and pour in 1 C almonds. Let it boil for 45 seconds.
- Strain almonds, and pour out water.
- Rinse almonds in cold water.
- Put 1/2 C water into blender with almonds and blend until very creamy.
- Add 1 C cold water, and keep adding water until you have 1/2 gallon of milk.
- Pour milk through cheesecloth into a bowl. Then, squeeze excess liquid out of cheesecloth into bowl.
- Chill and serve.
- Use leftover almond pulp in waffles, loaf, or burger.

SERVING SUGGESTIONS

- Our most simple milk recipe with a lovely, light flavor.
- This one is delicious just for a nice, cool drink in the evening.
- You can dress up this milk in any way you like, using honey, vanilla, maple, or any other flavors!

Tropical Delight Milk

Makes 7   1 C Servings

Blend until VERY creamy:

- ☐ 1 .... 20 oz. can, crushed, sliced, or diced pineapple, with juice
- ☐ 1 C .... Raw cashews[13]
- ☐ 2 C .... Water
- ☐ 2-3 Tb .... Honey

- •Pour milk into pitcher, and add enough water to make 7-8 cups total. You can add less water for a thicker, creamier milk.
- •Stir well before each use.
- •Refrigerate between use.
- •Better if served cold.

SERVING SUGGESTIONS

- •This milk is delicious over any dry cereal, but especially granola.
- •Try making a thicker batch as a cream to pour over fresh strawberries, and sprinkle a little coconut on top.
- •This creamy milk also really dresses up a fruit salad, especially if you have a little chopped cranberry in the salad!
- •Frozen in ice cube trays, this milk is delicious served in lemonade on a hot summer evening, or frozen as popsicles for the children.
- •For a tasty change, try it over toast and bananas with raisins sprinkled on top, or over steamed rice with a sprinkle of granola or coconut garnish.

Well Done! Waffles

Makes 12 Waffles

- ❑6 C .... Oats (rolled or quick)
- ❑1/4 C .... Cornmeal
- ❑1 C .... Wheat germ
- ❑1/2 C .... Dates
- ❑2 Tb .... Vanilla or maple extract
- ❑1 tsp .... Salt
- ❑1/3 C .... Soy flour
- ❑1/2 C .... Walnuts or pecans

- •Mix ALL ingredients in a large bowl.
- •Add water to make batter that will blend in blender.
- •Fill blender halfway with batter and blend well. The batter should pour easily, but not be watery.
- •Pour into another bowl. Repeat process until all batter is blended.
- •Pour batter onto hot, sprayed waffle irons.
- •Bake 8-10 minutes, or until golden brown.

SERVING SUGGESTIONS

- •Any oat waffle will have a better consistency the next day. To reheat, simply place directly on the oven rack at 250° until crisp and hot.
- •These waffles are light and fluffy, with a delicious flavor.
- •They are wonderful with Better Butter and maple syrup.
- •Try them with Better Butter and fresh fruit sliced on top.
- •Or, try topping them with Festive Fruit Topping and Tofu Whipped Cream for a delightful birthday breakfast.
- •These also make excellent sandwiches! You can use any burger or spread, or, of course, peanut butter and apple slices.

Golden Waffles

Makes 10 Large Waffles

- 8 C .... Rolled oats
- 3/4 C .... Soy flour
- 1/2 C .... Cornmeal (optional)
- 1/2 C .... Dates OR 1/3 C Honey
- 2 tsp .... Salt
- 4 Tb .... Vanilla OR 3 Tb Maple extract

- Put all ingredients in large bowl.
- Add 10-12 C water, or enough to make it blendable.
- Blend mixture, 3 C at a time, until smooth; add water if necessary to help mixture blend.
- Transfer blended batter into another bowl as you go.
- Cook for 8-10 minutes in a sprayed waffle iron.
- Cool on rack and, if possible, wait until next day to eat.

SERVING SUGGESTIONS

- Golden Waffles are a favorite with many. Remember, as the batter sits, it will thicken, so you may have to add some water. If your waffles are too crispy and thin, your batter is too thin. If waffles are heavy and solid, you did not add enough water. Either way, though, these waffles are still GRRReat! The consistency of the batter should be a little thinner than a cake mix.
- These waffles freeze well, and are delicious as a main breakfast dish or as toast with cereal. We love to make sandwiches from them for picnics.
- To heat, just pop them into the toaster or heat in a low-heat oven right on the rack.

Nutty Crisp Waffles

Makes 10 Waffles

- ❏ 10 C .... Oats
- ❏ 1 C .... Cornmeal
- ❏ 2 tsp .... Salt
- ❏ 1 C .... Walnuts or pecans
- ❏ 2 Tb .... Vanilla
- ❏ 1/2 C .... Honey

- • Mix ingredients in a bowl.
- • Add enough water to make batter blendable.
- • Cook on hot, sprayed waffle iron for 10 minutes.

SERVING SUGGESTIONS

- • See the Serving Suggestions for Well Done! Waffles and Golden Waffles on the previous pages.

Belgian Best Waffles

Makes 8 Waffles

(Designed for Belgian wafflers, but great for regular ones, too!)

☐ 4 C .... Quick oats
☐ 2 C .... Yellow cornmeal
☐ 1/3 C .... Soy flour
☐ 1/2 C .... Wheat germ
☐ 1/2 C .... Walnuts or pecans
☐ 1/2 C .... Pitted dates
☐ 1 1/2 tsp .... Salt
☐ 1 Tb .... Maple or vanilla flavoring
☐ 5 C .... Water

- **Mix ALL ingredients in a large bowl.**
- **Blend a little at a time in blender and pour into another bowl.**
- **When blending is complete, ladel batter onto hot, sprayed Belgian waffle iron, filling well. DO NOT over-fill!**
- **Bake for 9-10 minutes or until golden brown.**
- **Spray waffle iron after each waffle to prevent sticking.**

SERVING SUGGESTIONS

- You won't "waffle" on your feelings about these waffles! They're delicious! They can be used in many different ways.
- Try them with hot applesauce, maple syrup, Festive Fruit Topping or fresh fruit on top. You can even layer whole waffle rounds with Festive Fruit Topping and whipped cream for a delightful strawberry shortcake!
- Take them to work or school in the form of a sandwich using tahini and apple slices.
- Try one with a bowl of hot soup and a salad, or pop the whole batch in the freezer for later use.

Incr-edible Crepes!

Do ½   *Makes 27 1/3 C Crepes*

❏ 3 C .... Rolled oats
❏ 1/2 lb .... Soft tofu, crumbled
❏ 1 tsp .... Salt
❏ 1 Tb .... Vanilla
❏ 1/3 C .... Honey
❏ 1/4 C .... Oil
❏ 1/4 C .... Whole wheat flour
❏ 1/4 C .... White flour

Optional:
❏ 1 C .... Chopped pecans to blended batter

• Mix ingredients in large bowl. For fluffy pancakes, add
  3 Tb Ener-G Health baking powder (calcium carbonate).
• Add 4 C water and stir well.
• Blend batter by cupfuls until very smooth and pour into
  a separate container.
• Let blended batter sit 10-20 minutes to thicken.
• Drop by 1/4 or 1/3 cupfuls onto hot, nonstick griddle.
• Cook on medium-high heat until bubbles appear on top
  of pancakes and undersides are brown.
• Flip over and cook until undersides are brown.
• Transfer to baking dish and keep in warm oven until
  ready to serve.

SERVING
SUGGESTIONS

• Some people say these pancakes taste even better the
  next day.
• Try them with Festive Fruit Topping or one of the crisp
  filling recipes in this section, topped with Dreamy
  Cream Whip (see Desserts).
• My son likes them cold with a little fresh fruit sliced
  on top for a light supper.

Quick Crepes / Pancakes

Add ½ - ⅔   *Makes 18   1/3 C Crepes / Pancakes*

Stir together:

- ☐ 2 C .... Whole wheat flour
- ☐ 2 C .... Rolled oats
- ☐ 1tsp .... Salt

Add:

- ☐ 4 C .... Water or soy milk
- ☐ 2 Tb .... Oil
- ☐ 2-4 Tb .... Honey
- ☐ 1 Tb .... Vanilla

- Let stand for 5 minutes; blend mixture until smooth.
- Place 1/3 C portions of batter onto a sprayed, hot skillet.
- Add water if batter is too thick to make a thin pancake.
- They will be ready to flip when the underside is golden brown, and bubbles appear in the center.
- DO NOT undercook.
- Flip and cook until both sides are golden brown, turning again if necessary.
- Place in oven to keep warm for your meal, or, if you are not using them right away, place on a cooling rack.
- For extra "fluff," add 2 Tb ENER-G powder. Don't overmix.

SERVING SUGGESTIONS

- You can turn these into German blintzes by making a recipe of our fruit topping, using blueberries or strawberries. Make the crepes a little bigger, using a 1/2 C measure. Place a generous amount of fruit topping in the middle of the crepe. Roll it up and place a spoon of Dreamy Cream Whip (see Desserts) on top. Your family will love them—and you!
- They're delicious with almond butter and applesauce, or peanut butter and maple syrup!
- Try stacking them on your plate, alternating them with strawberry sauce and whipped cream. Strawberry Short-crepes!

Viva La French Toast

Makes 16 Slices

- ❑ 2/3 C .... Raw cashews[13]
- ❑ 1 2/3 C .... Water
- ❑ 2 tsp .... Vanilla or maple extract
- ❑ 1/2 C .... Milk powder (soy, tofu, or rice)
- ❑ 1 tsp .... Salt
- ❑ 2 Tb .... Honey
- ❑ 1/2 C .... Whole wheat flour
- ❑ 1 C .... Oats (rolled orquick)
- ❑ 1/4 C .... Soy flour
- ❑ 16 slices .... Whole wheat bread

- • Blend ALL ingredients except flours and bread. Blend very well.
- • When ingredients are blended well, add flours and continue blending.
- • Pour batter into bowl. Add more water if too thick.
- • Dip bread one slice at a time into batter, covering completely.
- • Quickly place dipped bread onto sprayed, hot Teflon-coated griddle. Brown on both sides; don't undercook.
- • Place on plate in warm oven until ready to serve.

- • This is a mild, versatile recipe.
- • Serve with nut butter or Better Butter and maple syrup, or make a recipe of our Festive Fruit Topping (see Breakfasts) and use it instead of syrup.
- • French toast is also great with hot applesauce on top.
- • Great cold or toasted the next day for a doughnut taste!
- • You can make sandwiches using nut butter of your choice and apple slices or banana rounds. Enjoy!
- • This toast is lovely served plain and warmed with a little fruit for a light supper.
- • It makes especially delicious sandwiches for active youngsters who need "stick-to-my-ribs" lunches for outdoor adventures and energy!

SERVING

SUGGESTIONS

Festive Fruit Topping

Makes 6   1/2 C Servings

- ☐ 1/2 C .... Frozen white grape/raspberry juice concentrate (100% juice)
- ☐ 2 Tb .... Cornstarch
- ☐ 1 .... 12 oz. bag, frozen strawberries or blueberries
- ☐ 1/2 C .... Water

> - **Dissolve cornstarch in cold water, then thicken with juice in a saucepan, stirring constantly.**
> - **When thick, add frozen fruit.**
> - **Simmer for 2 minutes; turn off heat.**
> - **If using more fruit (14 or 16 oz bag), add 1 Tb additional cornstarch.**

SERVING SUGGESTIONS

- For a tasty twist, use 1/2 C frozen white grape/peach juice and peaches.
- You can also try it with 1/2 C frozen apple juice concentrate and add 3 C of peeled, sliced, fresh apples. Also add 1/2 C of raisins, 1 tsp of corriander, then simmer for 10 minutes to soften apples.
- This is great over waffles or granola, or used as a topping for Creamy Millet Pudding (see Breakfasts).
- This recipe is a family favorite on waffles, french toast, or pancakes. It makes a wonderful filling for strawberry shortcake, blueberry tarts, or as a topping for lemon pie.
- Try it layered with whipped cream, granola, or lemon pudding in a parfait glass for a wonderful breakfast!

Tofu Super Scramble

Makes 12 1/2 C Servings

Sauté in a little olive oil or water in a large pan:

☐ 1 .... Onion, small, diced **OR**
                         1 tsp onion powder
☐ 2-3 .... Cloves, crushed garlic **OR**
                         1 1/2 tsp garlic powder
☐ 2 pounds .... Tofu, extra firm or hard
       (Drain, rinse, and crumble into small pieces into a skillet.)

Stir in well:

☐ 2 Tb .... Chick-it seasoning[4]
☐ 4 Tb .... Nutritional yeast flakes[10]
☐ 1/4 tsp .... Turmeric
☐ Vegetable Salt[20] or salt to taste
☐ Sprinkle with parsley to garnish (optional)

- •Cover and simmer for 10 minutes.
- • (Optional): Add 2 medium peeled, diced, cooked baked potatoes. (Leftover potatoes work great!)
- •Cover and simmer until all flavors have blended.
- •Sprinkle with dry parsley to garnish.

SERVING SUGGESTIONS

- •This recipe is delicious over toast for breakfast, topped with Kwick Country Ketchup (see Dressings.)
- •We love this scramble in steamed corn tortillas with Tangy Cheese Filling (see Cheeses), or with steamed broccoli or kale and a baked yam.
- •It is delicious cold in a pita pocket or a whole wheat sandwich with sprouts and Marvi-whip Mayonnaise, or served hot on toast.
- •For a zesty flair, try dicing 1/2 green or red bell pepper and adding it to the onion when you sauté.

Cheesy Tofu Scramble

Makes 10 1/2 C Servings

Crumble in a skillet:

- ☐ 4 C .... Tofu, extra firm or hard

Add:

- ☐ 1 1/2 C .... Cracker Barrel Cheddar or other cheese recipe (see Cheeses)
- ☐ 2 Tb .... Nutritional yeast flakes[10]
- ☐ 1 tsp .... Salt

> • Simmer until melted and flavors are blended, usually about 15 minutes.
> • Serve.

- • Rolled in a burrito with Kwick Country Ketchup (see Dressings), this makes a hearty breakfast.
- • It is delicious cold in a pita pocket or a whole wheat sandwich with sprouts and Marvi-whip Mayonnaise, or served hot on toast.
- • For a zesty flair, try adding 1/2 diced red or green bell pepper and 1/2 C chopped green onion.
- • For a south-of-the-border flair, add 1/4 C fresh chopped cilantro.
- • Try having it cold for your next picnic, stuffed in a French roll! Serve with shredded cabbage and Totally French Dressing (see Dressings), then...Scramble out for a hike!

Healthy Hashers

Makes 6   1 C Servings

- ❏ 5 .... Potatoes, peeled, cubed, cooked
- ❏ 1 tsp .... Onion flakes
- ❏ 1/2 tsp .... Garlic powder
- ❏ 1 tsp .... Parsley flakes
- ❏ 1/2 tsp .... Chick-it Seasoning[4]
- ❏ 1 Tb .... Nutritional yeast flakes[10]

- Place ALL ingredients in a bowl and mix well.
- Place HALF the mixture into an iron skillet and brown on both sides.
- Repeat with other half.
- Serve hot.

SERVING SUGGESTIONS

- We love this recipe with a generous serving of scrambled tofu (recipes on previous pages).
- It is delicious cold with baked beans and a fresh green salad.
- Try them in a burrito with diced, lightly steamed vegetables and a mayonnaise of your choice (see Dressings).

Breakfast Pizza

Have ready in the desired amount:

- ❏ Pizza crust, pita pockets, or English muffins
- ❏ Cracker Barrel Cheddar Cheese (see Cheeses)
- ❏ Spaghetti sauce
- ❏ Scrambled tofu
- ❏ Olives
- ❏ Artichoke hearts, if available (water packed)

> •Spread spaghetti sauce on chosen bread (pizza base).
> •Add scrambled tofu liberally.
> •Top with olives, artichoke hearts, and last with cheese.
> •Place in 350° oven until thoroughly warm and crisp.
>   Total time will depend on size of pizza.
> •You've got to try this! It's DEEEEElicious!!!

SERVING

SUGGESTIONS

- •This pizza is easy to make ahead of time in any size and freeze.
- •You can take one to work and enjoy it with a nice green salad and dressing (see Dressings).
- •You can substitute the cheese with any other cheese for a nice variety (see Cheeses).
- •Try this pizza topped with Hey! Hey! Hummus (see Dressings) instead of cheese for a tasty change.

Elegant Entrees

Better Burgers

Makes 15   1/3 C patties

- ❏ 2 C .... Cooked millet[9]
- ❏ 1/4 C .... Chopped nuts
- ❏ 1/2 tsp .... Garlic powder
- ❏ 2 Tb .... Flour
- ❏ 1 .... Medium onion, chopped fine
- ❏ 1/2 C .... Soft bread crumbs
- ❏ 1 C .... Firm tofu[18] (well mashed)
- ❏ 1 Tb .... Vegetable salt[20]
- ❏ 1 Tb .... Molasses
- ❏ 1/2 tsp .... Salt   ½ t. sage

> - **Mix thoroughly and form into patties. Use 1/3 C measure, or mason jar lid and ring (see procedure under Perfect Patties recipe in this section).**
> - **Bake at 350° on a sprayed cookie sheet until golden brown on both sides. (Usually takes about 20-25 minutes per side.)**

SERVING SUGGESTIONS

- These burgers make great sandwiches and are delicious hot with brown gravy or spaghetti sauce. They are also wonderful broken on top of pasta and spaghetti sauce as "meatballs."
- Try them crumbled over steamed rice topped with your favorite sauce. They are also a hearty addition to Mexican beans (break over the hot beans just before serving).
- I even love these versatile burgers broken up in cold pasta and vegetable salads or hot soups.
- My family also enjoys them broken over baked potatoes with choice of mayonnaise (see Dressings) on top. (DO NOT pre-mix with sauces too long before serving as the grains swell and become too moist.
- Remember to try them in your favorite burrito, tostado, "sloppy joe," or haystack recipe.

Tofu Croquettes

Makes 24   1/4 C Balls

☐ 1 lb .... Tofu[18], firm
☐ 1 .... Baked potato, large, cold, peeled & grated
☐ 1/2 .... Onion, chopped fine
☐ 3/4 C .... Bread crumbs
☐ 1/4 C .... Walnuts, finely chopped
☐ 2 Tb .... Olive oil
☐ 1 Tb .... Parsley, dried
☐ 1/2 tsp .... Onion powder
☐ 1/2 tsp .... Marjoram
☐ 1/2 tsp .... Oregano
☐ 1 tsp .... Salt
☐ 1 1/2 Tb .... Nutritional yeast flakes[10]

- **Put ALL ingredients into a bowl and mash together very well, using your hands.**
- **Use a small ice cream scoop to form balls. Use a tea spoon to push balls off scoop onto a sprayed cookie sheet. Make sure balls are packed firmly.**
- **Bake at 350° for about 25-30 minutes or until golden brown.**
- **Leave croquettes on cookie sheet to cool. They will get firmer as they cool. Or serve directly from oven.**

SERVING SUGGESTIONS

- These croquettes freeze beautifully, and are great to pack in a lunch.
- Try them with a little spaghetti sauce on a bed of rice, or cold topped with your favorite mayonnaise (see Dressings).
- They are delicious stuffed in a pocket bread, or as a cold side dish with beans and cole slaw.

Tender Gluten Steaks

❏2-3 C .... Gluten flour
❏2 Tb .... White flour
❏2 Tb .... Soy flour
❏2 Tb .... Nutritional yeast flakes[10]
❏2 C .... Water

- Place 2 C of gluten flour along with ALL other ingredients EXCEPT water, in a bowl.
- Add water and quickly mix with a fork.
- Sprinkle more gluten flour and press and knead until a soft ball is formed.
- Roll out into a long sausage-shaped roll.
- Slice into 1/4" or 1/2" discs, or desired size, and drop into boiling broth (see recipe below).
- Cook for 30 minutes on low boil.
- When cooled enough to handle, dip in milk and roll in cornmeal breading (see recipe on next page).
- Brown on sprayed Teflon grill, both sides.
- Top with gravy of your choice and serve.

Broth

Simmer:

❏ 2 Quarts .... Water
❏ 1 .... Onion, sliced
❏ 1 Tb .... Onion powder
❏ 2 Tb .... Nutritional yeast flakes[10]
❏ 2 .... Bay leaves
❏ 1 Tb .... Salt
❏ 1 stalk .... Celery, cut into pieces

Breading for steaks

Mix in a bowl:

- ❑ 3 C .... Cornmeal
- ❑ 1/2 C .... Nutritional yeast flakes[10]
- ❑ 1 tsp .... Salt
- ❑ 1 Tb .... Onion powder
- ❑ 1 tsp .... Paprika (optional)

SERVING SUGGESTIONS

- These steaks are fun for special occasions like Thanksgiving.
- They freeze beautifully and can be chopped in small pieces and used in cream sauces for stroganoff or over rice.
- They are wonderful served over steamed brown rice with Peanut Gravy (See Gravies).

Garden Lentil Patties

Makes 27   1/3 C patties

- ☐ 1 C .... Dry lentils, cooked in 2 C water
- ☐ 1 C .... Carrots, shredded or finely diced
- ☐ 1 .... Medium onion, finely chopped
- ☐ 1 C .... Bell pepper or zucchini, finely diced
- ☐ 1 C .... Celery, diced
- ☐ 2 C .... Quick oats
- ☐ 1/4 C .... Olive oil
- ☐ 3/4 C .... Tomato paste
- ☐ 1 Tb .... Italian seasoning
- ☐ 2 Tb .... Chick-it Seasoning[4]
- ☐ 1 tsp .... Salt

- •Simmer lentils, covered, until fully tender
- •Mix ALL ingredients together in a bowl.
- •Form into patties and place on a sprayed cookie sheet, pressing each pattie firmly together
- •Bake at 350° until golden brown— about 20-25 minutes on each side.

SERVING SUGGESTIONS

- •These burgers are wonderfully simple, low in fat, and inexpensive. They have a great flavor, too.
- •Try them with your choice of gravy or spaghetti sauce, served with green beans and a tossed salad.
- •They make great sandwiches, too. Just pop one into a pita pocket with sprouts, Kwick Country Ketchup, mayonnaise (see Dressings), and lettuce for a great to-go lunch.

Oh, Boy! Oat Burgers

Makes 12 patties

- ☐ 1 C .... Cooked oatmeal, cold and firm
- ☐ 1 .... Raw potato, grated
- ☐ 4 tsp .... Olive oil
- ☐ 1/2 C .... Ground walnuts
- ☐ 1 C .... Toasted bread crumbs
- ☐ 1 tsp .... Salt
- ☐ 1 pinch .... Sage
- ☐ 1 tsp .... White flour
- ☐ 1/4 C .... Nutritional yeast flakes[10]
- ☐ 1 tsp .... Chick-it Seasoning[4]
- ☐ 1/4-1/2 C............ Soy or nut milk (just enough to moisten)

- **Mix ALL ingredients together.**
- **Add just enough soy milk to moisten and bind mixture.**
- **Form into patties (see procedure under Perfect Patties).**
- **Place on sprayed cookie sheet.**
- **Bake at 350° for 20 minutes, then turn over and bake on the other side until golden brown.**

SERVING SUGGESTIONS

- This is one of our favorite picnic burgers. They are fabulous with the typical hamburger fixings (see Dressings).
- They're delicious plain served with baked beans and potato salad (made with Marvi-whip Mayonnaise—see Dressings.)
- These patties freeze very well and hold up nicely in sandwiches, making them a great item to have in the freezer for school or work lunch boxes.

Perfect Patties

Makes 24   1/3 C patties

- ☐ 4 C .... Rolled oats
- ☐ 1 .... Onion, medium, finely chopped
- ☐ 1/2 C .... Walnuts, chopped
- ☐ 1/2 C .... Raw sunflower seeds[14]
- ☐ 2 Tb .... Vegetable salt[20]
- ☐ 1 Tb .... Molasses
- ☐ 3 Tb .... Nutritional yeast flakes[10]
- ☐ 1 Tb .... Italian seasoning
- ☐ 1/2 Tb .... Oregano
- ☐ 1/2 Tb .... Basil

- Boil 4 C of water.
- Mix with other ingredients; let sit in bowl for 20 minutes.
- Shape into patties using 1/3 C measure or wide-mouth mason jar lid and ring. (To form patties with lid, place lid inside ring and fill with pattie mix. Invert ring and lid on cookie sheet. Place fingers around ring and put both thumbs on the lid, then press lid down through the ring. It will form a perfect pattie!)
- Bake on prepared cookie sheet at 350° for 25 minutes on one side, then 20 minutes on the other. Time may vary according to pattie size and oven heat.
- Let cool on rack.
- These patties taste better the next day and freeze well.

SERVING SUGGESTIONS

- This is a favorite picnic burger. We love them on whole wheat buns with homemade mayo, Kwick Country Ketchup, Miracle Mustard (see Dressings), and lemon pickles.
- Try stuffing them in pita pockets.
- They're also excellent broken up as a topping over rice, potatoes, or noodles with spaghetti sauce.
- Simply put, these are, well...Perfect Patties!

Soy Great! Patties

Makes 10 patties

- ❑ 1 C .... Soaked* soy beans[16]
- ❑ 2 Tb .... Nutritional yeast flakes[10]
- ❑ 1/2 tsp .... Salt
- ❑ 1/2 tsp .... Onion salt
- ❑ 1/4 tsp .... Garlic powder
- ❑ 1/2 C .... Water
- ❑ 1 Tb .... Chick-it Seasoning[4]
- ❑ 3/4 C .... Rolled oats
- ❑ 1 tsp .... Italian seasoning

* Soak 1 C Soy beans in 4 C water overnight. Drain and use 1 C for recipe and freeze remainder for future use.)

- •Combine all ingredients EXCEPT oats in blender and grind to fine consistency.
- •Pour over oats, stir, and let stand for 10 minutes.
- •Form into patties (see method under Perfect Patties).
- •Brown on both sides on a lightly sprayed teflon griddle. Cover while browning.
- •Transfer to a sprayed cookie sheet and bake at 350° for about 10 minutes on each side.

SERVING SUGGESTIONS

- •These patties are great cold in sandwiches with Marvi-whip Mayonnaise (see Dressings).
- •Serve them over rice with gravy or spaghetti sauce.
- •Try breaking them up over a baked potato topped with a dollup of Marvi-whip mayonnaise for a delicious, quick entree.
- •Make up a double recipe of these, and freeze all the extra patties for future use.
- •You can even try them plain. They're great as an entree with vegetables. For an extra taste treat, top them with a dab of our mustard or ketchup (see Dressings). Your tongue will LOOOVE you!

Tasty Tofu NeatBalls

☐ 1 C .... Coarsely chopped walnuts OR pecans, toasted at 200° for 15 minutes

☐ 1 1/2 C .... Soft bread crumbs

☐ 1 16-oz. block.... Tofu, firm or extra firm

☐ 3 Tb .... Gluten flour

☐ 2 Tb .... Onion powder

☐ 3 Tb .... Dried parsley

☐ 2 tsp .... Salt

☐ 1 tsp .... Sage

☐ 1 tsp .... Marjoram

☐ 1/4 C .... Nutritional yeast flakes[10]

- Mix ALL ingredients together and mash or knead thoroughly with hands.
- Roll into balls and place on sprayed cookie sheet.
- Bake at 325° for 30 minutes.
- Makes approximately 40 tofu balls (8 balls per cup).

SERVING SUGGESTIONS

- This one is delicious baked in a casserole with spaghetti sauce, served over rice or toast.
- These fabulous "meat" balls are great as an entree, too. Just smother them with some gravy or spaghetti sauce and serve with potatoes and vegetables.
- Try slicing them cold into a hot dog or hamburger bun, topped with Campfire Bar-B-Que (see Gravies/p 11 Sauces section) for a quick, wholesome lunch.
- Anything you can do with meatballs you can do better with NeatBalls!

Tater' NeatBalls

Makes 20   1/8 C Neatballs

❑ 2 C .... Potatoes, raw, ground
❑ 1 Tb .... Soy flour
❑ 1 .... Onion, medium, finely chopped
❑ 1 tsp .... Sage
❑ 1 tsp .... Basil
❑ 1 C .... Whole wheat bread crumbs
❑ 1 C .... Ground walnuts
❑ 1 1/2 tsp .... Salt
❑ 2 Tb .... Nutritional yeast flakes[10]

- Grind walnuts in blender, then place in a bowl.
- Cube potatoes and grind in blender.
- Mix all ingredients thoroughly with walnuts.
- Let mixture sit for 10 minutes.
- Form into balls and place in a sprayed baking dish.
- Bake 30 minutes at 350°.
- Cover with gravy or spaghetti sauce and bake an additional 15 minutes, covered.

SERVING SUGGESTIONS

- I like to top these with the simple sauce in the Lebanese Lentil recipe (see it in this section). It's fantastic! p. 54
- These are delicious over pasta with spaghetti sauce or baked in a casserole with spaghetti sauce, served over rice or toast.
- This is a great entree, too! Just cover the neatballs with some gravy or spaghetti sauce and serve with potatoes and vegetables.
- Try slicing them cold into a hot dog or hamburger bun, or hollow out a French roll and fill it with the neatballs. Then, top with Campfire Bar-B-Que Sauce (see Gravies/Sauces) for a quick, wholesome lunch. p. 113

Terrific Tofu Patties

Makes 24 burgers

- ☐ 1 lb .... Tofu, extra firm, mashed
- ☐ 2 .... Zucchini, grated
- ☐ 3 C .... Bread crumbs
- ☐ 1/4 C .... Olive oil
- ☐ 1/4 C .... Cornmeal
- ☐ 1/4 C .... Nutritional yeast flakes[10]
- ☐ 1 Tb .... Chick-it Seasoning[4]
- ☐ 1 tsp .... Vegetable salt[20]
- ☐ 2 tsp .... Onion powder
- ☐ 1 tsp .... Garlic powder

- •Mix ALL ingredients.
- •Form into patties using a 1/3 C measure.
- •Brown and bake for 25 minutes in 350° oven.

SERVING SUGGESTIONS

- •For a real meal, serve these in pita pockets with ketchup, mayonnaise, cheese, and lettuce.
- •Serve with gravy or mayonnaise (See Dressings) on top with a green salad, steamed broccoli, and 5th Avenue Carob Cream pie for desert (see Desserts).

Wheat Germ Patties

Makes 20 1/3 C burgers

☐1 1/2 C .... Wheat germ
☐1 C .... Oats (rolled or quick)
☐1 1/2 C .... Chopped walnuts
☐1 Tb .... Chick-it Seasoning[4]
☐3 Tb .... Nutritional yeast flakes[10]
☐1/2 tsp .... Salt
☐1/4 tsp .... Sage
☐1 .... Onion, finely chopped
☐1 1/2 C .... Milk of your choice (no vanilla flavor)
☐1 tsp .... Garlic powder

- **Mix ALL ingredients well in a bowl.**
- **Let sit for 10 minutes.**
- **Form into patties.**
- **Brown on a sprayed cookie sheet at 350° (about 20-25 minutes on each side).**

SERVING SUGGESTIONS

- These are great little sandwich burgers. Slap one on a slice of bread and add Cracker Barrel or All Star Cheddar Cheese (see Cheeses), mayonnaise (see Dressings), and lettuce for a great sandwich!
- If you're not sure your children will like it, just put one on a plate with some spaghetti sauce on top, and they'll soon be asking for more!
- Try them broken up into rice with cheese melted on top.
- These patties are delicious broken up in a steamed corn tortilla with Marvi-whip Mayonnaise or Kwick Country Ketchup (see Dressings)—or both!
- They also freeze well. So make a lot!

Wonderful Walnut Timbales

Makes 16   1/2 C servings

- ❑4 C .... Cubed toast or very hard bread
- ❑1 C .... Chopped walnuts
- ❑1/2 C .... Finely chopped onion sautéed in 2 Tb water
- ❑1 tsp .... Sage
- ❑1/2 tsp .... Thyme
- ❑1/2 tsp .... Oregano
- ❑1/2 tsp .... Garlic powder
- ❑1/2 tsp .... Onion powder
- ❑1 Tb .... Nutritional yeast flakes[10]
- ❑1/2 Tb .... Soy or wheat flour
- ❑2 C .... Plain soy milk (not vanilla flavored)
- ❑1 tsp .... Salt

- •Place bread in a bowl and pour milk over it. Let it stand for 10 minutes.
- •Add remaining ingredients.
- •Stir and scoop into sprayed muffin tins, firmly pressing mixture down (about 1/2 C per timbale).
- •Bake at 350° until set and brown, about 25-30 minutes.
- •Let sit in tins about 10 minutes before removing.
- •Serve topped with your choice of gravy.

SERVING

SUGGESTIONS

- •These timbales taste very much like a light stuffing, and are delicious with a gravy of your choice.
- •They are delicious cold, and eaten plain. They pack well in a lunch box.
- •During the holiday season, they are a nice replacement for stuffing.

Zucchini Tofoo Yung

Makes 14   1/3 Cup Burgers

- ❏ 1 lb .... Tofu, firm
- ❏ 1 C .... Bread crumbs   *Add 1 c. Oats (quick) or oat flour*
- ❏ 2 C .... Grated zucchini, OR zucchini / summer squash combination
- ❏ 1/2 .... Onion, finely chopped
- ❏ 1/2 C .... Walnuts, finely chopped
- ❏ 3 Tb .... Olive oil
- ❏ 1 1/2 Tb .... Nutritional yeast flakes[10]
- ❏ 1 tsp .... Salt

- •Mix ALL ingredients thoroughly, squeezing together with your hands.
- •Form into patties using 1/3 C measure.
- •Press onto sprayed cookie sheet, pressing and shaping patties with your hands.
- •Bake in 350° oven for 25 minutes.
- •Turn patties <u>carefully</u> and bake another 25 minutes.

SERVING SUGGESTIONS

- •These patties are an excellent way to use garden zucchini.
- •They are delicious cold in a sandwich, or served hot with rice and stir-fried vegetables.
- •Try stuffing them into a pita pocket with fresh lettuce and tofu mayonnaise.

Couscous

Makes 12 1 C servings

Sauté in a little olive oil or water in a large pan:

- ❑1 .... Medium onion, chopped fine
- ❑2 .... Stalks, celery, diced
- ❑1/2 tsp .... Garlic powder   OR 1 clove, crushed garlic

Have ready to add to couscous:

- ❑2 Tb .... Parsley
- ❑1 tsp .... Savory
- ❑1/2 tsp ,............... Basil
- ❑3 .... Shredded carrots
- ❑2 C .... Chopped steamed spinach, kale, or collards, well drained
- ❑1/4-1/3 C .... Olive oil

In a separate pot, bring 6 C water to boil and add:

- ❑3 C .... Couscous
- ❑1/4 C .... Nutritional yeast flakes[10]
- ❑1/4 C .... Chick-it Seasoning[4]
- ❑2 tsp .... Vegetable salt[20] OR salt to taste
- ❑Stir and simmer covered for 5 minutes

- •Add sautéed ingredients to couscous pot.
- •Add steamed greens.
- •Add olive oil.
- •Stir well and serve.

SERVING

SUGGESTIONS

- •This colorful, tasty dish needs no additions! I usually serve it with a fresh salad and homemade bread.
- •A nice alternative is to replace the steamed greens with either peas or green beans.

Crunchy Noodle Casserole

Makes 20　3/4 C servings

- ☐ 1 lb .... Noodles (bow-tie or seashell)
- ☐ 1 recipe .... Cashew milk gravy (see below)
- ☐ 3 Tb .... Chick-it Seasoning[4]
- ☐ 1 tsp .... Garlic powder OR 2 cloves, crushed
- ☐ 2 tsp .... Onion powder
- ☐ 3/4 C .... Frozen peas, uncooked
- ☐ 4 C .... Cornflakes, crushed or enough to cover bottom of dish and sprinkle top

Recipe for Cashew Milk Gravy

- ☐ 3/4 C .... Raw cashews[13]
- ☐ 5 C .... Water
- ☐ 1/4 C .... Cornstarch
- ☐ 1/2 tsp .... Salt
- ☐ 1/4 C .... Sesame tahini[15]

- • Cook noodles and drain water.
- • Make cashew milk gravy in blender. Use 1/2 C of water called for first, blend, then add remainder.
- • Thicken milk gravy in a saucepan, stirring constantly.
- • Add milk gravy, peas, seasonings to noodles, and stir.
- • Cover bottom of casserole dish with crushed cornflakes.
- • Pour noodles into casserole dish and top with crushed cornflakes.
- • Bake at 350° until heated through and bubbly. Corn flakes should be lightly browned.

SERVING

SUGGESTIONS

- • This casserole is a favorite of children!
- • It's good hot or cold, and makes a great cold entree for school or work lunches.

Garbanzo-Spinach Pasta

Serves 12

1 lb.	☐1 1/2 lbs	Pasta (your choice), cooked
4 oz.	☐2 C	Chopped, fresh spinach, in a pan OR
		6-oz. frozen, chopped spinach
2 C.	☐3 C	Cooked garbanzo beans
3 C.	☐1 qt	Tomato sauce
1 qt	☐1 1/2 qts	Tomatoes, canned, chopped
3	☐5	Garlic cloves
2 T.	☐3 Tb	Olive oil (optional)
1 T.	☐1 1/2 Tb	Italian seasoning
1 t.	☐1/2 Tb	Basil
1/2 t.	☐1 tsp	Vegetable salt[20] or regular salt to taste

- Grind or crush all garlic.
- Simmer garlic in a little water for a few minutes.
- Add ALL ingredients (except pasta).
- Simmer for approximately 1 hour.
- Serve over pasta.
- Top with nutritional yeast flakes[10].
- Tastes even better the next day.

SERVING SUGGESTIONS

- For a nice change, replace spinach with zucchini slices.
- Instead of using pasta, put it over French rolls. Just cut the rolls length-wise and scoop out some of the bread and fill it with the recipe. Then, top it all with nutritional yeast flakes. Talk about GOOOOOD!

Other Garbanzo recipes:
  Tasty Tofu Gravy   117
  Hey! Hey! Hummus   134
  Chickee Cheese Spread 146
  Where Have You Bean? Stew 83

Greek-style Veggi-lini

Serves 8

- ❑ 1 C .... Orzo (pasta that looks like rice), cooked in salted boiling water
- ❑ 2 .... Garlic cloves, crushed
- ❑ 1 .... Onion, large, chopped
- ❑ 1 Tb .... Olive oil
- ❑ 2 C .... Carrots, diced
- ❑ 1 .... Red or green pepper, chopped
- ❑ 1 .... Zucchini, diced
- ❑ 1 tsp .... Mint, dried
- ❑ 1 tsp .... Dill
- ❑ 1 pinch .... Marjoram
- ❑ 1 .... 14 oz. can, artichoke hearts (water packed), drained and chopped
- ❑ 1 .... 15 oz. can, Cannellini beans, drained
- ❑ 1 .... 14 oz. can, Italian-style stewed tomatoes
- ❑ 2 tsp .... Salt, or to taste

- • Sauté onion and garlic in a little water, then separate from pasta.
- • Add diced carrots and chopped pepper.
- • Dice zucchini and add into the skillet of vegetables.
- • Add seasonings and olive oil.
- • Add artichoke hearts, beans, and stewed tomatoes.
- • Simmer several minutes, stirring occasionally.
- • When pasta is done, drain and stir into vegetables.

SERVING SUGGESTIONS

- • Serve with a tossed green salad, bread and Better Butter for a wonderful, wholesome meal.
- • Thanks, Charlene Anderson, for this great recipe!

Macaroni & Cheese, Please!

Makes 10   3/4 C servings

Cook:

- ❏ 12 oz. bow-tie, seashell, or elbow noodles by directions

Blend in blender:

- ❏ 1 C .... Raw cashews[13]
- ❏ 1 1/2 C .... Water
- ❏ 1/4 C .... Lemon juice
- ❏ 3 Tb .... Sesame tahini[15]
- ❏ 4 Tb .... Nutritional yeast flakes[10]
- ❏ 1 1/2 tsp .... Salt
- ❏ 2 tsp .... Onion powder
- ❏ 1 tsp .... Garlic powder OR 2 cloves garlic
- ❏ 1 .... 4 oz. jar, pimientos (1/2 C)

- •Drain and rinse cooked macaroni and place back in pot.
- •Stir in cheese mixture and pour into sprayed casserole dish.
- •Top with crushed corn flakes if desired.
- •Cover with foil, and bake for 30-40 minutes at 350°, or until heated through.

SERVING SUGGESTIONS

- •This recipe is great for kids because it's so easy to eat! It's great for Mom, too, because it's so easy to fix.
- •It's great with 1/2 C green peas thrown in before you bake it, or with 1/2 a fresh tomato blended with the cheese. Talk about a great flavor!
- •If you want some quick cuisine for your next picnic, this one is a natural. Just serve it with carrot and celery sticks, baked beans, and your favorite melon and you've got a perfect picnic!

Spinach-ini Toss

Serves 8

- 8 oz. .... Fettuccini noodles
- 4 .... Garlic cloves, crushed
- 1 tsp .... Salt
- 1 tsp .... Basil
- 1 tsp .... Onion powder
- 1 box .... Tofu, silken, 12.5-oz.
- 2 C .... Soy or rice milk (plain, not vanilla)
- 2 Tb .... Flour
- 2 C .... Spinach, chopped/frozen, thawed and well-drained
- 1/3 C .... Parsley, fresh/chopped

- **Cook noodles in salted water until tender; drain.**
- **In a separate pan, sauté spinach and garlic in 1/4 C water or a little olive oil for about 2 minutes.**
- **Add salt, basil, and parsley.**
- **Blend tofu, milk, and flour in a blender, then stir lightly into spinach mixture.**
- **Cook 2 more minutes, and toss spinach mixture with noodles.**
- **Garnish with pimientos if desired.**

SERVING SUGGESTIONS

- Great with a raw veggie plate with dip and garlic bread.
- Is excellent for cold lunches or for picnics, too.
- Thanks, Charlene Anderson, for another great recipe!

Lebanese Lentil Loaf

Makes 9   2/3 C servings

- ❏ 1 .... Onion, diced
- ❏ 2 Tb .... Olive oil
- ❏ 1/2 C .... Wheat germ
- ❏ 2 1/2 C .... Cooked lentils (to package directions)
- ❏ 1/2 C .... Bread crumbs
- ❏ 1/2 C .... Ground walnuts
- ❏ 1/2 tsp .... Sage
- ❏ 2 Tb .... Nutritional yeast flakes[10]
- ❏ 1/2 C .... Mashed tofu[18]
- ❏ 1/2 C .... Water or vegetable broth
- ❏ 2 cloves .... Garlic, crushed
- ❏ 2 tsp .... Vegetable salt[20] or regular salt

- • Preheat oven to 350°.
- • Lightly simmer onion and garlic in oil on low heat.
- • Mix ALL loaf ingredients together, with oil and garlic, and stir well.
- • Pack into sprayed loaf pan or ring mold.
- • Bake until brown and firm, about 40-45 minutes.
- • When done, let cool 10 minutes, then turn onto serving plate and cover with Tomato Sauce Topping (below).

Tomato Sauce Topping

Mix together:

- ❏ 1 .... 12-oz. can, tomato sauce
- ❏ 1 .... 12-oz. can, whole, chopped tomatoes
- ❏ 1 tsp .... Basil
- ❏ 1 tsp .... Oregano
- ❏ Salt to taste

SERVING SUGGESTIONS

- • This loaf is great served hot or cold.
- • It also freezes very well.
- • Try it sliced cold in sandwiches or stuffed in a pita pocket with lettuce, Kwick Country Ketchup and choice of mayonnaise (see Dressings).

Mock Salmon Loaf

Serves 10

- ☐ 1 qt .... Tomatoes
- ☐ 3 Tb .... Peanut butter
- ☐ 2 C .... Yellow cornmeal
- ☐ 1 .... Onion, cut in pieces
- ☐ 2 cloves .... Garlic
- ☐ 2 tsp .... Vegetable salt[20]

- •Put tomatoes in the blender; add other ingredients, then blend 2 minutes, until creamy.
- •Place blended ingredients in a bowl. Mix well and put in a sprayed baking dish.
- •Cover and bake at 350° for 30 minutes and uncover.
- •Bake for another 30-45 minutes.
- •Will set as it begins to cool.
- •Serve with mayonnaise.

SERVING SUGGESTIONS

- •There's nothing "fishy" about this loaf—it tastes GREAT! Try it in sandwiches for a new taste treat for the lunch box. Just mash some on a slice of bread, add your favorite mayonnaise (see Dressings), lettuce, and tomato. You can't help but enjoy it!
- •Try spreading it on crackers or Zwieback.
- •It's a great picnic item, too. Serve it with baked beans or potato salad—and don't forget the carrots, celery, and olives! Why not take a watermelon along, too?
- •This loaf is also good with Spanish rice.

Rice-Pecan Loaf

Makes 12 2/3 C servings

- ☐ 4 C .... Cooked brown rice
- ☐ 1 C .... Pecan meal
- ☐ 2 C .... Bread crumbs
- ☐ 1 .... Large onion, chopped
- ☐ 2 tsp .... Salt
- ☐ 2 Tb .... Nutritional yeast flakes[10]
- ☐ 1 tsp .... Garlic powder, or 2 cloves, crushed
- ☐ 1 tsp .... Oregano
- ☐ 1 tsp .... Celery seed
- ☐ 1 Tb .... Basil
- ☐ 1/2 C .... Hot water OR soy milk

- •Place ALL ingredients in a bowl and mix very well. (I just use my hands for mixing.)
- •Pack firmly into sprayed casserole dish OR into several sprayed bread pans.
- •Bake at 350° for 45-55 minutes.
- •Serve hot with gravy or sauce of your choice.

SERVING SUGGESTIONS

- •This makes a large casserole for company. It can be placed into several smaller loaf pans that can be cooled and frozen for future use.
- •It's great with gravy or spaghetti sauce.
- •Try this one as a spread for sandwiches. And don't forget to top the sandwiches with Country Ketchup and the mayonnaise you like (see Dressings).
- •For great sandwich slices, let loaf cool completely and refrigerate. Then, cut into slices and top with mayonnaise and ketchup of your choice (see Dressings).

Caribbean Curry

Makes 8   1/4 C servings

☐1 box .... Quick brown rice **OR**
                    6 C cooked brown rice
☐1 .... Onion, large, chopped
☐1 .... Green pepper, chopped
☐1 Tb .... Olive oil
☐1/4 C .... Orange juice **OR** 2 Tb   lime juice
☐1 lb .... Tofu, cubed
☐12 oz. .... Black beans, drained
☐1 .... Tomato, large, diced
☐1 tsp .... Cumin
☐1 tsp .... Coriander
☐1 tsp .... Turmeric
☐2 cloves .... Garlic, crushed
☐1/2 C .... Cilantro, fresh, chopped (optional)
☐2 tsp .... Vegetable salt[20] or salt to taste

- Cook rice according to package instructions.
- Saute' onion, garlic and green pepper in a little water.
- Add juice, olive oil and tofu.
- Add seasonings (except cilantro) and cook until tofu takes on yellow color.
- Add black beans and tomato and cook until thoroughly heated.
- Add cilantro and serve over a bed of brown rice.

SERVING
SUGGESTIONS

- A tasty entree indeed, especially when complemented with raw vegetable sticks and / or a tossed green salad.
- Thanks, Charlene Anderson, for this island treat!

Stuffed Bell Peppers

Can also use zucchini   *Makes 12   1/2 pepper servings*

To prepare:

- ☐ Slice off top of 6 medium bell peppers and clean out white ribs and seeds. OR, if using zucchini, slice in half long way and spoon out and discard the pulp.

Mix in a bowl:

- ☐ 2 C .... Brown rice (cooked)
- ☐ 2 C .... Burger Delight (recipe in this section)
- ☐ 1/2 C .... Bread crumbs
- ☐ 1/3 C .... Nutritional yeast flakes[10]
- ☐ 1 Tb .... Chick-it Seasoning[4]
- ☐ Salt to taste
- ☐ 1/3 C .... Olives, chopped
- ☐ 1/2 .... Onion, chopped
- ☐ 1 C .... Spaghetti or tomato sauce to moisten
- ☐ Basil to taste

- Stuff peppers or zucchini and place in casserole with 1/2-inch of water on the bottom
- Cover and bake about 40 minutes at 350°, or until tender, then 10-15 minutes uncovered to firm up on top.

SERVING SUGGESTIONS

- Delicious topped with extra spaghetti sauce and a dab of Cracker Barrel Cheddar Cheese (see Cheeses).
- These peppers freeze beautifully and are lovely cold for picnics. Serve them with tomato salad and carrot sticks.
- For an entree, they are attractive served with baked sweet potatoes and corn.
- Always remember to begin the meal with a raw vegetable plate or salad.

Hey! Stacks

Serves 4

- ❏ 4 C .... Baked corn chips
- ❏ 2 C .... Chopped lettuce
- ❏ 3 C .... Cuban Black Beans or other bean (like Chow Down Chili Beans or pinto beans)
- ❏ 1 C .... Marvi-Whip mayonnaise
- ❏ 1 C .... Cracker Barrel Cheddar
- ❏ 1/2 C .... Chopped onions
- ❏ 1/2 C .... Olives
- ❏ 1 .... Avocado (optional)
- ❏ 1/2 C .... Chopped bell peppers
- ❏ 1 C .... Chopped tomatoes

- • Begin with corn chips. Crush chips on your plate and add lettuce.
- • Top with beans, mayonnaise, cheese, onion, olives, avocado, peppers, and tomatoes.
- • Makes a delicious meal!

SERVING SUGGESTIONS

- • This will become a family favorite in your home!
- • It's great for birthday dinners or for a family get-together.
- • This recipe is easily expanded to feed large groups and is also a very fun picnic item. Try it!

Tantalizing Tofu Rolls

12 Slices

- ❏ 1 recipe .... Perfect Pie Crust
- ❏ 1/2 C .... Raw cashews[13]
- ❏ 1 Tb .... Onion powder
- ❏ 1/2 Tb .... Vegetable salt[20] OR salt to taste
- ❏ 3 Tb .... Nutritional yeast flakes[10]
- ❏ 2/3 C .... Water
- ❏ 2 lbs .... Tofu, firm or hard

- Crumble tofu in skillet.
- Blend ALL remaining ingredients in blender, and pour over tofu.
- Simmer until hot and bubbly.
- Turn off heat.
- Divide dough in half.
- Roll out into two rectangles according to pie crust recipe directions.
- Divide tofu between the two rectangles, placing it in the middle section from the top to the bottom.
- Cut 1-inch wide strips (cut from edge in toward the center) all the way down, not cutting too close to the tofu in the center.
- Pull ends over the tofu, then braid the 1-inch strips over the tofu all the way down.
- Can also simply fold dough over tofu, without cutting or braiding.
- Bake at 350° for 30 minutes, or until light brown.

SERVING SUGGESTIONS

- This is not only pleasing to the tastebuds, but when braided, is also very pleasing to the eyes!
- It's great with soup and salad.
- It makes a wonderful holiday main dish.
- It's a nice change in lunches for the office or school.
- This recipe freezes well.

Soy-egg Salad

16 3/4 Cup Servings

- ☐ 3 pounds .... Tofu[18], hard or extra firm (not silken)
- ☐ 3/4 C .... Green onion, minced
- ☐ 1 C .... Celery, diced
- ☐ 1 C .... Lemon pickles, diced
- ☐ 1/2 tsp .... Garlic powder OR 1 clove, crushed
- ☐ 1/2 tsp .... Tumeric
- ☐ 1 1/2 tsp .... Salt
- ☐ 3 Tb .... Nutritional yeast flakes[10]
- ☐ 3 C .... Marvi-whip Mayonnaise (see Dressings)
- ☐ 1/2 tsp .... Paprika

- •Crumble tofu and mix ALL ingredients in a bowl.
- •(For chicken salad texture, freeze tofu first, then squeeze water out completely and then crumble.)
- •Chill.
- •Best if served the next day.
- •For variation add 1/2 C diced red bell pepper.

SERVING SUGGESTIONS

- •This "egg" salad is a great cholesterol-free alternative to the traditional type!
- •We love to stuff whole wheat rolls with this tofu mix on picnics or other outings.
- •This is also an excellent recipe for stuffing in a pita pocket with some lettuce and tomato!
- •It is delicious served cold with baked tortilla chips, baked beans, and watermelon for a refreshing lunch!

Baked Chicken Tofu

Makes 10 slices

☐ 1 lb .... Tofu[18], firm or extra firm
☐ 2 tsp .... Chick-it seasoning[4]
☐ 2 tsp .... Sesame (dark) OR olive oil

- Cut tofu into 1/2 inch slices.
- Layer in 9" x 13" casserole dish and sprinkle with Chick-it Seasoning[4].
- Drizzle with sesame or olive oil, then brush.
- Turn and repeat process on other side.
- Let marinate (anywhere from 30 minutes to overnight in the refrigerator).
- Bake at 350°, turning over after about 20-25 minutes.
- Let bake until firm and light brown (an additional 20 minutes or so—it will depend on the water content of the tofu.
- Let cool and store in a covered container.
- Keeps about one week in the refrigerator.

SERVING SUGGESTIONS

- I love to steam brown rice, stir in steamed peas, and layer this tofu on top for a delicious hot main dish. Use a little additional chicken seasoning and yeast flakes to season the rice, or even a little spaghetti sauce.

Bar-B-Que Tofu Ribs

Makes 20 ribs

❏ 2 .... 1 pound bricks Tofu[18], extra-firm or hard

Blend:

❏ 2 .... 6-oz. cans tomato paste
❏ 4 Tb .... Nutritional yeast flakes[10]
❏ 1 Tb .... Sesame tahini[15]
❏ 2 tsp .... Salt
❏ 3 Tb .... Molasses
❏ 1 Tb .... Sesame oil (dark)
❏ 2 tsp .... Garlic powder OR 3-4 cloves garlic
❏ 2 tsp .... Onion powder
❏ 3 Tb .... Lemon juice
❏ 4-5 C .... Water, (for spaghetti sauce thickness)

- Slice tofu (water-packed in 1-pound tubs) into 1/4 inch strips.
- Arrange slices on a sprayed cookie sheet and bake at 400° until browned and firm on both sides, about 10 minutes on each side.
- Layer tofu and sauce in a sprayed casserole dish and bake, covered, at 350° for about 30 minutes, or until bubbly and firm.
- If desired, use Campfire Bar-B-Que Sauce (see Sauces) instead of sauce recipe above.

SERVING SUGGESTIONS

- If they were bent, you'd think these "ribs" were the real thing!
- These "ribs" are delicious served over rice or noodles.
- Try them as a side dish with a green salad, steamed vegetables and hot whole wheat rolls with Better Butter.
- Another favorite is a "rib" sandwich. Just place a few on a slice of bread with lettuce and mayonnaise and send it to school or to the office.
- They're a great picnic treat, too. Serve them warm or cold. Here's a new standard for finger lickin' good!

Garden Gourmet Quiche

Makes 1   12" quiche

- ☐ 2 lbs .... Tofu[18], hard, extra firm or firm
- ☐ 1 .... 12-oz. pack frozen, chopped spinach
- ☐ 3 C .... Grated zucchini **OR** 1 1/2 C each grated zucchini and yellow summer squash
- ☐ 1/3 C .... Nutritional yeast flakes[10]
- ☐ 1/4 C .... Chick-It Seasoning[4] (see Miscellaneous)
- ☐ 1/4 C .... Olive oil
- ☐ 1/2 C .... Finely sliced green onions

- •Make 1 recipe of Perfect Pie Crust (in Desserts section) and line one 12" quiche dish **OR** two 9" pie plates. **DO NOT PREBAKE!**
- •Thaw spinach, and squeeze out ALL excess water.
- •Mash tofu in a bowl.
- •Add ALL ingredients and mix very well. (I use my hands.)
- •Pack quiche mixture firmly into unbaked shell(s).
- •Bake at 350° for 45-55 minutes, or until firm with moisture gone.

SERVING SUGGESTIONS

- •This quiche is delicious hot out of the oven or cold the next day.
- •It's a wonderful alternative to sandwiches at lunch.
- •Even those who don't like tofu can't resist this recipe!
- •Make your next picnic a memorable occasion with cold vegetable salad, topped with the mayonnaise of your choice and dill, with this quiche as the main dish.

Mexic-Enchiladas!

Makes 12 enchiladas

Freeze, thaw, squeeze dry, and tear into small pieces : (set aside)

- ☐ 1 1/2 lbs .... Tofu[18], firm

Have ready:

- ☐ 12 .... Corn OR flour tortillas (6- or 8-inch)

Prepare tomato sauce. Start by sautéing:

- ☐ 2 Tb .... Water
- ☐ 1 .... Onion, large, chopped
- ☐ 3 cloves .... Garlic, crushed

When onions are clear, stir in:

- ☐ 2 .... 15-oz. cans Tomato sauce, unseasoned
- ☐ 2 C .... Water
- ☐ 3 Tb .... Cumin
- ☐ 2 Tb .... Paprika
- ☐ Salt to taste
- ☐ Simmer for 20 minutes

Preheat oven to 350º, and mix together:

- ☐ 2 Tb .... Chick-it Seasoning[4]
- ☐ 1 Tb .... Peanut or almond butter
- ☐ 2 tsp .... Onion powder
- ☐ 1 tsp .... Cumin
- ☐ 1/3 C .... Water

  Mix well with thawed, squeezed tofu pieces

Recipe continued on next page.

Recipe continued from previous page.

- Lay tofu on a sprayed cookie sheet and bake for 15 minutes.
- Pour a thin layer of tomato sauce into a 9" X 13" sprayed pan.
- Dip tortilla in remainder of sauce and place on a plate.
- Spread about 1/3 C filling across tortilla, roll up, and place in pan.
- Repeat with remaining tortillas.
- Cover wrapped tortillas with rest of sauce and bake at 350^{0} until bubbly—about 25 minutes.
- Serve with mayonnaise dollops on top. Delicious!!!

SERVING SUGGESTIONS

- These enchiladas freeze very well.
- They are delicious and colorful with Spanish rice and steamed, fresh corn.
- Baked tortilla chips with Tangy Cheese Sauce (see Cheeses) is a nice complement.

Fiesta Mexicana

Serves 8

- ❑ 1 C .... Marvi-Whip mayonnaise (see Dressings)
- ❑ 2 C .... Salsa Maravillos (see Sauces)
- ❑ 4 C .... Frijoles Perfectos (see Beans)
- ❑ 4 C .... Freshly grated lettuce
- ❑ 8 .... Tortillas OR burritos

- •Heat tortillas or burritos in a hot skillet. Iron is best. No oil needed.
- •Fill burritos or tortillas with mayonnaise, frijoles, and lettuce, and salsa.
- •Can top with cheese sauce of your choice (see Cheeses), and chopped onions.

SERVING

SUGGESTIONS

- •This is a quick, nutritious, delicious meal that your children will love!
- •Serve it with a side dish like Spanish rice or a steamed vegetable.

Luscious Lasagna

Serving size will vary.

In a large, deep casserole dish, layer in order given:

- ❏ Spaghetti sauce (have 2 quarts available)
- ❏ Lasagna noodles
- ❏ Spaghetti sauce
- ❏ Thinly sliced onion and bell pepper
- ❏ Lasagna noodles
- ❏ Spaghetti sauce
- ❏ Thinly sliced zucchini or eggplant
- ❏ Lasagna noodles
- ❏ Spaghetti sauce
- ❏ Burger Delight OR Ricotta-style filling (see Entrees)
- ❏ Chopped olives
- ❏ Lasagna noodles
- ❏ Spaghetti sauce

Top with:

- ❏ Creamy Cheese Sauce (see Cheeses), chopped olives, bell pepper garnish. Sprinkle lightly with nutritional yeast flakes[10].

- • Cook lasagna noodles until tender, but not totally cooked, then rinse with cold water, and begin to layer ingredients as given above.
- • Cover the casserole and bake at 350° until noodles are soft and casserole is bubbly, about 45 minutes.
- • Then, uncover and bake until cheese is golden brown, about 15-20 minutes.

Serving Suggestions

- • This lasagna freezes beautifully and is delicious with a nice tossed leaf lettuce and raw vegetable salad, and fresh rolls. Try it also with steamed broccoli and Italian coleslaw (lemon, garlic, and a little chopped onion, olive oil, and salt) with cornbread.
- • This is an excellent "company" dish—we have never had any dinner guests turn up their noses at this one! People love it—especially non-vegetarians!

Pizzaz Pizza!

Serves 8

❑ 8 .... Whole wheat pita pockets, OR 4 English muffins, OR 1 large pizza crust

❑ 1 1/2 C .... Burger Delight OR Not-Cotta filling (see Entrees)

❑ 3/4 C .... Cracker Barrel Cheddar Cheese, frozen or chilled and grated (see Cheeses)

❑ 2 C .... Spaghetti sauce

❑ 1/2 C .... Onions, chopped

❑ 1/2 C .... Bell pepper, chopped

❑ 2/3 C .... Olives, chopped

❑ 1/4 C .... Nutritional yeast flakes[10]

- Spread desired amount of spaghetti sauce on half-baked pizza crust, or top of pita pockets, or halved English muffins.
- Add desired amount of bell pepper and onions. For milder flavor, you can sauté these in a little water first.
- Add desired amount of Burger Delight and grated or sliced cheese.
- Top with sliced olives and sprinkle nutritional yeast flakes on top.
- Bake in 350° oven until crisp and hot, about 20-30 minutes.

SERVING SUGGESTIONS

- This pizza makes up beautifully to freeze ahead of time for any special occasion.
- I make several at a time using round pizza trays or edged cookie sheets.
- I make my own pizza dough using any bread recipe, like the Nice-n-lite Dinner Rolls recipe (see Breads). After rolling out dough, let it sit for 10 minutes, poke with a fork and bake for 10 minutes. Let cool and freeze for later use.

Sloppy Joes

Serves 6

*H*ave ready:

☐ 4 1/2 C .... Burger Delight (in this section)
☐ 3 C .... Bar-b-Que Sauce (see Sauces)
☐ 6 .... Whole wheat hamburger buns OR
                         6 slices of toast

- Heat Bar-b-Que Sauce and burger. Mix together (if desired) and place on toast or buns.
- Enjoy with steamed vegetable of your choice.

SERVING SUGGESTIONS

- A fun camp-out meal, or great for parties and picnics.
- This one is good hot or cold.
- Make a double batch—it freezes beautifully!
- This recipe is great for work lunches—just pack what you want on the sandwich in separate containers and build it right on a paper plate. Then warm it in the microwave. Don't forget your salad—and a napkin or two!

Not-cotta Filling

Makes 28 2 Tb servings

1 pkg	❑ 3 lbs	Tofu[18], firm or hard, drained & mashed
1 t	❑ 1 Tb	Garlic powder OR 3 garlic cloves, crushed
½ t.	❑ 2 tsp	Oregano
½ t.	❑ 2 tsp	Basil
½ t	❑ 2 tsp	Salt
1 t.	❑ 1 Tb	Onion powder
2 t.	❑ 2 Tb	Parsley
1 T.	❑ 2 Tb	Fresh lemon juice
2 T	❑ 1/2 C	Raw cashews[13], blended with
	2 T	1/2 C water

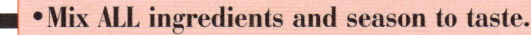

• **Mix ALL ingredients and season to taste.**

SERVING SUGGESTIONS

• This filling is excellent for manicotti or as a filling for lasagna.
• Try it in eggplant parmesan, too.
• It's very versatile and freezes very nicely.
• Thanks, Charlene Anderson, for another great recipe! Now I know why your husband is always smiling!

Burger Delight

18 2/3 C servings

- ☐ 2 C .... Bulghur wheat (not fine ground)
- ☐ 1 qt .... Canned tomatoes, with juice
- ☐ 1/2 .... Medium onion, cut in pieces
- ☐ 2-3 .... Garlic cloves
- ☐ 1 C .... Walnuts (may substitute pecans or raw sunflower seeds)
- ☐ 1 Tb .... Vegetable salt[20] OR 2 tsp salt
- ☐ 2 Tb .... Molasses

- •Place the wheat in a saucepan.
- •Blend ALL other ingredients until smooth.
- •Add blended ingredients into saucepan, mix with wheat, and simmer for 20 minutes, stirring ocassionally.
- •Spread mixture evenly on a sprayed cookie sheet, and bake at 250-275° for 45-60 minutes, until it is a loose, burger-like consistency.
- •Stir occasionally, and be careful NOT to overcook.
- •Remove from oven while it is still moist.

SERVING SUGGESTIONS

- •This burger is a staple in our home. It is very versatile and saves a lot of time in the kitchen.
- •Bake a potato and top it with this recipe, Cracker Barrel Cheddar Cheese or choice of mayonnaise (see Dressings) and chives for a wonderful, filling, nutritious meal. Serve it with a tossed salad and steamed broccoli.
- •Try serving on a bed of rice smothered with spaghetti sauce.
- •For a meal every child will love, serve it on hamburger buns as Sloppy Joes! (see recipe)
- •This one is a natural as "meat" in your spaghetti sauce, or mix it with chili beans for a really "filly" chili!
- •The uses for this burger are almost limitless! Use your imagination. Burger Delight freezes beautifully.

Savory Soups

& Beans

Luscious Lentil Soup

Serves 14

- ❏ 1 .... 16 oz. package, dry lentils
- ❏ 2 cloves .... Garlic, crushed
- ❏ 2-4 Tb .... Olive Oil
- ❏ 1 .... Medium, chopped onion
- ❏ 1/2 C .... Diced celery
- ❏ 2 C .... Baby carrots, or regular diced carrots
- ❏ 3 Tb .... Tomato paste
- ❏ 2 .... Medium potatoes, peeled and cubed
- ❏ 2 .... Bay leaves
- ❏ Salt to taste (Vegetable salt[20] or regular)
- ❏ 3/4 tsp .... Oregano
- ❏ 1/4 tsp .... Savory
- ❏ 1/4 C .... Parsley
- ❏ 1 .... 12-oz. can, tomatoes, chopped

> - **Cook lentils according to package instructions.**
> - **Reduce heat to medium.**
> - **Add potatoes and simmer until tender.**
> - **Add the rest of the ingredients; simmer for 20 minutes.**
> - **Add more water to desired consistency.**

SERVING SUGGESTIONS

- •This soup is delicious by itself with baked corn chips crushed on top.
- •It is also wonderful on a potato, a bed of rice, or just poured over toast for a quick, wholesome, tasty meal.

Persian Lentil Stew

Sauté in a little water in a large pot:

- ☐ 1 .... Onion, chopped
- ☐ 2 cloves .... Garlic, crushed
- ☐ 1 .... Bell pepper, chopped OR 1/2 green pepper and 1/2 red bell pepper, diced

Add:

- ☐ 4 C .... Red lentils
- ☐ 1 .... Small can, tomato paste (1/2 C)
- ☐ 1 .... Bay leaf
- ☐ Enough water to cover the lentils by about 1 1/2 inches
- ☐ Stir mixture and let it simmer until lentils are almost cooked—usually about 30 minutes.
- ☐ Be sure there's enough liquid to let lentils continue to cook.

Add to lentils:

- ☐ 2 .... Medium potatoes, peeled and cubed
- ☐ 2 C .... Cabbage, finely cut
- ☐ Allow to simmer until potatoes are tender
- ☐ Add more water if needed

When potatoes are cooked, add:

- ☐ 2 .... Medium-sized carrots, peeled/shredded
- ☐ 3 Tb .... Chick-it Seasoning[4], or to taste
- ☐ 2 tsp .... salt, or to taste
- ☐ 1/2 tsp .... Marjoram

SERVING SUGGESTIONS

- • This soup is wonderful with crushed baked chips or nutritional yeast flakes[10] on top.
- • Try it over potatoes or rice, too.
- • Turn it into Mazridra by serving it on a bed of rice with chopped chives, tomatoes, olives, and cucumbers.
- • Let you imagination go with this one. It's grrrreat!

Tofu Gumbo

Serves 14

- ☐ 1 .... Onion, medium, chopped or sliced thin
- ☐ 3 cloves .... Garlic, large, crushed
- ☐ 2/3 C .... Celery, diced
- ☐ 2 .... Carrots, medium, peeled and sliced
- ☐ 1 C .... Cabbage, shredded OR cubed
- ☐ 1 C .... Corn, frozen or fresh, cut off cob
- ☐ 1/3 C .... Peanut butter
- ☐ 1 .... 4-oz. can, tomato paste
- ☐ 1 lb .... Tofu[18], hard or extra-firm, cubed
- ☐ 2 Tb .... Extra virgin olive oil, optional
- ☐ 1 .... Bay leaf, large
- ☐ 1 Tb .... Chick-it Seasoning[4]
- ☐ 2 Tb .... Nutritional yeast flakes[10]
- ☐ 1 tsp .... Basil
- ☐ 2 tsp .... Salt, or to taste

- • Sauté onions, garlic, and celery in a little water, until tender.
- • Add ALL other vegetables.
- • Blend tomato paste and peanut butter in 1 qt. of water, then add to vegetables.
- • Add 1 qt. more water.
- • Simmer with 1 Bay leaf added until carrots are tender, then add the other seasonings and olive oil, if desired.

SERVING SUGGESTIONS

- • This gumbo is similar in flavor to a Ghanian (African) vegetable soup—rich in flavor and very aromatic!
- • It is delicious with corn crackers (see Breads) and salad.
- • This one packs well in a thermos for school or office lunches.
- • Like most soups, this recipe tastes better the next day.

Suddenly...Soup!

Makes 10   1 C servings

- ☐ 1 .... Onion, chopped
- ☐ 3 .... Potatoes, peeled and cubed
- ☐ 1/2 C .... Corn
- ☐ 1/2 C .... Peas
- ☐ 1/2 C .... Greens of your choice, cooked
- ☐ 1/2 C .... Lima beans
- ☐ 1/2 C .... Kidney beans (optional)
- ☐ 1/2 C .... Olives
- ☐ 3 Tb .... Chives
- ☐ 1/2 C .... Carrots, shredded
- ☐ 1 C .... Tomato, canned, crushed
- ☐ 1/2 C .... Cabbage, cut into small pieces
- ☐ 4 Cloves .... Garlic, crushed
- ☐ 2 tsp .... Onion powder
- ☐ 2 tsp .... Chick-it Seasoning[4], or to taste
- ☐ 1 tsp .... Cumin
- ☐ 1/3 C .... Tomato paste
- ☐ 1/2 tsp .... Oregano
- ☐ 1 tsp .... Basil
- ☐ 2 Tb .... Olive oil

- •Chop all your vegetables to desired size.
- •Sauté onions in a little water.
- •Add your tomatoes, tomato paste, and 3 quarts of water.
- •Add vegetables that take longer to cook (like potatoes and carrots.
- •When vegetables are halfway cooked, add the rest of the vegetables, herbs, and olive oil.
- •Simmer until done; then add yeast flakes or salt to taste.
- •Serve hot and call it...Suddenly—Soup!

SERVING SUGGESTIONS

- •This is a great way to use up leftovers or vegetables that you can't eat all at once by themselves.
- •Try it with side dishes of hummus and breadsticks.
- •The yeast flakes give it a rich cheesy flavor.

Very Veggie-mato Soup

Makes 12 1 C servings

- 2 qts .... Water
- 1 .... Bay leaf
- 2 Tb .... Chick-it Seasoning[4]
- 1 Tb .... Parsley flakes, dried
- 1 tsp .... Summer savory[17]
- 1 clove .... Garlic, crushed
- Vegetable salt[20] to taste
- 1/2 C .... Cooked rice
- 1 .... Onion, chopped
- 2 .... Potatoes, peeled, medium, cubed
- 2 .... Carrots, grated
- 2 C .... Tomato puree
- Optional: .... Shredded cabbage, zucchini, or corn.

- •Sauté onions and garlic in a little water.
- •Add other vegetables after 5 minutes.
- •Add water, rice, and seasonings, then boil until vegetables are tender.
- •Add tomato puree; simmer until flavors are blended.
- •Serve hot!

SERVING SUGGESTIONS

- •This is a very simple soup to make—and to eat!
- •Try it with breadsticks and a wonderful green salad.
- •It's a perfect choice for a cold winter's day.
- •For extra "good mood" food for the work day, pour this soup into a thermos. Then, enjoy your day—and your lunch!

Italian Style

Tomato Rice Soup

Makes 8   3/4 C servings

- ☐ 2 Tb .... Olive oil
- ☐ 1/2 C .... Onion, chopped
- ☐ 1/2 C .... Celery, chopped
- ☐ 28 oz. .... Tomatoes, canned
- ☐ 1 1/2 C .... Water
- ☐ 1 1/2 tsp .... Chick-it Seasoning[4]
- ☐ 1/2 tsp .... Marjoram
- ☐ 1/2 tsp .... Basil
- ☐ Salt to taste
- ☐ 1/3 C .... Brown rice, raw

- • Sauté onion and celery in 3 Tb water.
- • Blend canned tomatoes with onion, celery and water.
- • Add oil, herbs and rice. Bring to a boil.
- • Simmer, covered until rice is cooked. Then add salt.

SERVING SUGGESTIONS

- • Put this soup steaming hot into a big mug and crumble some baked chips on top!
- • You can substitute alphabet noodles for the rice and have a wonderful, tasty change that childen will love eating!
- • Thanks, Cindy Gonzalez, for this great recipe!

Creamy Tomat-ew Soup

Makes 8   1 C Servings

- ❏ 6 C .... Tomato juice
- ❏ 1 1/2 Tb .... Onion powder
- ❏ 1 pinch .... Oregano powder (about 1/16 tsp)
- ❏ 1/2 tsp .... Sweet basil
- ❏ Vegetable salt to taste[20]
- ❏ May season with Chick-it Seasoning[4] if desired

Blend for 1 minute:

- ❏ 1 C .... Raw cashews[13]
- ❏ 1 C .... Water
- ❏ 3 Tb .... Honey
- ❏ 1 Tb .... Nutritional yeast flakes[10]

> - Combine blended ingredients with ALL other ingredients in a large pot, stirring constantly.
> - Bring to a boil and serve, or remove from burner to prevent burning.
> - May add 1 C mixed vegetables if desired.

SERVING

SUGGESTIONS

- This soup is great for someone with a cold. It's very simple and very nourishing, and the flavor is quite appealing.
- Try it with the same serving ideas as our Very Veggie-mato Soup recipe.
- It is excellent served in a soup mug with crackers crumbled on top.

Potato Supreme Soup

Makes 10 1 C servings

- ☐ 1 Tb .... Olive oil
- ☐ 1 .... Onion, chopped
- ☐ 2 .... Garlic cloves, chopped
- ☐ 2 .... Celery stalks, chopped
- ☐ 6 C .... Water (approximately)
- ☐ 3-4 .... Potatoes, raw, cubed
- ☐ 2 Tb .... Nutritional yeast flakes[10]
- ☐ 1 tsp .... Chick-it Seasoning[4]
- ☐ 1 tsp .... Salt
- ☐ 1 tsp .... Celery powder
- ☐ 1/2 C .... Raw cashews[13]
- ☐ 3 Tb .... Flour
- ☐ 1/4 C .... Parsley, fresh, minced

- Sauté onions, garlic, and celery in a little water, until tender.
- Add potatoes and seasonings with enough water to cover and simmer until potatoes are soft.
- In a blender, process cashews with 1 C hot water until completely smooth and creamy.
- Add to potatoes and stir until well blended.
- Combine flour with a small amount of water and mix until smooth.
- Stir into soup and cook until thickened.
- Garnish with fresh parsley, etc.

SERVING SUGGESTIONS

- This is delicious in a mug with garlic bread or corn bread (see Breads).
- This soup packs well for lunches, too.
- Thanks to Kathryn and Gerard McClane for this delicious recipe!

Crock-it Barley Stew

Makes 15 1C servings

☐ 1 1/2 C (2)	....	Water
☐ 1/2 C	....	Barley
☐ 1/2 C	....	Lentils , *rinsed*
☐ 2 cloves	....	Garlic, crushed
☐ 3 C	....	Additional water
☐ Salt	....	To taste
☐ 1	....	Onion, large, diced
☐ 2 C	....	Tomatoes, canned and chopped
☐ 3 *medium*	....	Carrots, shredded or sliced
☐ 2	....	Potatoes, large, cubed
☐ 1 Tb	....	Sweet basil
☐ 2	....	Bay leaves

- Place water in a crock pot and add the barley and lentils.
- Turn on high heat and cook for one hour.
- Add 2 additional cups of water and remaining ingredients.
- Cook until all vegetables are tender; approximately 3-4 hours.
- Add more water or some tomato sauce as desired.

SERVING SUGGESTIONS

- This hearty stew sticks to your ribs and warms your heart on a cold wintery day.
- It packs well in a thermos for work or school.
- You can round out your stew meal with a pita pocket stuffed with a fresh green salad and your favorite dressing (see Dressings).
- This stew is great topped with croutons.
- I like adding some corn (off the cob) to give it a sweet flavor.

Where Have You Bean? Stew

Makes 8   1 C servings

- ☐ 1 .... 15 oz. can tomatoes, cut with juice
- ☐ 1 1/2 C .... Uncooked, small pasta shells
- ☐ 1 .... Onion, chopped
- ☐ 1/2 C .... Green pepper, chopped
- ☐ 2 tsp .... Basil
- ☐ 2 cloves .... Garlic, crushed
- ☐ 2 cans .... Kidney beans, drained (15 oz. can OR 2 1/2 cups
- ☐ 1 can .... Garbanzo beans (15 oz. can OR 1 1/4 cup
- ☐ 3 tsp .... Chick-it Seasoning[4]

> - **Cook noodles separately until almost tender.**
> - **Mix ingredients.**
> - **Heat to boiling in a pot, stirring occasionally.**
> - **Reduce heat.**
> - **Cover and simmer 15 minutes.**
> - **Stir periodically until noodles are fully tender.**
> - **Add more tomatoes or a little water, as needed.**

SERVING SUGGESTIONS

- This soup is wonderful with a tossed green salad and a baked sweet potato with Better Butter (see Dressings) and salt.
- Try using potatoes or cooked rice instead of pasta for a nice, tasty change.
- Experiment with different seasonings to add new taste sensations—try cumin, marjoram, oregano, paprika, and others.

Aye! Aye! Navy Bean Chowder

Makes 8   1 C servings

Cook:

❑ 2 lb .... White navy or great northern beans

Add:

❑ 1 .... Onion, chopped & sautéed in water

Blend:

❑ 3 C .... Bean & onion mix (with some water)
❑ 1 C .... Raw cashews[13]
❑ Add additional water to blend, if necessary
❑ Return this cream sauce to the beans

Add:

❑ 1 .... 4 oz. jar diced pimientos (1/2 C)
❑ 1 tsp .... Onion powder
❑ 2 Tb .... Parsley
❑ 1 tsp .... Basil
❑ 1/2 tsp .... Sage
❑ 2 pinches .... Fine's Herbs[8] (optional)
❑ 3-4 Tb .... Chick-it Seasoning[4], or to taste
❑ 3 Tb .... Nutritional yeast flakes[10]
❑ Salt to taste

> • Simmer for 30 minutes and serve hot.
> • If not eating right away, let it cool before storing.
> • Omit onion if using for breakfast beans with a fruit meal.
> • Variation: May use white lima beans.

SERVING SUGGESTIONS

• These beans are great for breakfast over toast. It's one of our family favorites.
• They're also wonderful alone with crushed baked corn chips on top.
• This dish has a creamy, pleasing taste and is perfect for company.
• Try serving it over rice with a green salad and steamed broccoli on the side.

Old English
Navy Bean Chowder

Makes 8   1 C servings

- ☐ 1 .... 12-oz. package, navy beans
- ☐ 1 .... Onion, medium, chopped
- ☐ 2 .... Bay leaves, large
- ☐ 2 tsp .... Marjoram (dried leaves) OR   1 tsp marjoram powder
- ☐ 1 tsp .... Basil
- ☐ 2-3 cloves .... Garlic, crushed
- ☐ Salt to taste
- ☐ 3 C .... Cabbage, cut in small pieces or cubes
- ☐ 1 .... Carrot, shredded

- • Cook beans with bay leaves until tender.
- • Add ALL other ingredients and simmer until cabbage is tender.
- • Adjust water to desired thickness.
- • Optional: Can add crushed tomatoes, bell pepper, or cubed peeled potatoes for a delicious variation.

Serving Suggestions

- • We love this chowder over toast for breakfast.
- • Try it over a bed of steamed brown rice for lunch, or over a big baked potato.
- • For a sweet essence, add 1/2 C of diced red pepper.
- • It is lovely served with bright yellow sweet potatoes.

Corn Chow-der

Makes 12   1 C servings

- ❑ 1 C .... Raw cashews[13]
- ❑ 4 C .... Frozen corn, or fresh off cob
- ❑ 1 .... Onion, chopped, sauteed in water
- ❑ 6 C .... Potatoes, peeled, cubed and cooked
- ❑ 1/4 C .... Chick-it Seasoning[4]
- ❑ 1/4 C .... Nutritional yeast flakes[10]
- ❑ Vegetable salt[20] or regular salt to taste
- ❑ 1 tsp .... Basil
- ❑ 1/2 tsp .... Fine's herbs[8] (optional)
- ❑ 1/2 tsp .... Savory OR sage
- ❑ 1 .... Bay leaf
- ❑ 1 tsp .... Onion powder

- • Cook onions and potatoes together in a little water.
- • Blend 2 C of the onion/potato mixture with the cashews and 1/2 C corn.
- • Add enough water to blend smoothly to a thick, creamy chowder. Blend by cupfulls if your blender is small.
- • The remainder of the corn and potatoes should be left chunky.
- • Add more water to entire mixture to desired consistency.
- • Add ALL other ingredients and simmer. DO NOT boil!

SERVING SUGGESTIONS

- • This soup is one of our favorites. It is wonderful as an entree, served with a green salad, fresh bread, or baked corn chips crushed on top.
- • Try it served over steaming rice or toast.

Cream of Spinach Soup

Makes 16   1 C servings

Sauté in water until tender:

- ❑ 1 1/2 .... Onions, chopped
- ❑ 4-5 cloves .... Garlic, crushed

Add:

- ❑ 4-5 .... Potatoes, large, peeled and cubed
- ❑ 12 C .... Water

Cook until potatoes are done, then add:

- ❑ 2-3 bundles .... Fresh spinach, chopped

Continue to cook until spinach is tender, then add:

- ❑ 3 Tb .... Chick-it Seasoning[4]
- ❑ Salt to taste
- ❑ 3 T .... Olive oil (optional)

> • **Blend soup in blender and pour into another pot.**
> • **Heat and serve.**

SERVING SUGGESTIONS

- • This is a great dish for a cold, snowy day. It's tasty and easy to make—and to eat! Little children love this soup.
- • Serve it with a salad and toast with cheese for a wonderful, warming meal.
- • Thanks, Cindy Gonzalez for sharing this recipe with us!

Very Veggie
Cheese Chowder

Makes 20   3/4 C servings

Steam until tender in 4 C of water:

☐ 5 .... Potatoes, medium, peeled, cubed
☐ 1 .... Onion, large, cut into small pieces
☐ 4 .... Carrots, large, peeled, sliced OR
                     6 medium carrots, peeled, sliced
☐ 1 C .... Raw cashews[13]

In a separate pot, steam until barely tender:

☐ 4 C .... Broccoli, diced into small pieces, OR
                     6 C Cauliflower

- Blend cashews and ALL ingredients (including the liquid), except the broccoli (or cauliflower), until very smooth and creamy. You will have to add some water to achieve smooth blending.
- Blend 2-3 Cups at a time.
- Pour blended vegetables into the pot with the broccoli.
- Add the following seasonings:

☐ 3 Tb .... Nutritional yeast flakes[10]
☐ 3 Tb .... Chick-it Seasoning[4]
☐ Salt to taste
☐ 1 tsp .... Basil
☐ 1/2 tsp .... Fine's Herbs[8] or marjoram
☐ 1/2 tsp .... Summer Savory[17] or sage
☐ 2 tsp .... Onion powder

- Stir well and simmer — DO NOT boil!

SERVING SUGGESTIONS

- This soup is a family favorite. I serve it over a little steamed rice in a bowl, or just by itself with a sprinkle of dry parsley over each serving.
- Delicious topped with croutons or crushed corn chips.
- The second day it is even thicker, and is delicious as a topping over baked potatoes or toast.
- You'll be amazed at the cheesy flavor, and you are getting wonderful potatoes and carrots as the base, along with delicious cancer-fighting vegetables!

Cream *of the* Crop Chowder

Makes 16   3/4 C servings

Steam until tender in 4 C of water:

- ☐ 4 .... Potatoes, medium, peeled, diced
- ☐ 1 .... Onion, large, cut into small pieces
- ☐ 1 C .... Raw cashews[13]

In a separate pot, steam until barely tender:

4 C .... Yellow summer squash, sliced

- • Blend cashews and ALL ingredients (including liquid *and* squash), until very smooth and creamy. You will have to add some water to achieve smooth blending.
- • Blend 2-3 Cups at a time.
- • Add the following seasonings:

  - ☐ 2 Tb .... Chick-it Seasoning[4]
  - ☐ 2 Tb .... Nutritional yeast flakes[10]
  - ☐ Salt to taste
  - ☐ 1/2 tsp .... Basil
  - ☐ 1/2 tsp .... Fine's Herbs[8] or marjoram
  - ☐ 1/2 tsp .... Summer savory[17] or Sage

- • Stir well and simmer — DO NOT boil!

SERVING SUGGESTIONS

- • Even folks who are not necessarily fond of summer squash love this thick, creamy soup. I use it in the same way I use the Very Veggie Cheese Chowder (recipe in this section)—and with the same wonderful results!
- • Try serving this soup with garlic bread and a pretty leafy-green salad with Totally French Dressing (recipe in Dressings section).
- • This one will really warm you up and give you the energy you need on a cold winter's day!

Chow Down Chili Beans

Makes 20   3/4 C servings

- ❏ 2 1/2 C .... Dry pinto beans
- ❏ 1 Tb .... Vegetable salt[20] OR salt to taste
- ❏ 1 .... Medium, chopped onion
- ❏ 1 .... Bell pepper, diced
- ❏ 2-3 .... Large cloves garlic, crushed
- ❏ 1 Tb .... Cumin
- ❏ 1/2 Tb .... Sweet basil
- ❏ 1 1/2 C .... Tomato puree
- ❏ 3/4 C .... Burger Delight (recipe in Entrees)
- ❏ Salt to taste

- •Soak pinto beans over night in a large pot, then rinse beans thoroughly.
- •Cover with about 2 inches of water and bring to a boil.
- •Reduce heat and simmer until tender.
- •Add water if needed
- •Add all other ingredients, except Burger Delight, and simmer until beans are well-flavored and sauce is thickened. Then add Burger Delight.

SERVING SUGGESTIONS

- •For a real international taste treat, try these beans over rice, baked potatoes, or polenta.
- •They're delicious served in a bowl topped with chopped olives and diced green onion, with steaming hot corn tortillas on the side.
- •And don't forget to get out your cornbread for these beans. They taste great blanketing some golden cornbread.
- •They're great topped with garlic-seasoned croutons.

Bountiful Baked Beans

Makes 12   3/4 C servings

- 1 lb .... Navy beans (or baby white lima beans cooked per package instructions)
- 1 .... Medium onion, chopped
- 2 Cloves .... Garlic, minced
- 1 C .... Tomato puree
- 1/2 C .... Dates, blended with 1 C water
- 1/3 C .... Molasses
- 1 tsp .... Onion powder
- 1 tsp .... Vegetable salt[20]
- 1/2 tsp .... Salt

- Cook beans until tender.
- Add ALL other ingredients and bake in a sprayed, covered 9" x 13" casserole dish at 350° for 1 hour.
- Uncover and bake about 30 more minutes, or until golden brown and bubbly.
- Tastes even better the next day.

SERVING SUGGESTIONS

- I love these baked beans with patties and cole slaw or potato salad at a picnic.
- Try them over toast for a great entree.
- You can pack them in a thermos for a wonderful hot lunch in the winter.

Frijoles Perfectos!

Cook 1 1/2 pounds pinto or black beans by directions, then add:

- ☐ 2 Tb .... Garlic cloves, crushed
- ☐ 1/2 .... Onion, small, diced fine
- ☐ 1/2 C .... Olive oil
- ☐ 1 Tb .... Postum or Roma[12] (optional)
- ☐ 2 Tb .... Chick-it Seasoning[4]
- ☐ 2 Tb .... Vegetable salt[20]
- ☐ 1 Tb .... Oregano
- ☐ 1 C .... Tomato, crushed
- ☐ 1 Tb .... Cumin (optional)

- •Mash beans slightly.
- •Heat and serve.
- •This is an original Mexican recipe! Thanks, Abuelita Mina Harding for sharing this recipe with her Chica Gina!

SERVING SUGGESTIONS

- •These are so easy and versatile, not to mention tasty!
- •I love to serve them over steamed polenta (very thick, coarse-ground steamed cornmeal).
- •It is also good cold as a tortilla-chip dip with sliced avacados.

Mexi-Beans

☐3 C .... Dry Pinto beans, cooked until done

Add:

☐1 .... Onion, chopped & sautéed in water
☐1 qt..................... Tomatoes
☐3-4 cloves .... Garlic
☐1 tsp .... Onion powder
☐1/4 C .... Nutritional yeast flakes[10]
☐2-3 Tb .... Extra virgin olive oil (optional)
☐Vegetable salt[20] or regular salt to taste
☐1 Tb .... Paprika
☐1 Tb .... Cumin

- Simmer for 20 minutes.
- Add water to desired consistency.
- Optional: add 1/2 diced bell pepper and 1/2 C chopped olives.

SERVING SUGGESTIONS

- This is another easy bean recipe, and it's great for feeding a large crowd.
- You can top it with Picnic Salsa (see Sauces) or Nacho Cheese (see Miscellaneous).
- Don't forget, these can be served over hot potatoes, rice, or toast as a meal-stretcher.
- Also delicious made with 15 bean mix in place of pinto beans.

Chili-Con Tofu

Have Ready:

- ❑ 3 C .... Cooked kidney beans
- ❑ 1 lb .... Tofu[18], frozen, thawed, squeezed and torn into bite-sized pieces

In a separate bowl, mix the following seasoning for the tofu:

- ❑ 1/3 C .... Water
- ❑ 2 Tb .... Chick-it Seasoning[4]
- ❑ 1 Tb .... Peanut OR almond butter
- ❑ 1 tsp .... Onion powder
- ❑ 1/2 tsp .... Cumin
- ❑ 1/4 tsp .... Garlic powder OR 1 Clove, crushed

Mix together well:

- ❑ Tofu and seasoning
- ❑ Place on a sprayed cookie sheet and bake 20 minutes at 350⁰, and turn to brown on the other side for 10 more minutes, or until brown on both sides.

Sauté the following in a little water in a soup pot:

- ❑ 1 .... Green pepper, large, diced
- ❑ 1 .... Onion, large, diced
- ❑ 2-3 Cloves .... Garlic, crushed

Add the following to the soup pot:

- ❑ Cooked kidney beans and baked tofu pieces
- ❑ 2 tsp .... Paprika
- ❑ 2 Tb .... Olive oil
- ❑ 1/2 C .... Tomato paste
- ❑ 2 Qts .... Water
- ❑ Salt to taste

• Simmer and serve piping hot!

TIPS ON BUYING AND PREPARING PRODUCE

Three Cheers for Salad

1. Choose fresh, red or green leaf lettuces, not iceberg.

2. Cut off the ends, wash and blot, and then layer lettuce with paper towels or Viva type towels in a plastic sealed container. They will stay fresh and perky, and last almost a week.

3. Have a plastic container for broccoli, cauliflower, and cabbage that is easy to get to, for adding raw veggies to your salad. Peel broccoli stems for more tenderness. Stems can be sliced and cut into salad or used as "sticks" for dips. Crookneck squash and zucchini can be used the same way.

4. Don't forget to have raw carrots (baby carrots are nice and quick) for salads also.

5. Try several types of cabbage: red, savoy Napa, even Bok Choy. Cut into slivers for best flavor. Savoy cabbage is our family favorite. Young, fresh kale is great shredded into a salad.

6. Try peeling and grating some raw beets for your salad. Keep in a separate container. Grated carrots in a salad adds moisture and sweetness.

7. Red bell pepper adds a lovely color, as does green. Vary your ingredients so you don't get bored, having the "same thing" every day.

Raw!

8. Try arranging a raw veggie platter on a bed of sprouts. Drizzle lemon juice, Seasoned Eatings[20] salt, and a little of your favorite dressing or extra virgin olive oil for a raw taste treat. Don't forget the juicy tomatoes and cucumbers on this one.

9. Finely shredded savoy cabbage is light and delicious. Toss with your favorite mayonnaise, tahini dressing, lemon and garlic dressing, or creamy Italian dressing. (SeeDressings). Toss in a few dry roasted peanuts for a change, or a little grated carrot, green onion, etc.

Raw!

10. Any salad combination is delicious tucked inside a hot tortilla with a little hummus or homemade mayonnaise.

11. Eat your raw foods first for improved digestion and absorption. Crackers, a few nuts, or bread is nice to complement this essential first course.

12. Avoid loading so many "extras" (garbanzo and kidney beans, crushed chips, olives, sesame sticks, for instance) on the salad if there will be other food served. These are all wonderful additions, but it is easy to overdo, unless the salad is the main course. If it is the main course, try stuffing it in a pita pocket. Great for an office lunch! Just package the salad and dressing in separate containers, take a pita pocket or two, and assemble at lunchtime.

ARTICHOKE: Steam in a steam rack for 25 minutes, or until tender when a knife is inserted into the middle. Delicious with any of our dressings or mayonnaise in this book.

ASPARAGUS: Trim tough ends; lightly steam in a steamer or covered pan with a small amount of water. Delicious with any dressing or cheese sauce with yeast flakes; or just lemon and salt.

BEANS: Lima or Green lima: Steam until tender; sprinkle Seasoned Eatings[20] salt and lemon juice. Green: Delicious steamed with crushed garlic, thin onion slices, Chick-it Seasoning[4] , Nutritional yeast flakes[10], and lemon juice.

BEETS: Scrub, cut off ends, slice in quarter inch rounds, and simmer in a little water with thinly sliced onion. Or, simmer and serve with lemon juice and salt.

BROCCOLI: Peel broccoli stems; slice in long sticks, lightly steam. Drizzle with choice of dressing (tahini dressing is nice), or sprinkle yeast flakes and lemon juice with Seasoned Eatings[20] salt. Or try with mayonnaise as a topping, or cheese sauce. Delicious steamed with thinly sliced onion.

BRUSSELS **S**PROUTS: Steam and season with Seasoned Eatings[20], lemon juice and yeast flakes. Or try with cheese sauce or mayonnaise.

CABBAGE: Delicious steamed and seasoned the same way as the broccoli. Can be done with broccoli and Brussels sprouts. Delicious steamed with thinly sliced onion.

CARROTS: Try cutting diagonally, steam with thinly sliced onion, basil, yeast flakes; add lemon juice and salt when done. Or, glaze with a little maple syrup or honey.

CAULIFLOWER: See broccoli.

CHARD: Delicious steamed plain, or with fresh slivered beet slices and sliced onion with lemon juice and salt. See also, Collards:

COLLARDS: Wash, cut off stem ends. Stack some leaves on a cutting board, and cut into three lengthwise strips, then cut horizontally into 1/2 inch strips. Makes nice little bite size pieces. Place in steamer or pot with a small amount of water. Steam until tender. Drizzle extra virgin olive oil and sprinkle with Seasoned Eatings[20] salt. Or, season with lemon juice and salt seasoning of your choice. Also delicious topped with our mayonnaise or Tahini dressing. Try steaming them with thinly sliced onion.

CORN: Steam whole in a pot; rub fresh lemon wedged on cob; sprinkle with salt. Also good with Better Butter spread on cobs.

For a Mexican flair, steam off the cob with diced red and green bell pepper and green onion. Season with salt.

KALE**:** See collards and chard.

PEAS**:** Try adding peas to our peanut gravy and serving over rice, potatoes, toast or pasta. Delicious with lemon juice and Seasoned Eatings[20].

POTATOES**:** Red or white potatoes are delicious steamed and topped with extra virgin olive oil, dill, yeast flakes, Chick-it Seasoning[4] or Seasoned Eatings[20]. Good cold the next day as a side dish with a salad. Try any potato baked or steamed, and topped with any mayonnaise, tahini, or other dressings; beans, cheese spaghetti sauce, Burger Delight, or broccoli and cheese sauce, peanut gravy or French dressing.

PEPPERS**:** See recipe for stuffed bell peppers. Try this: make a sandwich using tahini for spread. Slice a whole bell pepper; place a few slices on sandwich with sliced cabbage, lettuce, tomato, cheese and olives for a delicious sub sandwich.

SPINACH**:** See spinach tofu quiche recipe; try seasoned with lemon juice and salt. Good with dressings or mayonnaise too.

SQUASH**:** Crookneck, Zucchini, Acorn, Spaghetti, Butternut.

> •*Crookneck:* Cut off ends; slice into quarter inch slices; steam with thin onion slices; delicious with mayonnaise or lemon juice. See also our quiche recipe.

•*Zucchini:* See quiche recipe; delicious steamed with crook neck squash and seasoned with lemon juice and sprinkled with basil and or yeast flakes.

•*Acorn:* Cut in pieces; steam in covered pan with a little water; delicious with salt or Better Butter. May also sprinkle with basil.

•*Spaghetti squash:* Good baked or steamed, served with Better Butter, salt, or spaghetti sauce.

•*Butternut:* See acorn.

SWEET POTATOES OR YAMS: Peel with a potato peeler. Slice into half-inch rounds; steam until tender. Delicious plain, or with a drizzle of maple syrup and chopped pecans. See recipe. Try them baked with Better Butter on top.

TOMATOES: Absolutely wonderful stuffed with scrambled tofu, topped with mayonnaise. Also good mixed with cucumbers, seasoned with lemon juice, yeast flakes, salt, basil, and, if you wish, a little extra virgin olive oil and shredded lettuce.

*I*nteresting vegetable combos to try:

- corn & limas
- corn & diced red bell pepper
- peas & carrots
- Savoy cabbage and leeks with dill weed
- new potatoes & onion with olive oil and dill weed
- crookneck squash & zucchini with basil
- red cabbage & red onion with dill weed
- carrots, Brussels sprouts & onion with olive oil
- sweet potato and carrots
- carrots & red potatoes
- beets and onions with lemon and dill weed
- green beans, garlic, and onions with lemon
- tomato, cucumber, and onions with lemon
- zucchini and onion with basil
- collards or chard with lemon, onion, and olive oil

Succulent Salads

& Veggie Dishes

Peppy Potato Salad

Mix together:

3 1/2 C	Potatoes, peeled, cooked, cubed
1 C	Celery, finely diced
1/3 C	Black olives, sliced
2 Tb	Fresh parsley, chopped
1 tsp	Tumeric
2 1/2 tsp	Onion powder
1/2 C	Onion, diced (green onion is nice)
1 Tb	Lemon juice
1 C	Marvi-whip mayonnaise (see Dressings)
1 tsp	Salt, or to taste

- Mix well.
- Place in a glass bowl and chill before serving.

SERVING SUGGESTIONS

- This recipe is an old time favorite in our home! Yes, you CAN still eat potato salad! Try it in all the ways listed below. It will give you pep and energy!
- Take it on a picnic lunch with baked beans, stone ground corn chips, carrot and celery sticks, and a nice ripe watermelon.
- Stuff it in a pita pocket with tomato slices and leaf lettuce.
- It's also great mounded in the center of a fresh tossed salad.
- Why not serve it as a side dish with your favorite sandwich or soup?

Mediterranean Bean Salad

- ❏ 4 C .... Cooked brown rice
- ❏ 1 can .... Kidney beans, drained
- ❏ 1 .... Cucumber, sliced
- ❏ 1-2 .... Tomatoes, diced
- ❏ 1 can .... Artichoke hearts (water-packed), drained and sliced
- ❏ 1/3 C .... Lemon juice
- ❏ 2 Tb .... Olive oil (or less)
- ❏ Salt to taste
- ❏ Herbs to taste—Basil, oregano, garlic, etc.

> • Mix ALL ingredients well and chill before serving.

SERVING SUGGESTIONS

- This is one of my husband's favorites!
- It's a great "quick-fixer" for a picnic—just fix it, put it in the ice chest, and you're ready to go!
- This is a good lunch box main dish for school or for the office.

Christmas Fruit Salad

- ☐ 2 .... Granny Smith apples
- ☐ 2 .... Red Delicious apples
- ☐ 5 .... Kiwi fruit
- ☐ 1/2 tsp .... Almond extract
- ☐ 3 C .... Strawberries, fresh OR frozen
- ☐ 1 recipe .... Dreamy Cream Whip
- ☐ Shredded coconut

- • Slice strawberries while still frozen and place in a glass serving bowl.
- • Add peeled and sliced kiwi fruit.
- • Cut apples into bite-sized pieces and add to bowl.
- • Mix well.
- • Fold almond extract into Dreamy Cream Whip and fold topping into fruit mixture.
- • Sprinkle shredded coconut on top.
- • Chill and serve.

SERVING SUGGESTIONS

- • This salad—delightful, crisp, and tangy—is delicious with homemade crackers and Chickee Cheese (see Cheeses) for a light supper.
- • Try it with one of our seasoned popcorns (see Miscellaneous) for a real taste treat that everyone will love!

Great Greek Green Beans

Good

- ❑ 8 C .... Green beans, steamed OR canned
- ❑ 1/4 C .... Olive oil *only 1 T.*
- ❑ 1 .... Onion, large, chopped
- ❑ Juice of 1 lemon or lime
- ❑ 3/4 tsp .... Salt (less salt if using canned)
- ❑ 1/3 C .... Bread crumbs (grind toast or bread in blender or coffee mill)
- ❑ 3 pinches .... Savory[17], or sage
- ❑ 2-3 Cloves .... Garlic, crushed

> - Sauté onions, garlic, and savory in a little water.
> - Mix olive oil into the green beans.
> - Layer ALL ingredients in a medium-sized casserole dish.
> - Heat and serve, or enjoy at room temperature.

SERVING SUGGESTIONS

- These beans are wonderful served with spaghetti.
- If your children are feeling blue about green beans, this will get their interest RED HOT!

Potato Salad Supreme

- ❏ 4 .... Potatoes, large, cooked and peeled
- ❏ 1 .... Onion, medium-small minced
- ❏ 1 C .... Celery, diced
- ❏ 2/3 C .... Lemon pickles, diced
- ❏ 1/2 tsp .... Garlic powder
- ❏ 1/4 tsp .... Tumeric
- ❏ 3 Tb .... Chick-it Seasoning[4]
- ❏ 4 Tb .... Nutritional yeast flakes[10]
- ❏ 1 tsp .... Onion powder
- ❏ 3 C .... Mayonnaise (see Dressings)
- ❏ Salt to taste

> • **When potatoes are completely cold, cut into desired size cubes.**
> • **Mix ALL ingredients thoroughly in a bowl.**
> • **Chill.**
> • **Best if served the next day.**

SERVING SUGGESTIONS

- Talk about an exciting, nutritious, heart-friendly, brain-boosting buddy for lunches, this is it!
- Of course, it's excellent to take on picnics along with Better Burgers (recipe in Entrees section) and other picnic fixings.
- I like to add 1 C mashed extra firm tofu or scrambled tofu for an "egg" potato salad effect.
- This is also an excellent recipe for stuffing in a pita pocket with some lettuce!

Persian Broccoli

☐ 6 C .... Broccoli
☐ 1/2 .... Medium onion
☐ 2 Tb .... Pecans, chopped
☐ 1 Tb .... Nutritional yeast flakes[10]
☐ 1-2 tsp .... Vegetable salt[20]
☐ 1/2 C .... Lemon juice

- Lightly steam broccoli, peel outer skin and cut into strips, and thinly sliced onion.
- When done, lightly sprinkle with chopped pecans, nutritional yeast flakes, vegetable salt, and a little fresh lemon juice.

SERVING SUGGESTIONS

- When the veggies are "dressed up" (like this recipe does), I like to keep the entrees simple.
- This is delicious with plain steamed brown and wild rice or a baked potato, topped with a dollop of our sour cream (see Dressings) to moisten. You could leave off the sour cream and use a little spaghetti sauce, too!

Great Gravies

& Sensational Sauces!

Sicilian Spaghetti Sauce

- ☐1 qt .... Tomatoes, chopped
- ☐3 .... 12-oz. cans, tomato paste
- ☐1 .... Onion, large, chopped
- ☐1 .... Bell pepper, large, chopped
- ☐2 .... 6-oz. cans, pitted/sliced black olives
- ☐4-6 .... Cloves, crushed garlic
- ☐1/3 C .... Nutritional yeast flakes[10]
- ☐1 tsp .... Italian seasoning
- ☐Salt to taste
- ☐1 Tb .... Vegetable salt[20]
- ☐1/2 Tb .... Basil
- ☐1 tsp .... Oregano
- ☐1 tsp .... Marjoram
- ☐1/2 tsp .... Thyme
- ☐4 Tb .... Extra virgin olive oil (optional)

- •In a large soup pot, sauté onion, garlic, and green peppers in water.
- •Add tomato paste and WATER to desired consistency.
- •For sweeter sauce, add 1/4 C honey
- •Add ALL ingredients and simmer for about an hour— stir in a little olive oil for added flavor (optional).
- •Sauce always tastes better the next day.

SERVING SUGGESTIONS

- •Use it as a ketchup on sandwiches or fries.
- •I love it over rice or noodles.
- •For a great variation try this: Make a thick cornmeal in a crockpot (use 1 C cornmeal to 2 1/2 C water; pinch of salt; touch of olive oil). Serve it hot and cover with sauce, then top with Cracker Barrel Cheddar Cheese (see Cheeses). It's a great rib-sticker!
- •Try this one over veggies or bake (covered) with cooked garbanzos and diced zucchini.
- •Serve it over steamed rice or over any burger.
- •It's a tempting topping on any casserole.
- •Try adding diced zucchini or eggplant to the recipe.
- •I always have some in the freezer—just in case Uncle Luigi pays a surprise visit!

Campfire Bar-b-Que Sauce

Makes 6 Cups

☐ 1 .... Onion, medium, minced
☐ 2 cloves .... Garlic, crushed
☐ 4 C .... Tomato sauce
☐ 1/4 C .... Water
☐ 1/4 C .... Nutritional yeast flakes[10]
☐ 1 tsp .... Salt (if needed)
☐ 1 tsp .... Onion powder
☐ 1 1/2 tsp .... Dried parsley
☐ 1 Tb .... Vegetable salt[20] OR salt to taste
☐ 2 Tb .... Molasses
☐ 1 Tb .... Paprika
☐ 1/2 C .... Lemon juice

> • Sauté minced onion and garlic in a little water.
> • Add other ingredients and simmer until thickened.
> • Add 3 Tb Extra virgin olive oil (optional).
> • Tastes even better the next day!

SERVING SUGGESTIONS

• For a spectacular taste treat, use this sauce with the Burger Delight recipe (see Entrees) for FANTASTIC Sloppy Joe sandwiches. Put it in hamburger buns, or over baked potatoes or even over rice.

• Make glutten steaks, and marinate them in this sauce overnight in a casserole dish. The next day, heat and serve as your main course. Your family or guests will love it!

• This sauce can also be used when you make the Bar-b-Que Tofu Ribs (see Entrees).

• You'll love this one so much, you'll find excuses to use it!

NO PITS

Bar-b-Que Sauce

Makes 10 Cups

- ❑ 4 .... 6-ounce cans, tomato paste
- ❑ 7 C .... Water
- ❑ 1 .... Onion, medium, chopped
- ❑ 3 cloves .... Garlic, crushed
- ❑ 1/3 C .... Honey
- ❑ 1/2 C .... Molasses (DO NOT use blackstrap!)
- ❑ 1/4 C .... Lemon juice
- ❑ 1/8 C .... Olive oil
- ❑ 1/3 C .... Nutritional yeast flakes[10]
- ❑ 1/2 Tb .... Salt
- ❑ 1/2 Tb .... Chick-it Seasoning[4]
- ❑ 2 tsp .... Onion powder

> • Sauté onions and garlic in a little water.
> • Blend remaining ingredients, half at a time, and pour into pot with sautéed ingredients.
> • Heat and serve.

SERVING SUGGESTIONS

• See the Serving Suggestions for Campfire Bar-b-Que Sauce on the previous page.

Peanut Gravy

Makes 5 Cups

- ☐ 1/2 C .... Peanut butter
- ☐ 3 Tb .... Nutritional yeast flakes[10]
- ☐ 2 Tb .... Chick-it Seasoning[4]
- ☐ 1/3 C .... Whole wheat or white flour
- ☐ 2 Tb .... Soy milk powder (plain flavor, not vanilla)
- ☐ 1 1/2 tsp .... Onion powder
- ☐ 4 C .... Water

> • Blend all ingredients, pour into a saucepan and thicken over medium heat, stirring constantly with a whisk.
> • Serve.

SERVING SUGGESTIONS

- • This gravy is perfect over potatoes, rice, or toast.
- • It's wonderful as a gravy for pot pie filling, too.
- • Mix it with green peas and chick peas, and serve it over rice for "Chick-pea Ala King"!

Terrific Tartan Gravy

Makes 5 1/2 Cups

- ❑1 C .... Raw cashews,[13] *sunflower, seeds & peanuts*
- ❑1/3 C .... Unbleached white flour, *browned*
- ❑4 C .... Water
- ❑1/4 C .... Yeast flakes
- ❑2 tsp .... Onion powder
- ❑2 Tb .... Chick-it Seasoning[4]
- ❑1/4 C .... Sesame tahini[15]

- Blend ALL ingredients 2-3 minutes in blender.
- Pour into saucepan and thicken, stirring constantly.
- Remove from heat and serve.

SERVING SUGGESTIONS

- Pluck that chicken gravy recipe out of your recipe box! This one is ten times better! It has a rich, creamy flavor and is very versatile.
- Try it on a baked potato for a delicious, fast lunch, or on toast for a savory breakfast.
- This can also be used for pot pie gravy (see recipe).
- Serve it over cooked brown rice for a real taste treat.

Tasty Tofu Gravy

Makes 5 Cups

- ☐ 1 C .... Soft tofu[18]
- ☐ 1 1/2 C .... Water
- ☐ 1/2 tsp .... Garlic powder OR 1-2 cloves garlic
- ☐ 1 C .... Cooked garbanzo beans
- ☐ 1 tsp .... Onion powder
- ☐ Salt to taste (Vegetable salt[20] OR regular)
- ☐ 2 tsp .... Chick-it Seasoning[4]

- •Blend ALL ingredients until creamy, then place in sauce pan and heat to just below boiling.
- •Dissolve 2 Tb of cornstarch in 1/4 C water, and add to other ingredients to thicken.
- •Add more dissolved corn starch if gravy is too thin.

SERVING SUGGESTIONS

- •This gravy is superb over patties, rice, pasta, or vegetables.
- •It's also wonderful for breakfast poured over toast or biscuits.
- •Pour it over baked potatoes for a wonderful entree.

Chick'mmm Gravy

1/2 recipe   *Makes 8 Cups*

- ❏ 1 1/2 C .... Raw cashews[13]
- ❏ 1/3 C .... Cornstarch
- ❏ 3 Tb .... Chick-it Seasoning[4]
- ❏ 1/3 C .... Yeast flakes
- ❏ 2 tsp .... Onion powder
- ❏ Salt to taste (Vegetable salt[20] OR regular)

- •Grind ALL ingredients in blender until fine.
- •Bring 1 quart of water to a boil.
- •Add another quart to the dry mixture in the blender, then blend until very creamy.
- •Add mixture in blender to boiling water and thicken on medium heat, stirring constantly.

SERVING SUGGESTIONS

- •Delicious served over toast, rice, or baked potatoes. I like to sprinkle a little dry parsley on top to add color.
- •For a great variation, add steamed peas and cooked garbanzos for an "a-la-king" entree. Add about 1 C peas and about 1 1/2 to 2 C garbanzos.

ANY WODI COOKBOOK - CHICKEN STYLE GRAVY p.8

Blend smooth: 1c. watER 3/4 c. Cashews
Add & Blend: 1c. Water   2T. chicken-style seasoning
6T. ubleached flour
2T. onion powder 1/3 t. garlic powder
3/4 t. salt   1-2 T. yeast flakes
Bring 2c. water to a boil. Add blended mixture
and stir often. Cook 5-10 min.
Yields   4 cups

Picnic Salsa

Makes 6 Cups

- ❑ 1 qt .... Tomatoes, chopped, with juice
- ❑ 1 C .... Tomato sauce
- ❑ 1 C .... Green onions, diced
- ❑ 1 Clove .... Garlic, crushed (optional-this will make it hot)
- ❑ 1 .... Bell pepper, medium, diced
- ❑ 1 .... Cucumber, diced (remove seeds)
- ❑ 1 .... Celery stalk, diced
- ❑ 3 Tb .... Cilantro, fresh, chopped
- ❑ 1/4 C .... Lemon juice
- ❑ 1 1/2 tsp .... Salt

- • Mix ALL ingredients in a bowl and let chill.
- • DO NOT Cook!
- • Best the next day.

SERVING

SUGGESTIONS

- • This salsa is cool and filled with garden flavor.
- • Delicious in a burrito with shredded lettuce or savoy cabbage and mayonnaise or hummus. (see Dressings)
- • Great over scrambled tofu, or as a garnish for potato salad.
- • Try a spoonful over hot black or chili beans, or stuffed in a veggie pocket with raw fresh veggies.

Salsa Maravillosa

Makes 6 Cups

- ☐ 1 .... Cilantro, medium bundle, chopped
- ☐ 1 Tb .... Garlic, crushed
- ☐ 8 .... Tomatoes, chopped
- ☐ 1/2 C .... Onion, chopped
- ☐ Juice of one lemon
- ☐ 1 Tb .... Vegetable salt[20]

> - Mix ALL ingredients together well and chill before serving.
> - Delicious!

SERVING SUGGESTIONS

- This easy, cool, refreshing recipe can be adjusted to fit any taste.
- It is lovely over shredded savoy cabbage, or rolled into a burrito with any of our black or pinto bean dishes (see Beans).
- Try it as a garnish over Scrambled Tofu (see Breakfasts), or over steamed rice for a low-fat fiesta.
- Thanks, Abuelita Mina Harding, for this wonderful recipe!

Here's a tasty tip for keeping your herbs such as cilantro fresh:

- After buying herbs, cut off 1 inch of stalk.
- Place the herbs stems down into a large-mouthed one-pint mason jar with 1" of water and no lid. Add 1/2 teaspoon of sugar to the water, and place the jar in the refrigerator.
- Herbs will stay fresh for at least a week. But be sure that you change the water every few days.

Delightful Dressings & Sensational Spreads

Tahini Tang Dressing

Makes 1 1/2 Cups

Place in a blender:

- ☐ 1/2 C .... Sesame tahini[15]
- ☐ 1/2 C .... Water
- ☐ 1/4 C .... Lemon juice, or to taste
- ☐ 1 tsp .... Salt
- ☐ 1-2 Tb .... Honey
- ☐ 1 tsp .... Garlic powder OR 1 clove fresh
- ☐ 1/2 tsp .... Onion powder

> •Blend until very creamy and smooth.
> •Pour into a pint jar, cover and chill.

SERVING SUGGESTIONS

- •This salad dressing is one of our family favorites. It is wonderful over any green salad or coleslaw.
- •Try it as a spread for sandwiches. Just spread some on a slice of bread with mayonniase or cheese on the other slice. Then, put sliced red or green peppers, lettuce, cucumber, tomato and sprouts on top, close it up and you've got a super veggie sandwich!
- •This dressing is also great as a raw vegetable dip or on top of steamed broccoli or cabbage!
- •You can't run to the corner market to get some dressing as fast as you can make this one! Besides, you won't find a dressing this tasty or this healthy anywhere! Any salad covered with this dressing is "dressed for success"!
- •For a great tasting, sour-cream-like dip, use less water and let it sit for several hours until it becomes thickened. You'll love it!

That's Italian! Dressing

Makes 2 1/2 Cups

Blend until very smooth and creamy:

- ☐ 2 C .... Water
- ☐ 1 C .... Raw sunflower seeds[14]
- ☐ 1/4 tsp .... Celery seed
- ☐ 3 tsp .... Onion powder
- ☐ 1 tsp .... Garlic powder OR 1 clove fresh
- ☐ 1/2 C .... Lemon juice
- ☐ 1 tsp .... Salt

- •While blending above ingredients, slowly add 1/4 to 1/2 C olive oil (optional).
- •After blending is complete, add:

  - ☐ 1 Tb ....Parsley
  - ☐ 2 tsp ....Basil

- •Chill and serve!

SERVING SUGGESTIONS

- •This is one of our richer recipes, so I make it a special treat.
- •It is delicious over any salad, and also tastes great over steamed broccoli, cabbage, or green beans.
- •Try it in sandwiches instead of mayonnaise for a real taste treat!
- •Don't miss trying this as a dip for a raw veggie plate. Your friends will be begging you for the recipe!
- •We even enjoy this dressing on a baked potato, or over steamed red potatoes with cooked carrots and cabbage for an Irish treat.

Viva La French Dressing

Makes 4 Cups

Blend until very smooth and creamy:

- ☐1 .... 12 oz can tomato paste
- ☐2 tsp .... Onion powder
- ☐1 tsp .... Garlic powder OR 1 clove fresh
- ☐2 Tb .... Honey
- ☐1/3 C .... Olive oil OR 1/2 C Raw cashews[13]
- ☐1 tsp .... Salt
- ☐1/3 - 1/2 C .... Lemon juice (the more the tangier)
- ☐2-3 C .... Water, or to desired consistency

> •Chill after blending.
> •That's it!

SERVING SUGGESTIONS

- •This dressing is delightful not only for salads, but also as a dressing for raw vegetable plates.
- •I love to use it in the place of ketchup in sandwiches, or as a topping for haystacks. It tastes "eiffel" good over steamed broccoli or cabbage, too.

Sun Seed Dressing

Makes 3 Cups

Blend until very smooth and creamy:

- ❑1 C .... Cooked brown rice or millet
- ❑1 C .... Raw sunflower seeds[14]
- ❑1 tsp .... Dill weed
- ❑1 tsp .... Salt
- ❑1-2 cloves .... Garlic
- ❑1 tsp .... Onion powder
- ❑1/4 C .... Lemon juice

> •Blend until creamy with less water for thick mayonnaise.
> •Blend with more water for salad dressing thickness.

SERVING

SUGGESTIONS

- •This dressing is delightful not only for salads, but also as a dressing for raw vegetable plates.
- •An excellent topping over baked potatoes and Burger Delight (See Entrees).
- •This is also a great spread on bread with Perfect Patties (See Entrees) or other sandwich stuffers.
- •It's great for a spread in your pita pocket sandwiches, too.
- •Try it over hot asparagus, broccoli or cauliflower. Either form, thick or thin, is great!

Golden Salad Dressing

Makes 2 Cups

Blend until very smooth and creamy:

- ☐ 1/2 C .... Extra virgin olive oil
- ☐ 1/4 C .... Lemon juice
- ☐ 2 Tb .... Honey
- ☐ 1 Tb .... Chick-it Seasoning[4]
- ☐ 1 .... Onion, medium-small, cut in pieces
- ☐ 1 C .... Water, or more, for desired consistency.

SERVING SUGGESTIONS

- Chill in refrigerator.
- This dressing is delightful not only for salads, but also as a dressing for raw vegetable plates.
- Delicious drizzled over shredded, raw savoy cabbage.
- Great drizzled into a vegetable-tofu stuffed pita pocket for a take-away lunch.
- Tasty over steamed Brussels sprouts, asparagus, broccoli, or cabbage.
- This makes a lovely dip for artichokes, too.

Sunny Salad Dressing

Makes 2 Cups

Blend until very smooth and creamy:

- ☐ 1 C .... Water
- ☐ 2/3 C .... Raw sunflower seeds[14]
- ☐ 1/2 tsp .... Salt
- ☐ 1 tsp .... Onion powder
- ☐ 1/2 tsp .... Garlic powder OR 1 clove fresh
- ☐ 1/8 tsp .... Thyme
- ☐ 1 tsp .... Basil
- ☐ 3 Tb .... Lemon juice (or more, for more tang)

SERVING SUGGESTIONS

- •Chill in refrigerator.
- •This dressing is delightful not only for salads, but also as a dressing for raw vegetable plates.
- •It's very light and delicious.
- •This recipe is adapted from the Country Life cookbook.

Superior Sour Cream

Makes 1 1/2 Cups

- ☐ 1 C .... Raw cashews[13]
- ☐ 1 C .... Well-cooked rice
- ☐ 1 tsp .... Dill weed
- ☐ 1 tsp .... Salt
- ☐ 1/2 tsp .... Chick-it Seasoning[4]
- ☐ 1 1/2 tsp .... Onion powder
- ☐ 1 tsp .... Garlic powder
- ☐ 4-5 Tb .... Lemon juice

- •Add just enough water to blend.
- •Blend until very creamy.
- •Chill.

SERVING SUGGESTIONS

- •This is great with pretzels or on potatoes or sandwiches.
- •It's absolutely fantastic as a raw vegetable dip.
- •My husband loves this on his French fries, too!

Marvi-whip Mayonnaise

Makes 3 Cups

*B*lend until very smooth and creamy:

- ❑ 2 C .... Soft tofu[18]
- ❑ 2 Tb .... Nutritional yeast flakes[10]
- ❑ 1 tsp .... Salt
- ❑ 1/4 C .... Lemon juice
- ❑ 1 tsp .... Onion powder
- ❑ 1/2 tsp .... Garlic powder OR 1 clove fresh
- ❑ 1/3 C .... Olive oil OR raw cashews[13]
- ❑ 1/4 C .... Water, if using cashews in place of oil

- • To make a creamy Italian dressing, just add 1/2 tsp EACH of dill weed, basil, and Italian seasoning.
- • For a tangy dip or salad dressing, add 1 tsp dill weed.
- • Chill and serve.

SERVING SUGGESTIONS

- • This delightful, light mayonnaise is delicious on salads or as a dip for raw veggies. You can also use it as a great topping for steamed asparagus, artichokes, cabbage, or broccoli.
- • We love it over Mexican beans, on haystacks, or as a taste-tempting topping over baked potatoes with a sprinkle of dill and chopped scallions.
- • Try it also as a sandwich spread, or as a filling in pita bread. It is even good as a topping for many savory casseroles such as those made from rice, lentils, or garbanzo beans.
- • Try a dollop in the center of our Cuban Black bean stew or other hearty bean soup for a tart accent.

Kwick Country Ketchup

Makes 1 1/2 Cups

- ☐ 1 .... Small can, tomato paste
- ☐ 1 tsp .... Salt
- ☐ 3 Tb .... Olive oil
- ☐ 3 Tb .... Lemon juice
- ☐ 2 Tb .... Honey
- ☐ 1/2 tsp .... Garlic powder OR 1 clove fresh
- ☐ 1 tsp .... Onion powder
- ☐ 1/2-3/4 c .... Water

- • Place ALL ingredients in a container and stir very well.
- • Place in refrigerator.
- • Eat!
- • Now, that's quicker than going to the store to buy some!

SERVING SUGGESTIONS

- • Put some on your next batch of Healthy Hashers (see Breakfasts).
- • You'll love this recipe! It stores in the refrigerator nicely.

Miracle Mustard!

Makes 2 Cups

- ❑ 1 pound .... Tofu[18] (soft)
- ❑ 2 Tb .... Lemon juice
- ❑ 1 tsp .... Salt
- ❑ 1 1/2 tsp .... Turmeric
- ❑ 1/2 tsp .... Garlic powder
- ❑ 1/2 tsp .... Paprika

> • **Place ALL ingredients in a blender; blend until smooth.**
> • **Place in a pot and bring to a boil.**
> • **Let cool to set up.**
> • **Add more lemon juice for a sharper mustard taste.**

SERVING SUGGESTIONS

- • This tastes great anywhere you've used mustard in the past.
- • Don't forget to take this one on picnics!

Hey! Hey! Hummus

Makes 3 Cups

- ☐ 2 C .... Cooked garbanzo beans
- ☐ 1/4 C .... Lemon juice
- ☐ 1/3 C .... Sesame tahini[15]
- ☐ 2 tsp .... Garlic powder OR 2 cloves fresh
- ☐ 1 tsp .... Salt
- ☐ 1/2 C .... Water

- Blend ALL ingredients thoroughly.
- If you are using a conventional blender and not a stronger machine like a Bosch or VitaMix, blend recipe half at a time.
- Stop blender and use spatula to stir, if necessary.
- Continue to blend until a creamy consistency.
- Chill.

SERVING SUGGESTIONS

- This is a wholesome, versatile, quick, tasty recipe you'll find yourself using—and eating!—often.
- Stuff it in a pita pocket with alfalfa sprouts, tomato and green peppers for a delicious, nutritious sandwich.
- Put it on baked potatoes with chives and olives.
- Try putting a generous scoop of it on your green salad with chips, carrots, onions, and tomatoes. And don't forget to squeeze some fresh lemon on top.
- It's also delicious as a chip or cracker dip.
- As a variation add these to the above recipe:
  - ☐ 1 stalk Celery, finely diced
  - ☐ 1/4 C Green onion, finely chopped
- Hey! Hey! Hummus anyone?

The Best! Bean Spread

Makes 2 1/2 Cups

- ❏ 1 C .... Pinto beans, cooked, mashed
- ❏ 1/2 C .... Burger Delight (see Entrees)
- ❏ 1/2 C .... Marvi-Whip Mayonnaise (see Dressings)
- ❏ 1/3 C .... Olives, sliced
- ❏ 1 tsp .... Onion powder
- ❏ Salt to taste

- •Mix ALL ingredients well.
- •Chill and use for spread.

SERVING SUGGESTIONS

- •This packs a punch in terms of portability, versatility, and taste.
- •It is a family favorite in pita pockets or in a hollowed French roll, topped with lettuce and mayonnaise (see Dressings).
- •It is also great as a spread on Corn Crackers (see Breads).

Better Butter

Makes 2 Cups

- ❑ 1/2 C .... Uncooked cornmeal
- ❑ 1/2 C .... Shredded, unsweetened coconut
- ❑ 1 tsp .... Salt
- ❑ 2 Tb .... Nutritional yeast flakes[10]
- ❑ 2 C .... Water
- ❑ 1 tsp .... Butter flavor (optional)

- • Place cornmeal, coconut, and water in a small saucepan. Simmer until thoroughly cooked (about 25-30 minutes).
- • Add all other ingredients PLUS 1/4 to 1/3 C more water.
- • Blend until very creamy and smooth.
- • Pour into a sprayed mold and let cool uncovered.
- • When cool, place in the refrigerator until firm. Turn out of dish if desired. Use a butter knife to loosen around the edges.
- • Will last in the refrigerator for about one week.

SERVING SUGGESTIONS

- • This butter is a wonderful alternative to the *udder butter*! It's great on toast, too!
- • Try serving cooked summer squash with a little Seasoned Eatings[20] and Better Butter on top.
- • You can also mix it into rice and top it with Nutritional yeast flakes[10].
- • For a real treat, put it on hot sweet potatoes or on a baked potato with mayonnaise and chives.
- • For a "cheesy" flavor, add 1 Tb of nutritional yeast flakes.[10]
- • For a grrrreat garlic spread, add the nutritional yeast flakes[10] PLUS a clove (or two!) of garlic.
- • If you want a delicious maple spread, simply omit the yeast flakes and add 1 Tb Maple extract and 1/2 C Honey. Your toast will never be the same again!
- • Try pouring it hot, like hollandaise sauce, over vegetables.

Pineapp-ricot Jam

Makes 5 Cups

☐ 1 1/4 C .... Prunes, pitted and dried
☐ 1 C .... Apricots, dried
☐ 1/2 C .... Pineapple, unsweetened, crushed

- Simmer prunes and apricots in enough juice or water to cover fruit.
- Blend with pineapple until smooth and creamy. If you like chunky jam, blend less.

SERVING SUGGESTIONS

• This is a wonderful replacement for regular jam. Use it on toast, hot cereal, waffles, french toast, pancakes, or bread for a nutritious, delicious spread.

Notes

Now, you can safely say...

Cheese

Cracker Barrel Cheddar

Makes 3 Cups

- ☐1/2 C .... Sesame tahini[15]
- ☐1/4 C .... Lemon juice
- ☐4 Tb .... Nutritional yeast flakes[10]
- ☐1/2 C .... Pimiento
- ☐1 1/2 tsp .... Salt
- ☐1 tsp .... Onion powder
- ☐1/2 tsp .... Garlic powder
- ☐3 Tb .... Emes unflavored gelatin[6], dissolved in 1/2 C cold water

- •Bring an additional 1/2 C water to a boil.
- •Place ALL ingredients, including the gelatin and boiling water, into a blender.
- •Blend thoroughly, until mixture is smooth and creamy.
- •Pour into a sprayed mold and refrigerate. A small bread pan works great for a mold.
- •When thoroughly chilled and set, turn out onto a dish.
- •Slices and melts well.

SERVING SUGGESTIONS

- •This cheese is delicious melted on toast, vegetables, rice, or noodles.
- •A dollop over steaming black beans or chile beans is a mouth-watering taste treat!
- •Enjoy it in sandwiches or tortillas.
- •It is also delicious frozen, then grated on pizza, enchiladas, burritos, manicotti, or nut loafs.

All-Star American Cheese

Makes 2 1/2 Cups

*B*lend until smooth and creamy:

- ☐ 1/2 C .... Pimiento *or 8 oz. Tomato Sauce*
- ☐ 1/2 C .... Unbleached, white flour
- ☐ 1/2 C .... Nutritional yeast flakes[10]
- ☐ 1 C .... Water *1/4 cup*
- ☐ 3 Tb .... Sesame tahini[15] *+ 1/4 cup Sunflower Seeds*
- ☐ 2 Tb .... Lemon juice *3 T.*
- *1/2* ☐ ~~1 1/2~~ tsp .... Salt *1 t. Onion powder*
  1/2 t. Garlic powder

- •Pour into a small coated bread pan.
- •Bake at 350° for 30 minutes, or until firm-looking in the center. *use little toaster-oven*
- •It will settle and firm as it cools.
- •Refrigerate.
- •When cold, run knife around outer edges of pan and turn cheese out onto a serving plate.
- •Slice before serving.

SERVING SUGGESTIONS

- •This is my son's favorite cheese. He loves to roll it up in steamed corn tortillas with shredded lettuce and Marvi-whip Mayonnaise (Dressings and Spreads).
- •Try this cheese in your sandwiches or on crackers.
- •Sometimes I bake it with 1/2 C of sliced olives for a real tasty treat!

Tangy Cheese Sauce

Makes 3 Cups

- ❏ 1 C .... Water
- ❏ 2 Tb .... Sesame seeds (optional)
- ❏ 3 Tb .... Nutritional yeast flakes[10]
- ❏ 1/2 C .... Pimiento
- ❏ 2-4 Tb .... Lemon juice
- ❏ 3/4 C .... Raw sunflower seeds[14]
- ❏ 1 1/4 tsp .... Salt
- ❏ 1/2 tsp .... Garlic powder OR 1 clove fresh
- ❏ 1/4 C .... Rolled oats
- ❏ 1/2 tsp .... Dill weed

Do not use Vita Mix !!!

- •Blend the oats and seeds until powdery.
- •Add ALL other ingredients and blend until very smooth.
- •Put into saucepan and heat until thick, stirring constantly.

SERVING SUGGESTIONS

- •We love this cheese over regular potatoes, or in potatoes au gratin.
- •It's also great in sandwiches, and in a macaroni and cheese casserole.
- •Try it over rice, broccoli, pinto beans, or on tortillas, tacos, or crackers
- •We also love this cheese over cornbread and garnished with chopped onions and olives for an easy, cheesy main dish.
- • For a milder flavor, use equal parts sunflower seeds and raw cashews[13].

Creamy Cheese Sauce

Makes 3 Cups

*B*lend in blender:

- ❏ 1 C .... Water
- ❏ 3/4 C .... Raw cashews[13]
- ❏ 3 T .... Sesame tahini[15]
- ❏ 1 1/4 tsp .... Salt
- ❏ 4 Tb .... Nutritional yeast flakes[10]
- ❏ 2 tsp .... Onion powder
- ❏ 1/2 tsp .... Garlic powder
- ❏ 1/4 tsp .... Dill weed
- ❏ 1/2 C .... Pimiento
- ❏ 3-4 Tb .... Lemon juice

- • Pour into a saucepan and thicken over medium heat, stirring constantly.
- • Serve.

SERVING SUGGESTIONS

- • This cheese makes a wonderful topping for tortilla chips, rice, potatoes, or other dishes calling for cheese sauce.
- • It makes a wonderful filling with beans in tortillas or burritos!
- • Try it over steamed broccoli or cauliflower, too.
- • Use your imagination—then, use your tastebuds!

Chickee Cheese Spread

Makes 4 Cups

Blend in blender:

- 2 C .... Garbanzo beans, cooked
- 1/2 C .... Cashews, raw[13]
- 2 Tb .... Sesame tahini[15]
- 2 tsp .... Onion powder
- 1 1/2 tsp .... Salt
- 1/4 C .... Lemon juice
- 1/4 C .... Nutritional yeast flakes[10]
- 1/2 C .... Pimientos
- 1 tsp .... Garlic powder OR 1 clove fresh garlic
- 1 1/2 - 2 C .... Water (just enough to blend to thick consistency)

- Grind cashews in blender.
- Then add ALL other ingredients and blend with enough water to make it creamy and thick.
- If you are using a regular blender, do this recipe half at a time to ensure proper blending consistency.
- If using canned garbanzo beans, rinse first, and use 1/2 tsp less salt.
- Place in a container and chill.
- Serve.

SERVING SUGGESTIONS

- This one is great in sandwiches, burritos, or tortillas.
- Use it just like you would any other spread cheese.
- You've got to try this one on pizza, or baked on top of a pita bread with lightly steamed veggies on top!
- This is definitely one of our favorite cracker spreads.

Dream Cream Cheese

Makes 5 1/2 Cups

½ Recipe

- ☐ 2 C .... Blanched almonds
- ☐ 2 Tb .... Emes gelatin[6], unflavored
- ☐ 2 tsp .... Salt
- ☐ 2 Tb .... Lemon juice
- ☐ 3 1/2 C .... Boiling water

> • **Blend until very creamy and smooth.**
> • **Pour into bowl and chill until set.**

SERVING SUGGESTIONS

- If you like bagels, you'll LOVE them now! This is the perfect spread for them.
- Try speading this one in celery for a wonderful, wholesome appetizer.
- Use it to top a baked potato along with cream cheese, chives, and nutritional yeast flakes[10] for a wonderful, delicious, nutritious meal.

Beautiful

Bread

& Crunchy Crackers!

Nice-n-lite Bread or Rolls

Makes 5 Loaves

❑ 5 C .... Warm water
❑ 3 Tb .... Dry, active yeast
❑ 1/2 C .... Honey
❑ 1/3 C .... Molasses
❑ 2 Tb .... Salt
❑ 3/4 C .... Oil
❑ Whole wheat flour*
❑ White, unbleached flour*

(*You will use approximately 1/2 to 2/3 of a 5-pound bag of whole wheat flour and about 1/3 of a 5-pound bag of white flour.)

- Heat 3 C of water in a saucepan until very hot.
- Put molasses, honey, salt, oil, 4 C whole wheat flour, and 1 C white flour in a large bowl. Add hot water and stir well.
- Dissolve yeast in 2 C warm water and let stand for a few minutes.
- Add yeast mixture to large bowl and stir into flour.
- Add more wheat and white flour a little at a time until you cannot stir mixture with a spoon anymore.
- Begin kneading the dough with your hands, alternately sprinkling wheat and white flour, continuing to knead until the dough is elastic and firm, only slightly sticky, and springs back to the touch—usually takes about 10 minutes.
- I knead my dough right in the large bowl, or you can knead it on an oiled countertop.
- Be careful not to add too much flour at one time. Just keep sprinkling to keep it from being sticky so you can knead it. The proportion of wheat to white flour should be either 2/3 wheat to 1/3 white, or 3/4 wheat to 1/4 white, depending on how light you like your bread.
- Now, rub the lump of dough with some oil, place it in a large bowl, and cover with a cloth. Let the dough rise for 90 minutes in a warm room—DO NOT use a heated oven!

(Continued on the next page.)

- **NO cheating. Let it rise the full time—this conditions the dough.**
- **Remove the cloth and punch the dough down.**
- **Pre-heat oven to 350° (Important!)**
- **FOR BREAD, divide dough into 5 equal part, shape into loaves, and let rise in sprayed, 1-pound pans for 15-20 minutes, or until dough has risen about 1/2" to 1" above the pan.**
- **Bake for 50 minutes.**
- **FOR ROLLS, divide dough evenly into 4 lumps anduse a rolling pin to roll out each lump one at a time into a circle about 3/4 of an inch thick.**
- **Using a small mason jar lid ring, press out circle in dough, and place rolls side by side on sprayed cookie sheets. Let them rise until double in size—about 15-20 minutes.**
- **Bake for 30-35 minutes, until golden brown on the bottom. If using more than one oven rack, switch rolls to different rack every 10 minutes.**
- **Slip the rolls off the cookie sheets and let them cool on a rack.**

Jewish Caraway

❑Follow bread recipe above, but add:
❑1/2 C .... Caraway seeds
❑1/2 C .... Raw sunflower seeds

Other Variations

As you become more skilled in breadmaking, add other grains in small amounts (1/4 to 1/2 C measurements), like soy flour, cornmeal, 7-grain cereal, flax, etc. You'll discover some great-tasting—and very wholesome!—combinations!

Pumpernickel, Please!

Makes 2 Loaves

*M*ix together:

- ❑ 1 1/2 C .... Warm water
- ❑ 1/2 C .... Molasses
- ❑ 4 tsp .... Salt
- ❑ 1-3 Tb .... Caraway seed (optional)
- ❑ 2 Tb .... Oil
- ❑ 3 Tb .... Yeast

*S*tir until yeast is dissolved, then mix in:

- ❑ 3 1/2 to 4 C .... White flour
- ❑ 2 C .... Rye flour, coarse OR
- ❑ 2 3/4 C .... Regular rye flour

- • **Make a stiff dough, and let stand for 10 minutes.**
- • **Knead until smooth, usually about 10 minutes..**
- • **Let rise until doubled in size.**
- • **Punch down and divide into two loaves.**
- • **Sprinkle cookie sheet with cornmeal.**
- • **Cover with damp cloth and let rise about 45 minutes.**
- • **Brush lightly with cold water.**
- • **Bake 10 minutes in 450° oven, then 350° for 30 minutes.**

SERVING SUGGESTIONS

- • This is delicious with any of our spreads or dressings.
- • Make it into rolls for easy freezing and for using to make quick, easy lunch items.
- • It's great toasted with a little Better Butter (see Spreads) for breakfast or for a light supper.

Basic Muffin Mix

Makes 10 Muffins

Combine and let stand 5-8 minutes:

- ❑ 2 C .... Warm water
- ❑ 2 Tb .... Honey
- ❑ 1 1/2 Tb .... Dry yeast

Then add and mix well.

- ❑ 2 Tb .... Oil
- ❑ 1 tsp .... Salt
- ❑ 3 C .... Whole wheat flour
- ❑ 1/2 C .... White flour

> •Spray muffin tins and fill 2/3 full with batter. Can also
>   drop by spoonfuls onto sprayed cookie sheets if desired.
> •Let rise 10 minutes, and bake at 350° for 30-35 minutes.
> •Or place in sprayed 8" X 8" bread pan and let rise for
>   15 minutes and bake at 350° for 45-50 minutes.

SERVING

SUGGESTIONS

- •This recipe is quick, easy, and the variations listed on the next page make this a very versatile recipe.
- •These muffins freeze well, thaw quickly, and soften nicely when re-heated.
- •We're very thankful to JoAnn Rachor, author of *Of These Ye May Freely Eat* cookbook (it's one of my all-time favorites!) for this great recipe.

See muffin variations on next pages:

Muffin Variations

Use the BASIC MUFFIN MIX just as it is along with any of these variations. When recipe reads to leave out certain items, this pertains to the BASIC MIX recipe.

Jam Muffins

❑ 3/4 C .... Pine-apricot Jam or other fruit jam
❑ After filling muffin tins, drop 1 tsp jam on top of batter; let it rise as usual

Cornbread Muffins

❑ 1 3/4 C .... Cornmeal
❑ 3/4 C .... White flour
❑ 1 Tb .... Oil
(Use 1/2 C less water & 2 1/2 C less whole wheat flour)

Your Choice Muffins

Can make this with cranberries, carrots, zucchini, or apples!

❑ 1/2 C .... Honey
❑ 1/2 C .... Chopped nuts
❑ 1 1/2 tsp .... Coriander
❑ 1 1/2 tsp .... Dried orange peel
❑ 1 1/2 C .... Cranberries, briefly blended OR
   2 C .... Either Zucchini OR grated apple
                        OR grated carrot
(Use 1/2 C less water for the cranberry muffins and 3/4 C less water for the apple or zucchini muffins.)

Variations continued on next page:

Muffin Variations

Raisin-Orange Muffins

- ☐ 3/4 C .... Raisins
- ☐ 1 Tb .... Dried orange peel

Date-Bran Muffins

- ☐ 1/2 C .... Oat or wheat bran
- ☐ 2/3 C .... Dates, chopped

Blueberry Muffins

- ☐ 1 1/2 C .... Blueberries
- ☐ 1 tsp .... Vanilla
- ☐ 1/4 C .... Honey or other sweetener
  (Use 1/2 C less water)

Pineapple Muffins

- ☐ 1 .... 20-oz. can, pineapple, crushed, drained
- ☐ 1 tsp .... Vanilla
- ☐ 2 Tb .... Honey or other sweetener
  (Use 1/2 C less water)

Banana-Nut Muffins

- ☐ 2 C .... Banana, mashed
- ☐ 1/2 C .... Walnuts, chopped
  (Use 2/3 C less water)

 *Used by permission from* Of These Ye May Freely Eat *cookbook by JoAnn Rachor. Thanks JoAnn, for letting us share this favorite with our friends!*

Country Corn Muffins

Makes 10 Muffins

Blend until very smooth and creamy:

- ❏ 2 C .... Soaked soy beans[16]
- ❏ 1 tsp .... Salt
- ❏ 2-3 Tb .... Honey
- ❏ 2 C .... Water

Pour into a bowl and add:

- ❏ 3/4 C .... Cornmeal (regular, NOT self-rising)

> - **Stir and mix well. Then spoon into sprayed muffin tins, or into a 9-inch sprayed casserole dish or iron skillet.**
> - **Bake at 350° for 35-45 minutes, depending on what baking dish you're using.**
> - **Muffins should be brown on the sides and sound hollow to the tap when done.**
> - **DO NOT overbake!**

SERVING SUGGESTIONS

- This cornbread is delicious hot, right out of the oven, and served with beans or soup of any kind. We love to crumble the cornbread right on top of the soup!
- When baking in the iron skillet, just place it—skillet and all—right on the table for a festive feast your family will favor!
- We eat this cornbread as a main meal with Tangy Cheese Sauce (recipe in Cheese section) and chopped olives and onions on top. We also enjoy it covered with beans and Marvi-Whip Mayonnaise (see Dressings).
- Try it in a sack lunch with fruit, or crumbled hot in a bowl with Creamy Cashew Milk (recipe in Breakfast section) and peaches.

Delicious Corn Bread

Makes 10 Slices

- ☐ 2 C .... Cornmeal
- ☐ 1 1/2 C .... Unbleached white flour or oat flour
- ☐ 1 C .... Whole wheat pastry flour
- ☐ 2 Tb .... Soy flour (optional)
- ☐ 1 1/2 tsp .... Salt
- ☐ 1/4 C .... Oil
- ☐ 2 1/2 C .... Warm water
- ☐ 1 Tb .... Dry yeast
- ☐ 2 Tb .... Honey

> • Mix all DRY ingredients EXCEPT YEAST thoroughly.
> • Mix water, honey and yeast in separate bowl.
> • Let yeast rise 10 minutes. Then stir into flour mixture.
> • Pour into a sprayed iron skillet and bake at 350° for 40 minutes, or until golden brown and hollow to the tap.

ET RISE 15 MIN.
N PAN.
TURN OVEN ON
TO 400° HERE
THEN TO 350° TO BAKE

SERVING SUGGESTIONS

- • This cornbread is great served with any of our beans or entrees.
- • It is delicious crumbled on top of soup, or even lightly over a salad.
- • Crumble onto the bottom of a bowl and top with hot beans or spaghetti sauce for a real Mediterranean treat.
- • It's great with Better Butter (see Spreads) for breakfast, along with any scrambled Tofu recipe (see Breakfasts).

Corn Crackers

Makes 24 Crackers

*B*lend:

❑ 1 1/4 C .... Water
❑ 1 1/2 Tb .... Sesame tahini
1/2 t. ❑ ~~1 1/2~~ tsp .... Salt
❑ 3 Tb .... Nutritional yeast flakes[10]
❑ 1/2 C .... Cashews, raw[13]
❑ 1 Tb .... Coconut
❑ 1 tsp .... Garlic powder
❑ 1 tsp .... Onion powder

*W*hen smooth and creamy, ADD:

❑ 1/2 C .... Water
❑ 1 1/4 C .... Corn meal

• Blend briefly to mix.
• Pour onto sprayed cookie sheets with edges.
• Bake at 350° for 20 minutes.
• Score (lightly slice with a sharp knife into cracker-sized squares) and return to oven for 40-45 minutes.

SERVING SUGGESTIONS

• These crackers are fabulous with any of our soups, beans, or spreads.
• They "travel" well and are great for picnics.
• Use them for dips with fresh veggie sticks and Hey! Hey! Hummus (see Spreads) or any of our cheeses (see Cheeses).

Holiday Stuffing

Makes 15 Cups

- ☐ 2 loaves .... Light wheat bread, 1-pound size
- ☐ 1 .... Onion, chopped
- ☐ 4 stalks .... Celery, diced
- ☐ 1/3 C .... Chick-it seasoning[4]
- ☐ 1 Tb .... Sage
- ☐ 1/3 C .... Olive oil
- ☐ 3 Tb .... Parsley
- ☐ 1 1/2 C .... Chopped walnuts, pecans, or combination of both
- ☐ Salt to taste
- ☐ 4-5 C .... Water

- •Pinch bread loaves apart into small pieces. Let dry in a 150° oven for a few hours on cookie sheets or in a large roasting pan. Toss occasionally and continue to dry until no moisture can be felt in bread.
- •Pour the dry crumbs into a large bowl and add the chopped nuts.
- •Sauté the onions and celery in a little water.
- •Add all other seasonings, oil, and water to make a broth, and simmer for 10 minutes.
- •Cool broth for 20 minutes, then pour over bread and nut mixture, tossing lightly until well moistened and evenly damp.
- •Bake at 300° in a covered 9" X 13" casserole dish for about 40 minutes or until slightly crusty on the sides and well heated.

SERVING SUGGESTIONS

- •Put stuffing into your mouth, not into a turkey!
- •Top stuffing with the gravy of your choice, and serve with mashed potatoes, cranberry sauce, greens, and pumkin pie for a wonderful thanksgiving meal! And don't wait until November—you can be thankful now for such a wonderful, wholesome bounty.

Delicious Desserts

Oatmeal Raisin Cookies

Makes 40 Cookies

Not good!
Terrible!
Too hard!

- 1/2 C .... Honey
- 1 Tb .... Molasses
- 1/2 C .... Oil
- 1 Tb .... Vanilla
- 1 tsp .... Salt
- 1/2 tsp .... Lemon extract (optional)
- 1/2 C .... Soy milk
- 3/4 C .... Chopped walnuts
- 3/4 C .... Raisins, soaked in hot water (drain water)
- 2 1/2 C .... Quick oats
- 1/4 C .... Whole wheat flour
- 1/4 C .... Unbleached white flour

- In one bowl, beat together first seven ingredients.
- Mix remaining dry ingredients in another bowl.
- Combine liquid and dry ingredients, then stir together well.
- Let sit for 10 minutes or so to firm up.
- Drop by 2 Tb portions (1/8 C) onto sprayed cookie sheet.
- Flatten slightly and shape.
- Bake at 350° for 25 minutes.

SERVING SUGGESTIONS

- These cookies freeze well and are great for lunchboxes, picnics, birthdays, and any other special occasions.
- I like to crumble one over a smoothie (see Miscellaneous) for a great dessert or a light supper.
- This recipe is adapted from a Country Life cookbook recipe.

Date Apple Cookies

Makes 50   1 Tb Cookies

- ☐ 1 C .... Dates
- ☐ 1/2 C .... Water
- ☐ 1 C .... Apples, shredded, unpeeled
- ☐ 1/2 C .... Chopped nuts (walnuts, pecans, or other)
- ☐ 1/2 tsp .... Salt
- ☐ 1 tsp .... Vanilla
- ☐ 3 C .... Rolled oats
- ☐ 1/2 C .... Unsweetened coconut[19]

- **Cook dates in water in a small saucepan and mash with a fork.**
- **Add remaining ingredients and MIX together.**
- **Drop by tablespoons on a lightly sprayed cookie sheet.**
- **Bake at 375° for 25 minutes.**

SERVING SUGGESTIONS

- These cookies taste absolutely wonderful! But the best part is that they don't contain any damaging baking soda or baking powder!
- They're great for packing in lunches.
- They freeze well, so make a big batch and always have some on hand!

Nut Sandies

Makes 60 Cookies (8 per cup)

- ☐4 C .... Oat flour (blend enough oats for 4 C)
- ☐2 C .... Nut meal (grind pecans, or walnuts, cashews, brazil nuts, etc., until fine meal)
- ☐1 C .... Honey
- ☐1/2 C .... Oil
- ☐1/4 C .... Water with 1 Tb cornstarch dissolved in it
- ☐1/2 tsp .... Salt
- ☐2 Tb .... Vanilla

- • Mix flour and nut meal.
- • Mix liquid and dry ingredients together.
- • Let the dough sit for 10 minutes. It should be just firm enough to shape into balls with wet hands. Add flour or water as needed for proper consistency.
- • Roll into balls and place on sprayed cookie sheet. Bake for 20-25 minutes at 350° or until lightly browned.
- • Remove carefully from the cookie sheet to cool. They will be soft when you remove them, but will harden as they cool.

SERVING SUGGESTIONS

- • These cookies are a special treat for picnics, camping trips, and school lunches. They're delicious, and they don't fall apart easily.
- • During the holidays, get your young ones in the kitchen, give them the dough and some cookie cutters, and let them create-a-cookie! They'll love it!
- • The dough is easy to work with, and you can even make words or pictures with it for a beautiful edible centerpiece at any special occasion.
- • See next page for several variations that will make this recipe even "sweeter"!
- • Thanks to Joy Cafaro for sharing this recipe!

Nut Sandies Recipe Variations:

Jambos

Make recipe as usual. Form into balls. Place on a sprayed cookie sheet. Press thumb into the center of each cookie before cooking and fill the hole with the jam of your choice.

Candy Canes

Replace vanilla with peppermint extract if desired. Roll and shape dough into candy cane shapes. Bake. When cool, use a thin paint brush to paint stripes on the canes. Use food coloring or water from cooked beets.

Carob Coconut Balls

Follow basic recipe, substituting coconut instead of nut meal. Replace 2/3 C of oat flour with carob powder. No vanilla is needed. Form into balls and bake as usual.

Stuffed Dates

Stuff dates with walnut pieces. Using basic recipe, surround date with dough and bake.

Try other variations like cashew meal and anise, almond meal and maple extract, or sesame seed and orange extract. Use your imagination—then use your tastebuds!

Peanut Butter Cookies

Makes 40 Cookies

Cream together:

- ☐ 1 C .... Peanut butter
- ☐ 1 1/4 C .... Honey OR maple syrup
- ☐ 1/2 C .... Oil
- ☐ 3/4 tsp .... Salt
- ☐ 1 1/2 tsp .... Vanilla

Add and mix well:

- ☐ 1 C .... Whole wheat flour
- ☐ 1/2 C .... Oat flour
- ☐ 1/2 C .... Unbleached white flour
- ☐ 4 Tb .... Corn starch

- •Form into cookies; bake on sprayed cookie sheets at 350°
  for 10-15 minutes, until light brown.
- •Will harden as they cool.

SERVING SUGGESTIONS

- •If you want the kids to have some special fun BE-FORE they eat these cookies, just add enough flour to make rollable dough. Then roll it out and give them all some cookie cutters! They'll have a ball!
- •This recipe is adapted from a recipe in the Ten Talents cookbook.

Haystack Cookies

Makes 80 Cookies (8 per cup)

- ☐ 2/3 C .... Peanut butter
- ☐ 1/2 C .... Quick oats
- ☐ 4 C .... Coconut
- ☐ 1 tsp .... Salt
- ☐ 1 1/2 C .... Chopped nuts
- ☐ 2/3 C .... Honey
- ☐ 2 C .... Dates, softened and chopped
- ☐ 2/3 C .... Flour
- ☐ 2/3 C .... Cold water

- • Mix ALL ingredients together and place by spoonfuls onto sprayed cookie sheet.
- • Bake at 350° for 20-25 minutes.

- • This cookie recipe is quick, easy, nutritious and delicious for picnics and office or school lunches.
- • Great for a quick dessert option, too!

Brazil Nut Cookies

Makes 40   1/8 C cookies

- ☐ 1 1/2 C .... Brazil nuts, ground
- ☐ 3 C .... Oats, ground
- ☐ 1/2 C .... Coconut
- ☐ 1 1/2 tsp .... Salt

Cream together in a small bowl:

- ☐ 1/2 C .... Oil
- ☐ 3/4 C .... Honey
- ☐ 2 tsp .... Vanilla
- ☐ 3/4 tsp .... Lemon extract

- • Mix DRY ingredients together thoroughly. Cream liquids together well and add to dry ingredients.
- • Spoon onto a sprayed cookie sheet and bake at 350° until golden brown around the edges.
- • Let cool for 10 minutes before removing from cookie sheet.

SERVING SUGGESTIONS

- • These cookies are perfect for school or work lunches.
- • It's fun for kids to use cookie cutters with this recipe, too. Just add more flour if needed to make firmer dough.
- • Of course they're great for holiday desserts or family picnics.

Great Granola Bars

Makes 18 Bars

☐ 4 1/2 C .... Quick oats, or combination of regular and quick
☐ 1/2 tsp .... Salt
☐ 1 Tb .... Vanilla
☐ 1/2 C .... Oil
☐ 1/2 C .... Honey
☐ 2 Tb .... Molasses
☐ 1/2 C .... Nuts, finely chopped
☐ 1/2 C .... Dried fruit, finely chopped

- **Put ALL ingredients into a bowl and mix together well.**
- **Place into a sprayed 9" X 13" baking dish.**
- **Press down evenly and firmly with hands or metal spatula.**
- **Bake at 400° for 15 minutes.**
- **Reverse dish in oven and bake another 5 minutes, making sure the bars do not burn.**
- **Cool completely before cutting.**

SERVING SUGGESTIONS

- You can add various combinations of fruits and nuts to make several wonderful different bars. Try combining:
    - Apricots and walnuts OR
    - Dates and walnuts OR
    - Pecans and apples OR
    - Raisins and almonds

- This recipe is adapted from a Country Life cookbook recipe.

Nutty Carob Fudge Balls

Makes 25 Fudge Balls

- 2 C .... Brazil nuts
- 1/2 C .... Sesame tahini[15]
- 1/2 C .... Honey
- 1/3 C .... Carob powder[3]
- 1/2 tsp .... Salt
- 1 tsp .... Vanilla
- 1/2 tsp .... Peppermint flavoring

- **Blend brazil nuts until ground well.**
- **Empty ground nuts into bowl and ALL other ingredients.**
- **Mix together well and roll into 1/8 C balls.**
- **Place on wax paper and freeze.**
- **Thaw a few minutes before serving.**

SERVING SUGGESTIONS

- These freeze well and are lovely after a light meal.
- They pack well in a lunchbox and are great to take on a campout or a hike.
- Give these as a reward to the children for a job well-done—and look forward to more well-done jobs in the future!
- This recipe is adapted from a Country Life cookbook recipe.

Carob Nut Brownies

Makes 12 Servings

Cream together:

- 1 C .... Honey
- 4 Tb .... Oil
- 1 Tb .... Vanilla
- 2 tsp .... Lemon juice
- 2 Tb .... Soy milk powder
- 1 1/2 tsp .... Grated orange or lemon rind

Add and mix:

- 2/3 C .... Carob powder[3]
- 1/2 C .... Oat flour
- 1/2 C .... Unbleached white flour
- 1 C .... Walnuts, chopped

- • Pour into a sprayed medium-sized cake pan.
- • Bake in 350° oven for 35-40 minutes.
- • When cooled, cover with Carob Peanut Butter Icing (see Desserts) if desired.

SERVING

SUGGESTIONS

- • This is a really fun birthday treat!
- • They're delicious crumbled over Desert Date Smoothies (see Miscellaneous) for a really sensational taste treat!
- • These freeze well so make a big batch and have them handy!
- • This recipe is adapted from a recipe in Ten Talents cookbook.

Banana Nut Cake

Serves 12

Dissolve in a small bowl:

- ❑ 1/2 C .... Warm water
- ❑ 2 Tb .... Honey
- ❑ 2 Tb .... Dry yeast

In another bowl mix:

- ❑ 1/3 C .... Honey
- ❑ 1 Tb .... Vanilla
- ❑ 1/2 C .... Oil
- ❑ 4 .... Bananas, large, ripe

Add yeast mixture, which has begun to double, then blend in :

- ❑ 3/4 C .... Whole wheat flour
- ❑ 3/4 C .... White flour
- ❑ 1 C .... Walnuts, chopped
- ❑ 2 tsp .... Salt
- ❑ 1 C .... Raisins

- • Place in sprayed baking pan and let rise until double in size.
- • Cover and bake at 375° for 15 minutes, and then at 325° for 30-40 minutes.
- • Frost with Carob Peanut Butter Icing (see Desserts) or Coconut Frosting (see Desserts) when cooled, if desired.

- • This cake freezes well and is delightful baked in a bundt pan.
- • Try serving it with Christmas Fruit Salad (see Salads) for a wonderful holiday (or non-holiday!) treat.
- • Makes into great little cupcakes. Just spray your tins and bake for 35 minutes.

Date Nut Cake

Serves 12

Mix well in a bowl:

- ❑ 1/2 C .... Orange juice
- ❑ 1/3 C .... Dates, blended with enough hot water to make it smooth
- ❑ 2 tsp .... Vanilla
- ❑ 2 Tb .... Oil
- ❑ 1/2 tsp .... Salt
- ❑ 1/2 C .... Unbleached white flour
- ❑ 1/2 C .... Whole wheat flour
- ❑ 2 C .... Dates, chopped
- ❑ 2 C .... Walnuts, coarsely chopped

> • **Spoon into small sprayed loaf pan or bundt pan.**
> • **Bake at 350° for 45-60 minutes.**
> • **Serve with Lemon Sauce topping (recipe in this section).**

• See Serving Suggestions for Banana Date Nut Cake on previous page.

That's Nice! Spice Cake

Serves 12

- ☐ 1 1/2 C .... White, unbleached flour
- ☐ 1 C .... Whole wheat flour, sifted
- ☐ 1 tsp .... Salt
- ☐ 1 tsp .... Coriander
- ☐ 1 C .... Raisins
- ☐ 1/2 C .... Chopped walnuts
- ☐ 1 1/2 tsp .... Orange peel
- ☐ 3 Tb .... ENER—G[7] baking powder

Cream together in a small bowl:

- ☐ 1/2 C .... Oil
- ☐ 3/4 C .... Honey or sorghum
- ☐ 1 Tb .... Maple extract
- ☐ 1 Tb .... Vanilla
- ☐ 1/2 C .... Orange juice

- • Mix ALL ingredients together thoroughly.
- • Bake at 350° in a sprayed cake dish until done, about 35-40 minutes.
- • Cake will be cooked when a toothpick inserted in the middle comes out clean, with no cake sticking to it.
- • When cool, frost with maple or coconut frosting.

SERVING SUGGESTIONS

- • This is a great-tasting cake. It's great for birthdays as well as holidays.
- • For cupcakes, try pouring the batter into sprayed muffin tins and baking for 30 minutes or until golden brown.
- • This is a great one for packed lunches, camping trips, or for special gifts!

Carob Cake

Makes 20 Slices

*B*lend in blender:

❑ 1 C .... Water
❑ 1/2 C .... Oil
❑ 1 C .... Honey
❑ 1 tsp .... Vanilla
❑ 1/3 C .... Carob powder[3]

*P*our blended ingredients into bowl and add:

❑ 2 C .... Flour (Fresh ground whole wheat
                          flour makes a real difference, but half
                          white and half wheat works well, too.)
❑ 3 Tb .... ENER-G[7] baking powder

> •Place ALL ingredients into a sprayed medium-sized cake pan.
> •Bake in 350° oven for 25 minutes.
> •DO NOT overbake!

Icing on the Cake!

❑ 1 C .... Honey
❑ 3 Tb .... Oil

*B*ring to boil, then add:

❑ 1 1/2 C .... Toasted coconut
❑ 1 C .... Chopped walnuts

> •Cook ingredients for 1/2 minute after boiling.
> •Spread hot on carob cake.
> •Let cool before serving.

Thanks to Louise Killian for sharing this recipe.

Blueberry Cheesecake

Makes 2 pies

*P*repare two *Granola Crunch pie crusts:*

- ☐ 2 1/4 C .... Tofu[18], silken, extra firm, rinsed
- ☐ 1 20 oz. can ...... Pineapple chunks, well drained
- ☐ 1 3/4 C .... Banana chunks
- ☐ 1/4 C .... Honey
- ☐ 1 3/4 tsp .... Vanilla
- ☐ 1/2 tsp .... Salt

> • Place ALL ingredients in blender and blend until smooth and creamy.
> • Pour blended ingredients into pie crust.

*B*lueberry glaze:

- ☐ 2 C .... Blueberries (need 2 C more later)
- ☐ 1/4 C .... Honey
- ☐ 3 Tb .... Cornstarch
- ☐ 1/8 tsp .... Salt
- ☐ 1/2 C .... Water

> • Blend well in blender.
> • Pour into saucepan and cook over medium heat until thick, stirring constantly until thickened.
> • Remove from heat and ADD 2 C additional blueberries.
> • Fill pre-made Granola Crunch Crust (see Desserts) with the cheesecake filling.
> • Top with blueberry glaze and chill.

SERVING SUGGESTIONS

- • Be sure and use silken to avoid beany flavor.
- • Just try to find a better cheesecake—Anywhere!
- • Thanks, Cindy Gonzalez, for sharing this great recipe with us!

Pineapple Tofu Cheesecake

Makes 1 regular-sized pie

Soak:

- ☐ 3 Tb .... Emes[6] kosher gelatin (unflavored)
- ☐ 1/2 C .... Cold water

Place in blender:

- ☐ 3/4 C .... Pineapple juice
- ☐ 1/2 C .... Cashews
- ☐ 3/4 C .... Drained pineapple chunks
- ☐ 1/4 tsp .... Salt
- ☐ 1/4 tsp .... Maple extract
- ☐ 1/3 C .... Honey
- ☐ 1 tsp .... Lemon rind
- ☐ 2 C .... Tofu[18], silken, extra firm, rinsed
- ☐ 1/2 C .... Pineapple juice, heated

- •Add Emes mixture to blender ingredients.
- •Blend until very smooth and creamy.
- •Pour into pre-baked pie shell (recipe on next page).
- •Chill and serve.

SERVING SUGGESTIONS

- •This is a lovely light dessert which goes well with entrees like pizza, soups, and beans.
- •Packs well in a thermos for lunch.
- •Keep refrigerated.
- •Try topping with fresh kiwi slices, fresh strawberries, or blueberries.
- •Be sure to use the silken tofu so it won't have a beany flavor.

Crust recipe on next page.

The Crust
Pineapple Tofu Cheesecake

Blend:

- ☐ 1/2 C .... Walnuts
- ☐ 1 1/2 C .... Seven grain flakes OR granola
- ☐ 1/3 C .... White flour
- ☐ 1/2 tsp .... Coriander
- ☐ 1/2 tsp .... Salt
- ☐ 2 tsp .... Date sugar[5] OR Sucanat

Pour above ingredients, when blended, into bowl and add:

- ☐ 1/4 C .... Water

• Press into sprayed pie pan.
• Bake in 350° oven for 10 minutes, or until brown.

SERVING SUGGESTIONS

• This crust is nice for our lemon pies or for the carob pie.
• Another quick, delicious crust option is Granola Crunch pie crust (this section).

Simply Silky Cheesecake

- ☐ 2 pounds .... Tofu[18], silken, extra firm, rinsed
- ☐ 1/2 C .... Honey
- ☐ 1 Tb .... Lemon juice
- ☐ 1 tsp .... Lemon extract
- ☐ 1 tsp .... Lemon rind
- ☐ 2 Tb .... Eme's gelatin[6], dissolved in 6 Tb hot water
- ☐ Pinch of salt

- •Place ALL ingredients in a blender.
- •Blend until smooth and creamy.
- •Pour into pre-baked Granola Crunch OR Tropicana Pie Crust (see Desserts).
- •Chill and top with cold, thickened Festive Fruit Topping (see Desserts).
- •Refrigerate at least two hours before serving.

SERVING SUGGESTIONS

- •If you like cheesecake, you'll love this!
- •Be sure to use the silken tofu, so it won't have the beany flavor regular tofu can produce.

Fifth Avenue
Carob Cream Pie

*B*lend until very smooth and creamy:

- ❏ 1 C .... Water
- ❏ 1/2 C .... Raw cashews[13]
- ❏ 1 tsp .... Vanilla
- ❏ 1/2 tsp .... Salt

*A*dd and continue to blend:

- ❏ 1 C .... Pitted dates, softened in 1 C water (add both dates and water)
- ❏ 3 Tb .... Cornstarch
- ❏ 3 Tb .... Carob powder[3]
- ❏ 1 Tb .... Postum OR Roma[12] (optional)

- • **Pour into saucepan and thicken, stirring constantly.**
- • **Pour thickened mixture into baked Coconut Blizzard pie crust or Granola Crunch pie crust (see Desserts).**
- • **Chill and serve.**

SERVING SUGGESTIONS

- • This pie filling is delicious layered with granola and sliced bananas for a special breakfast treat.
- • It is also splendid layered with chilled Dreamy Cream Whip (recipe in this section) in a parfait glass, with a strawberry on top, or a few carob chips.
- • Try using this filling to top a dish of fresh strawberries for a real taste treat.

Lemon Chiffon Pie

Blend until very smooth and creamy:

- ❑ 1 1/2 C .... Pineapple juice
- ❑ 1/3 C .... Honey
- ❑ 1 Tb .... Orange juice concentrate
- ❑ 1 tsp .... Vanilla
- ❑ 1/4 tsp .... Salt
- ❑ 1/3 C .... Cornstarch
- ❑ 1/4 C .... Lemon juice
- ❑ 1 Tb .... Grated lemon rind

- •Cook over medium heat until thick. Keep stirring, don't let it burn or scorch.
- •Let it sit at room temperature for 10 minutes.
- •Mix in 1 C "Dreamy Cream Whip," (see Desserts).
- •Pour into a baked pie shell and chill.
- •Top with coconut or with more "Dreamy Cream Whip."

SERVING SUGGESTIONS

- •Use this in the same ways as Lemon Velvet Pie (recipe on the next page).

Lemon Velvet Pie

Blend until smooth and creamy:

- ☐ 1 .... 20-oz. can, pineapple, sliced, crushed, or chunk (with juice)
- ☐ 1/2 C .... Water
- ☐ 1 .... Medium orange, peeled and cut into little pieces (remove ALL seeds)
- ☐ 6 Tb .... Cornstarch
- ☐ 6-7 Tb .... Honey
- ☐ 1/2 tsp .... Lemon extract
- ☐ 4-6 Tb .... Lemon juice

> - Pour into a saucepan and thicken over medium heat.
> - Pour into baked Granola Crunch pie crust (see Desserts).
> - Top with coconut or carob chips as an added treat, or a dollop of Dreamy Cream Whip (see Desserts).
> - For an extra lemony taste, add 1 tsp of Lemon peel while blending the ingredients.
> - Chill and serve.
> - NOTE: Be certain to remove ALL the orange seeds. If you don't, the pie will taste very bitter.

SERVING SUGGESTIONS

- This pie filling is very delicious and extremely versatile. You can serve it in parfait cups layered with chilled Dreamy Cream Whip (see Desserts) and a peppermint sprig or a lemon wedge.
- I love to layer it in a cake pan with granola and sliced bananas.
- Try it as a topping over fresh fruit or granola, or even over waffles with fresh strawberries and coconut cream.
- Dress up your morning's hot millet cereal by pouring this pudding right on top. And add some fresh blueberries or peaches, too. Your kids will look forward to this breakfast.

Strawberry Pie

Makes 1 9" Pie

Have ready:

- ☐ 1 .... Granola Crunch Pie Crust, baked (see Desserts)
- ☐ 1 1/2 C .... Dreamy Cream Whip (see Desserts)
- ☐ 1 1/2 qt .... Fresh strawberries, or enough to mound in a pie dish
- ☐ 1/2 C .... Frozen White grape / raspberry juice concentrate (100% juice)
- ☐ 1/2 C .... Water
- ☐ 3 Tb .... Cornstarch

> • Dissolve cornstarch in water. Add juice concentrate and thicken in a saucepan.
> • Set aside and allow to cool to room temperature.
> • When cool, fold in fresh strawberries and pour into cooled crust.
> • Top with Dreamy Cream Whip (see Desserts).
> • Serve chilled.

SERVING SUGGESTIONS

- • A delightful light supper with one of our popcorn or nacho recipes (see Miscellaneous).
- • This is great for a fruit lunch with granola or a nut butter sandwich lunch away from home.

Pleasing Pumpkin Pie

Makes 2   9-inch pies

- ❏ 3/4 C .... Raw cashews[13]
- ❏ 1 1/2 C .... Soy or other milk
- ❏ 3 1/4 C .... Pumpkin OR 1 29-oz. can of solid pack, unflavored pumpkin
- ❏ 3 Tb .... Molasses
- ❏ 3/4 C .... Maple syrup
- ❏ 3/4 tsp .... Salt
- ❏ 3 tsp .... Coriander
- ❏ 1 Tb .... Vanilla
- ❏ 1/4 C .... Cornstarch

- • Blend first two ingredients on high until creamy.
- • Add ALL remaining ingredients and blend until very smooth. May have to blend in two batches.
- • Pour into unbaked Perfect Pie Crust (recipe in this section) and bake at 350° for one hour or until pie is set in center.

SERVING SUGGESTIONS

- • This filling is delicious made without crust, in muffin tins as a light custard dessert.
- • This pie freezes well and is a nice addition to any lunch, main meal, or supper.
- • This recipe is adapted from a Country Life cookbook recipe.

Carob P-B Icing

☐1/2 C .... Water
☐1/3 C .... Carob powder[3]
☐1/4 C .... Water
☐3/4 C .... Dates, blended with hot water until
                        smooth and thick
☐2/3 C .... Peanut or almond butter
☐1 tsp .... Vanilla
☐1/2 tsp .... Salt

- **Put first two ingredients in a saucepan and cook, stirring constantly until thickened.**
- **Remove from heat.**
- **Add ALL remaining ingredients and mix together well, adding more blended dates or peanut butter to thicken if needed.**

SERVING
SUGGESTIONS

- This recipe is nice on carob fudge brownies and is delicious even as a spread on toast, crackers, or waffles.
- This recipe is adapted from a recipe in the Country Life cookbook.

Coconut Blast Frosting

Makes 1 1/4 Cups

Blend until very smooth and creamy:

- [ ] 1 C .... Water
- [ ] 3/4 C .... Unsweetened coconut[19]
- [ ] 1 Tb .... Cornstarch
- [ ] 1/4 tsp .... Salt
- [ ] 3 Tb .... Honey

> • **Pour blended ingredients into a saucepan and thicken, stirring constantly.**
> • **Allow to cool before using.**

SERVING SUGGESTIONS

- You talk about a delicious frosting! This is one of the best you'll ever find! It can be used as a substitute for any of the Dreamy Cream Whip (see Desserts) serving suggestions, and is also delicious on cakes and cupcakes.
- I love it as a frosting for carrot cake, or layered with waffles and partially thawed frozen strawberries for the most delicious strawberry shortcake you can find—ANYWHERE!
- Don't let your kids lick the spoon every time—you enjoy it, too!

Dreamy Cream Whip

Makes 3 C (24 1 Tb servings)

*B*lend until very smooth and creamy:

- ☐ 2 pounds .... Tofu[18], extra firm, silken, rinsed
- ☐ 1/3 C .... Oil
- ☐ 2 Tb .... Vanilla
- ☐ 2/3 C .... Honey OR maple syrup
- ☐ Pinch salt

> • Put ALL ingredients into blender and blend.
> • Add SMALL amounts of water IF necessary while blending to keep mixture moving in blender.
> • Chill and enjoy!
> • Be certain to use silken tofu to avoid beany flavor.

SERVING SUGGESTIONS

- • This whipped treat is for special occasions and is superb on any pie, spooned on top of fruit salad cups, or even on a bowl of piping hot multi-grain cereal for a creamy, dreamy treat!
- • Try this spread as the crowning touch on Golden Waffles (see Breakfasts), smothered with fresh, juicy strawberries.
- • You can also try it over waffles and strawberries to make a luscious, delicious strawberry shortcake! Just layer waffles, berries and cream as high as you want. Oh, does that make me hungry!

Lemon Dream Cream

2 pounds .... Tofu[18], extra firm, rinsed
1/2 C .... Honey
1 Tb .... Lemon juice
1 tsp .... Lemon extract
1 tsp .... Lemon rind

- Place ALL ingredients into a blender.
- Blend until smooth and creamy.
- Chill and serve.

SERVING SUGGESTIONS

- This topping is sensational over our lemon pies.
- It is delicious as a topping over banana nut bread.
- Try it over a fresh fruit salad, or over steamed brown rice with fresh strawberries, bananas, and blueberries for a sweet breakfast treat.
- Try layering it with granola and our Pineapple Cream Pudding (see Breakfasts).

Lemon Sauce

*Blend together, pour into saucepan and bring to boil,
then simmer until thickened and clear in color:*

- ❑ 1 C .... Pineapple juice
- ❑ 1 .... Pinch, salt
- ❑ 2-3 Tb .... Cornstarch

Remove above from heat, then add:

- ❑ 3 Tb .... Lemon juice
- ❑ 1/2 tsp .... Lemon extract
- ❑ 1 Tb .... Honey

> • **Delicious on cakes, cereal, or fruit.**

SERVING SUGGESTIONS

- • This lemon sauce is delicious over banana nut bread or carrot cake (see Desserts).
- • I also enjoy this over steamed brown rice topped with fresh blueberries, strawberries, or sliced bananas for a tangy breakfast treat.
- • Try dizzling this one over a fresh fruit platter for an elegant flair!
- • Adapted from Country Life cookbook.

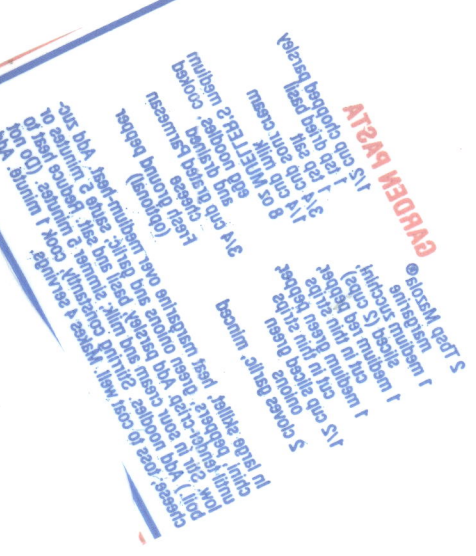

Perfect Pie Crust

Makes 2 9" or 1 12" Crust

Mix together in a bowl:

½ ❑1 C .... Whole wheat pastry flour
/ ❑1/2 C .... White flour
❑1/2 C .... Oat flour (blend oats in blender)
❑1 tsp .... Salt

Beat with a fork in a separate bowl:

❑1/3 C .... Oil
❑1/2 C .... Hot water
❑1 Tb .... Lecithin granules or liquid (optional)

- Beat, oil, water, lecithin in a bowl.
- Mix dry ingredients in a separate bowl. Add liquid ingredients to dry; pouring slowly into the middle of the flour and mixing lightly with a fork. DO NOT overmix or the dough will be tough.
- Rub a damp cloth on top of the counter and cover a 12" to 14" area with plastic wrap. Place half the dough in the center of the plastic wrap.
- Cover with another layer of plastic and roll with rolling pin to desired size and shape.
- Remove the top layer of plastic wrap and place pie pan upside down in center of dough.
- With one hand on the pie pan, put your other hand between the counter top and the plastic wrap under the dough, and flip dough & pie pan right side up.
- Press into shape in pan and flute edges.
- For pre-baked shells, prick dough with fork and bake at 350° for 20 minutes.

Serving suggestions are on the next page.

SERVING

SUGGESTIONS

- This crust is delicious and flexible for many recipes. It can be used in many ways, including pot pie crust, pumpkin pie crust, danish pastry dough, crackers, quiche crust, and double pie crusts for apple or peach pies (see recipes for exact instructions).
- Don't give up if it doesn't turn out just the way you want it to the first time you make it. Just be patient.
- Be sure you use HOT water.
- The real key is light, thorough mixing and learning the proper consistency of the dough.

Granola Crunch Pie Crust

☐ 1 1/2 C .... Granola
☐ 2 Tb .... Oil (or water)
☐ Pinch of salt

• Grind granola in a blender.
• Put granola in a bowl and add all ingredients.
• Sprinkle with more water if needed to moisten.
• Mix with a fork, adding a little more water if necessary.
• Press into pie plate with fingers.
• Bake at 350° for 10-15 minutes, or until firm and crusty.
• Try finding ANY other pie crust that's this simple—and this tasty!
• Use ONLY with pre-cooked fillings.

SERVING SUGGESTIONS

• Our easiest and most versatile pie crust.
• I use it for any of my uncooked pies and sprinkle left over crust on top of the pies for a nice flair.

Coconut Blizzard Pie Crust

☐ 1 C .... Unsweetened coconut[19]
☐ 2 Tb .... Cornstarch

• Mix with fork in a sprayed pie dish, adding just enough water or "nut milk" (recipes in miscellaneous), usually about 3 Tb, to hold it together. Press into pie dish firmly with hands.
• Bake at 375° for 10 minutes, or until crust is a light, golden brown.

SERVING SUGGESTIONS

• You can serve this pie crust with any type of pre-cooked filling. It tastes absolutely wonderful, too. And you can mix it up so fast you won't believe it. Try it soon. It will become your hands-down favorite!

Festive Cranberry Mold

Makes 12   1/2 C Servings

☐ 6 Tb .... Emes kosher gelatin[6] dissolved in 1 C raspberry or cherry /white grape juice concentrate
☐ 1 C .... Boiling water
☐ 1 1/2 C .... Chopped, raw cranberries
☐ 3/4 C .... Firm pear, diced into small pieces
☐ 2 .... Oranges, chopped, with seeds removed
☐ 2 .... Apples, finely chopped with skins (Red delicious taste wonderful!)
☐ 2/3 C .... Broken walnuts

- Mix ALL ingredients.
- Pour into sprayed mold and let chill for several hours.
- Salad will become firm, but will not turn out as a free-standing mold.
- Leave in mold and serve.
- This one is truly DELICIOUS!

Yule Fruit Salad

Makes 20 1/2 C Servings

- ☐ 2 .... Granny Smith apples
- ☐ 2 .... Jonagold or Gala apples (crisp / yellow)
- ☐ 5 .... Kiwi
- ☐ 1/2 tsp .... Almond extract
- ☐ 3 C .... Strawberries, fresh or frozen
- ☐ 1 recipe .... Dreamy Cream Whip (recipe in this section)
- ☐ 2/3 C .... Unsweetened coconut[19], shredded

- **Slice strawberries while frozen and place in glass serving bowl.**
- **Add peeled, sliced kiwi.**
- **Cut apples into bite-sized pieces and add to bowl.**
- **Mix well.**
- **Fold almond extract into whiped topping (see Desserts) and fold topping into fruit mixture.**
- **Sprinkle shredded coconut on top.**
- **Chill and serve.**

SERVING SUGGESTIONS

- This is great with Jambo cookies ^{p. 169} (recipes in this section) for a wonderful Christmas dinner.
- Try it with popcorn for a delightful, delicate dinner.
- For a special breakfast treat, try it over waffles or pancakes!
- This is a great tasting thermos filler for the office or school lunch box. It will calm the nerves and satisfy the tummy!

Caramel Corn Crunch

- ☐ 4 qts .... Popcorn (popped)
- ☐ 1/2 C .... Date sugar[5] **OR** Turbinado sugar
- ☐ 1/4 C .... Pure maple syrup **OR** molasses
- ☐ 1/2 tsp .... Salt
- ☐ 1/4 C .... Oil
- ☐ 1/2 tsp .... Vanilla
- ☐ 2 C .... Peanuts

NOT GOOD!

- •Mix ALL ingredients in a large bowl.
- •Place on sprayed cookie sheets.
- •Bake at 350° for 25-30 minutes.

SERVING SUGGESTIONS

- •What a wonderful treat this one is! It's great for a lunch box surprise, or a dessert for a special-occasion meal.
- •This is a favorite picnic desert.

Chick-it Seasoning

Blend:

- ☐ 1/4 C .... Salt
- ☐ 1/2 C .... Nutritional yeast flakes[10]
- ☐ 1/4 - 1/2 tsp .... Turmeric
- ☐ 1/2 - 1 tsp .... Garlic powder
- ☐ 1 Tb .... Onion powder
- ☐ 1/2 tsp .... Marjoram
- ☐ 1/2 tsp .... Sage or Summer savory[17]
- ☐ 1 Tb .... Parsley

> • **Blend thoroughly to a powder-like consistency.**
> • **Store in a sealed container in the refrigerator.**

SERVING SUGGESTIONS

- • This is an excitotoxin-free seasoning.
- • It is great in any of your recipes that call for chicken-like seasoning or chicken broth.
- • You can use it to season soups, sauces, gravies, burgers, loafs, or other savory dishes.
- • Keeps very well in the freezer, so make up a double recipe!

Seasoned Eatings! (Vegetable salt)

Blend in blender:

- ❏ 1/4 C .... Salt
- ❏ 1/3 C .... Nutritional yeast flakes[10]
- ❏ 1/4 tsp .... Oregano
- ❏ 1/4 tsp .... Garlic powder
- ❏ 1/2 tsp .... Onion powder
- ❏ 2 Tb .... Parsley
- ❏ 1/4 tsp .... Basil
- ❏ 1/8 tsp .... Dill weed
- ❏ 1/4 tsp .... Sage

- **Blend thoroughly to a powder-like consistency.**
- **Store in a sealed container in the refrigerator, or pour into a salt shaker with large holes in the cap. Store in a cool, dry place.**
- **Add or subtract herbs in this recipe to your own liking.**

SERVING SUGGESTIONS

- This is an excitotoxin-free seasoning.
- It's the perfect seasoning for salads—just sprinkle it on and add some lemon juice and Chick-it Seasoning[4].
- Use it just like you would any vegetable salt.
- It really adds the perfect flavor to vegetables, soups, and gravies.
- Try this to replace the salt in your popcorn, too!

Presto! Popcorn

*P*op enough popcorn to make 12 cups, and then:

- ❏ Place popped corn in a paper bag
- ❏ Drizzle in 3 Tb olive oil
- ❏ Shake well

*S*prinkle in:

- ❏ 1 Tb .... Nutritional yeast flakes[10]
- ❏ 2 tsp .... Chick-it[4] seasoning **OR** Vegetable salt[20]
  OR Salt to taste

> • **Shake bag thoroughly again.**
> • **Pour into a large serving bowl and enjoy!**

SERVING SUGGESTIONS

- • *Popcorn makes a great complement to a light fruit supper, and packs well in a lunch with your choice of sandwiches.*
- • *To keep fresh, store in plastic bags in the freezer*
- • *Try this popcorn as a delicious side dish for soups, chowders or beans*

*S*ee Mexican popcorn recipe on next page!

'M 'M Mexican Popcorn

*P*op enough popcorn to make 12 cups, then place in a large bowl and add:

❑ 3 Tb .... Tahini (Add 1 Tb at a time, tossing with hands before adding more tahini.

*S*prinkle on:

❑ 2 tsp .... Chick-it seasoning[4] OR salt to taste
❑ 1 Tb .... Nutritional yeast flakes[10]
❑ 1 tsp .... Cumin OR to taste
❑ 1 tsp .... Paprika
❑ 1 tsp .... Onion powder
❑ 1/2 tsp .... Garlic powder

- Toss with hands until seasonings are blended in well.
- Season to your taste—add more seasonings for a stronger tasting popcorn.
- This is a delicious recipe!

SERVING

SUGGESTIONS

See suggestions for Presto! Popcorn.

Nachos N' Cheese

❑ 1-2 bags .... Baked corn chips
❑ 1 recipe .... Cracker Barrel Cheddar Cheese (see Cheeses)

- Arrange chips on a cookie sheet in a single layer.
- Preheat oven to 400°.
- Lay cheese slices on top of chips and place in oven until melted.
- May broil for a minute or two to brown chips.

SERVING SUGGESTIONS

- This recipe is great with any of our bean dishes, and a nice juicy watermelon for dessert.
- We enjoy Nachos with fresh fruit for a light lunch or supper too!
- Try topping with chopped green onions and olives before you bake. Then add one of our salsas (See Sauces) for an easy, savory meal.

Desert Date Smoothie

Makes 6-7 Cups

- 1/3 C .... Date pieces
- 1/2 C .... Pecan pieces
- 1/3 C .... Milk powder (soy, rice, or other)
- 2 C .... Frozen bananas
- 2 C .... Ice
- 1 Tb .... Vanilla or maple extract (optional)
- 2 C .... Water

> • This recipe is designed for the Vita-mix Total Nutrition Center. For other blenders, simply process half of recipe at a time.
> • Grind nuts and dates, then add ALL other ingredients and blend until thick and smooth.

SERVING SUGGESTIONS

- This smoothie is even better than the date shakes I enjoyed as a girl at the Indio Date Festival in California. But this recipe doesn't cause the allergies, mucous, and other undesirable side effects that dairy-based shakes can.
- Enjoy this smoothie in a tall, frosty glass or pour it over a waffle, French toast, or granola on a hot summer day. (See Breafasts.)

Berry Blast Smoothie

Makes 6-7 Cups

☐ 2 C .... Frozen strawberries, blueberries, or cherries
☐ 1/4 C .... 100% juice concentrate, tropical blend OR orange juice concentrate
☐ 1 C .... Ice
☐ 1 C .... Frozen bananas
☐ 2 C .... Water
☐ 1/4 C .... Milk powder (soy, rice, or other), optional

- **This recipe is designed for the Vita-mix Total Nutrition Center. For other blenders, simply process half of recipe at a time.**
- **Blend ALL ingredients until thick and smooth.**

SERVING SUGGESTIONS

- Enjoy this smoothie in a tall, frosty glass or pour it over a waffle, French toast, or granola. (See Breakfasts.)
- It's a favorite treat of children on a hot summer day.
- It's a delicious alternative to sherbet or very sweet sorbets.

Banana Smoothie

Serves 3

*B*lend until very smooth and creamy:

- ❏ 2 .... Bananas, frozen
- ❏ 1 C .... Pineapple, crushed, with juice (chunk is OK, too)
- ❏ 6 .... Strawberries, frozen

> • Blend ingredients until they are thick like a milk shake.
> • Add more pineapple juice if the mixture is too thick and will not "turn" in the blender.
> • When the smoothie is the right thickness, pour it into glasses and top them with a frozen strawberry or other frozen fruit, and a mint leaf.
> • Always make enough for seconds—no one will refuse!

SERVING SUGGESTIONS

- • For some variety, instead of the 6 frozen strawberries, use frozen peach slices, or frozen blueberries, or...well, you get the picture, right?
- • Whatever you use with this recipe, it will always be a refreshing, smooth treat on a hot summer day! It's very nutritious because it's SUGAR free, and filled with fiber, vitamins, complex carbohydrates, and other wonderful ingredients!
- • Make it early and freeze it before a birthday for a wonderful "ice cream" replacement. Kids love it!
- • It makes a wonderful topping for waffles or pancakes, too.

The following items are a necessity to make your cholesterol-free adventure easier—and successful! (Not to mention tastier!)

Grains & Beans

- ❑ Whole wheat flour
- ❑ Oat, rice, millet, or barley flour
     (Can be made in a blender)
- ❑ Oats
- ❑ Brown rice
- ❑ Split peas
- ❑ Barley
- ❑ Lentils
- ❑ Beans (navy, soy, pinto, kidney, black, garbanzo, etc.)
- ❑ Millet

Seeds & Nuts

- ❑ Cashews
- ❑ Almonds
- ❑ Sunflower seeds
- ❑ Sesame seeds
- ❑ Coconut
- ❑ Walnuts

Dried Fruits & Yeasts

- ❑ Raisins
- ❑ Dates
- ❑ Nutritional yeast flakes[10]
- ❑ Dry, active yeast
- ❑ Dried apricots

Seasonings & Flavorings

- ❑ Oregano
- ❑ Basil
- ❑ Thyme
- ❑ Marjoram
- ❑ Sage
- ❑ Rosemary
- ❑ Garlic powder
- ❑ Onion powder
- ❑ Cardamom
- ❑ Coriander
- ❑ Vanilla extract
- ❑ Maple extract
- ❑ Butter extract
- ❑ Almond extract
- ❑ Fine's Herbs
- ❑ Summer savory
- ❑ Maple syrup
- ❑ Honey

Miscellaneous

- ❑ Crockpot
- ❑ Blender (Vitamix is best)
- ❑ Seed grinder
- ❑ Waffle iron (or two!)
- ❑ Large bowls
- ❑ *WILLING HANDS!*

Yes, it will cost some money to re-stock your kitchen. But remember, once you begin your cholesterol-free cooking adventure, you will save 20-30 percent on your food bill each month! Try re-stocking a little bit at a time—consider it an investment in your future, one that will reap you a healthy return!

Many *people want to have a more wholesome lifestyle but few know where to begin! When it comes to putting tasty, wholesome food on the table or in the lunchbox every day, many throw up their hands in despair and settle for fast, frozen, or nuked!*

What *to do? Where can you find help in planning a menu that you and your family will enjoy—without taking hours to prepare?*

Relax! *This menu guide has been written to help you plan easy, wholesome meals—that will save you time and money in the long run! There's a whole week's menus for breakfasts and light suppers, and 2 week's menus for main meals! Now, do you feel less stress? Just remember, this a menu idea guide to help stimulate your own creativity. Leftovers and lunch-on-the-go ideas are not figured in.*

 *Menu Maps*

Breakfast Bonanza

*H*ave A Nice Day?

*H*ave a nice day...without a good breakfast? Don't count on it! It is very important to start the day off right with a good breakfast.

A good breakfast isn't a cup of coffee, a sip of orange juice, and a cinnamon bun or Danish as you rush out the door to the office!

A good breakfast should include whole grain products such as hot cereals or breads, and lots of fresh fruit.

*H*ere are some ideas to help you start your day hearty...and have a NICE DAY!

✔ Fresh pineapple slices
✔ Kiwi
✔ Apple
✔ Waffle recipe of your choice, topped with:
  • Almond butter
  • Applesauce

✔ Grapefruit
✔ Banana
✔ Grapes
✔ Whole wheat toast with Better Butter
✔ Brazil nuts
✔ Hot 7-grain cereal with fortified soy milk and raisins

✔ Orange
✔ Cantaloupe
✔ Dried figs
✔ Granola with fortified soy milk
✔ Whole wheat muffins with peanut butter and all-fruit jam

Day 4

- ✔ Fresh strawberries or blueberries in season
- ✔ Honeydew melon
- ✔ Tangerine
- ✔ French toast with almond butter and your fresh fruit or Festive Fruit Topping with Dreamy Cream Whip

Day 5

- ✔ Banana
- ✔ Peach (in season)
- ✔ Kiwi
- ✔ Pineapple Cream Pudding
- ✔ Whole grain toast with Better Butter
- ✔ Almonds

Day 6

- ✔ Grapefruit
- ✔ Pear
- ✔ Grapes (any variety)
- ✔ Wheat Treat hot cereal with raisins and fortified soy milk
- ✔ Banana-Nut muffin with Better Butter and applesauce

Day 7

- ✔ Pear
- ✔ Plum
- ✔ Orange
- ✔ Pineapple slices
- ✔ Scrambled Tofu over whole wheat toast, topped with Kwick Country Ketchup
- ✔ Dried figs

Menu Maps

Main Meals

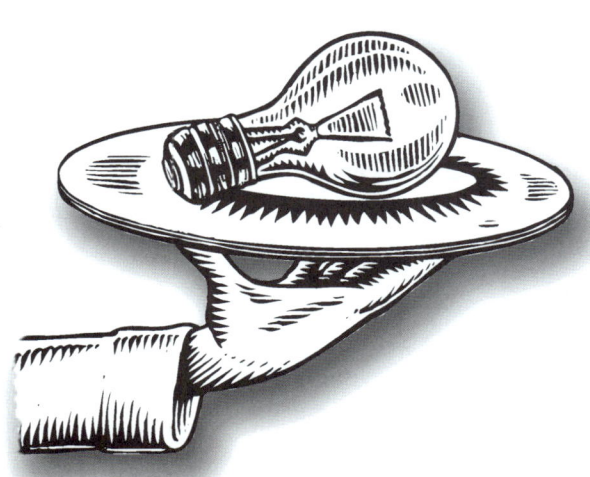

Snap Decisions?

Just as a good breakfast gives you a good start on the day, a good mid-day meal keeps you making those good snap decisions all day long—at home, at school, and at work!

A good mid-day meal isn't a ham and cheese sandwich and a bag of fried corn chips, either! And fast food is not the fuel fast decisions are made of—at least not successful ones!

A good meal should include whole grains, either fruits or vegetables (raw or cooked), green-leaf salads, and other tasty items.

Here are some ideas to help you keep your day hearty...and make those necessary, successful snap decisions! We've included ideas for meals at home—and away from home!

Day 1

- ✓ Tossed leaf lettuce salad with Tahini Dressing
- ✓ Persian Lentil Stew
- ✓ Corn crackers

Day 2

- ✓ Raw vegetable plate (carrot sticks, olives, celery sticks, bell pepper strips, raw cauliflower pieces)
- ✓ Marvi-Whip Mayonnaise for dip
- ✓ Macaroni and Cheese, Please!
- ✓ Steamed broccoli

Day 3

- ✓ Italian-style coleslaw
- ✓ Big Smack sandwich
- ✓ Greek-style Green Beans
- ✓ Garden salad

Day 4

✔ Tossed green salad
✔ Savory Boquet Dressing
✔ Brown rice topped with Peanut Gravy
✔ Oatmeal cookies

Day 5

✔ Raw carrot and celery sticks
✔ Tahini Tang Dressing
✔ Steamed collards
✔ Baked potato topped with Burger Delight and
✔ Marvi-Whip Mayonnaise

Day 6

✔ Shredded Savoy cabbage with lemon juice,
  olive oil, and Seasoned Eatings on top
✔ Chow-down Chili Beans
✔ Cornbread muffins with Better Butter
✔ Steamed green beans

Day 7

✔ Tossed green salad
✔ That's Italian dressing
✔ Pizzaz Pizza!
✔ Lemon Velvet Pie

We know you're busy at home and at work, and need as many meal ideas as possible. So, because we appreciate your confidence, we decided to give you a bonus—another 7 days worth of great-tasting, brain-boosting, less-stress, disease-disabling recipes! Enjoy!

BONUS Day 1

✔ Raw vegetable platter (carrot sticks, tomato slices, avocado slices, raw broccoli spears)
✔ Savory Boquet Dressing for dip
✔ Steamed corn
✔ Garden Gourmet Quiche

✔ Tossed green salad
✔ Tahini Tang Dressing
✔ Steamed kale
✔ Potato Corn chowder
✔ Whole wheat muffins or rolls

✔ Italian-style coleslaw
✔ Spaghetti
✔ Garlic bread
✔ Steamed peas

✔ Haystacks
✔ Steamed collards

Day 5

✔ Tossed green salad
✔ Totally French Dressing
✔ Suddenly...Soup!
✔ Corn crackers
✔ Carob Fudge Balls

Day 6

✔ Raw vegetable platter (zucchini and cucumber slices, cauliflower spears, red bell pepper strips, olives)
✔ Tahini Tang Dressing
✔ Brown rice topped with Tasty Tofu Neatballs and spaghetti sauce
✔ Steamed broccoli

Day 7

✔ Tossed salad
✔ That's Italian! Dressing
✔ Egg Shamwiches
✔ Steamed beets

Turn the page for some GREAT lunch-on-the-go ideas!

 *Menu Maps*

Pauper's Supper

Cultural...Or Natural?

Now that the hard part of your day is over, it's time to eat a big, delicious meal, right? WRONG! What are you going to do for the rest of the day? Very little, usually!

A big evening meal is cultural—not natural! The fact is, studies are now revealing that if you want to stay thin and healthy, your evening meal should be the smallest of the day!

A large evening meal, among other things, can reset your body clock, making it harder for you to go to sleep at night, and can add excess weight very quickly—even when you're eating all the right food!

Here are some ideas for an evening meal—if you even have one at all! Remember: if you do eat, be sure it's at least 2 hours before you plan to go to bed.

Day 1

✔ Popcorn
✔ Fruit salad

Day 2

✔ Cream of Spinach Soup
✔ Corn muffins

Day 3

✔ Berry Blast Smoothies over Granola

Day 4

✔ Toasted waffle pieces with applesauce
✔ Fresh fruit

Day 5

✓ Tomato Rice Soup
✓ Corn crackers

Day 6

✓ Mock Salmon loaf, mayonnaise, lettuce, and cucumber slices on whole wheat bread

Day 7

✓ Nachos n' Cheese
✓ Carrot sticks

*H*ere's an easy way to remember your daily meal plan:

Eat breakfast like a King
Eat lunch like a Queen
Eat supper like a pauper...

OR

Eat a breakfast of Gold
Eat a lunch of Silver...
Because your supper will be LEAD!

Brown Bag Buffet

Great Ideas for Lunch-on-the-go!

Tip 1 When I pack a sandwich, I like to make sure I get my raw veggies, because the vitamins and minerals are great stress-fighters. Raw vegetable consumption not only fights cancer, but magnesium absorption is enhanced, which helps such disorders as fibromyalgia and headache, as well as overall brain function. The fiber fills me up, without making me sleepy from taking in too large a load of carbohydrates. Get what you really need when you are on the go: fresh, fabulous fiber in colorful vegetable wrapping for less stress, more alertness, and a pleasantly satisfying meal!

Tip 2 All breads are not created equal. For best blood sugar control and sustained energy, try whole grain breads that contain multiple grains, and breads that contain cracked grains and seeds. This has been shown to be especially beneficial for diabetics. This type of bread, as free from additives and preservatives as possible, ministers not only to your taste buds, but also to your nervous system, by providing stress-fighting magnesium, vitamins, zinc, and other essential elements!

Tip 3 For maximum alertness, watch the total fat content of the meal. If you have a rich main dish, have a piece of melon or a couple of dates for dessert rather than cookies.

Tip 4 If you begin your meal with a large helping of raw fruits or vegetables, you will reduce the tendency to overeat carbohydrates, which tend to cause sleepiness later in the day.

Tip 5 Drink plenty of water between meals, and don't snack. You will be more alert, have better job performance, and experience better moods. When it is time for lunch, you will be ready and your digestive organs will not be overtaxed from an abusive "boss" who wont give them a break!

Tip 6 Try to pack lunches that focus on a vegetable or a fruit emphasis, which will promote better digestion. Melon, pineapple, and dates are fine with either a fruit or vegetable meal for most people.

Tip 7 Packing your lunch means more time for after-lunch exercise and less time sitting in a car or waiting in line! An invigorating walk, or hiking up a few flights of stairs after your meal will help ward off the midday "slump."

Tip 8 For quick, easy preparation, items like garbanzo beans, black beans, hummus (spelled "humous" on some packages), and lard-free refried beans can be purchased at grocery or health food stores.

Tip 9 Any pita or sandwich lunch is accented very nicely with a hot thermos of vegetable soup, or any of the bean stews, or cream chowders. If you're packing a bean sandwich, fill the thermos with a vegetable soup or cream chowder, not a bean soup!

Tip 10 Any of the main meal ideas in the Menu Maps section can be used all, or in part, for a portable lunch. For example, baked sweet potatoes travel nicely, as do any of the noodle or other casseroles presented in this book. Many of the dishes are good hot or cold. All recipes can be prepared in advance and many items can be frozen. So, use your imagination and experiment!

Pita Pockets & Sandwiches

Pita pockets are so easy to pack and fun to eat. Try to stay with the whole wheat variety. The following pocket fillings all work very nicely in sliced breads or buns, also. You can easily alter these ideas to your personal taste.

Power Pocket: Mix equal amounts of Burger Delight* and refried beans. Moisten with plenty of Marvi-whip Mayonnaise* and add chopped green or black olives. Season with a little salt and onion powder, or chopped onions, if desired. Stuff in a whole wheat pocket and enjoy a side salad, raw veggie plate, or coleslaw.

Persian Pocket: Stuff a pita bread pocket with hummus*, shredded cabbage (savoy is nice), mayonnaise*, green bell pepper slices, and thinly sliced cucumber.

Deep Pocket: Slice a piece of Savoy cabbage about 1/2 inch thick (it will look like a round disk), and drizzle fresh lemon juice on it. Sprinkle with vegetable salt or regular salt, and then drizzle the desired amount of sesame tahini. Slip this into the pita pocket, then layer with lettuce, carrot shreds, red bell pepper slices, and cucumber slices. (Thin purple or white onion slice is a nice addition).

Garden Pocket: Shred carrots and zucchini (and a little yellow crookneck squash if you have it). Then, stir in your favorite dressing (like Marvi-whip mayonnaise*, Totally French Dressing*, or another) or a little olive oil, salt, and lemon. Stuff into a pita pocket or hollowed French roll and add sliced red bell pepper, lettuce, and thinly sliced savoy cabbage. This is great with a little hummus spread inside the bread also!

Veggie-verde: Mash one ripe avacado in a bowl with a fork. Add a little salt, crushed garlic and lemon juice. Stuff a pita pocket or layer a sandwich with this mixture and add thinly shredded cabbage and carrots. If adding tomato to any sandwich, pack it separately and add it just before you eat. You can also layer this with red leaf lettuce, sprouts, and a little raw spinach and sliced cucumber for a refreshing meal.

Beanie Babies: Mash cold, cooked beans or lentils (use any of the recipes in this book) and stuff into your pita pocket. Add mayonnaise*, shredded cabbage or leaf lettuce.

Baked Chicken Tofu Sandwich: Layer desired selection of baked chicken tofu,* thin red bell pepper slices, snow peas, romaine lettuce or bok choy green tops, carrot shreds, and choice of mayonnaise,* catsup,* or mustard.*

American Cheese Salad Sandwich: Layer American cheese* with thin cabbage slice (savoy is best), red or leaf lettuce, raw spinach, thin onion slice, avocado and choice of mayonnaise,* catsup,* or mustard.* (Red or green bell pepper slices optional.)

Burger Break-up: Break up any cold, leftover burgers (i.e. *Country Best Burgers*, *Lentil patties**, or *Perfect Patties**) into bite-size pieces. Mix with tofu mayonnaise and stuff a pita pocket the same way you would use falafel. This also makes a fabulous topping for baked potatoes, steamed rice, or noodles. Surround burger mixture with shredded vegetables of your choice.

Egg Shamwich: Scoop a generous amount of Super Tofu Scramble* into a whole wheat pita pocket or a sandwich, topping with mayonnaise*, lettuce and sprouts. You can substitute cheese* or ketchup* for mayonnaise if desired. Don't forget to tote along a zesty garden salad with raw broccoli on top and a little potato salad!

Big Smack: Using our Country Best Burger* recipe (or any burger recipe in this book), make a sandwich using mayonnaise*, ketchup*, leaf lettuce, sprouts, cheese* of your choice, lemon dill pickles if desired and a whole wheat hamburger bun (or in a stuffed pocket bread).

*See recipe in appropriate section

The holiday season can be a time of happiness, fellowship, refreshment, and spiritual renewal. But all too often the flurry of high-geared activity results in stress, overspending, overindulgence, sickness, and depression. How can we gear the holiday season to maximize mental, physical, and spiritual health, and at the same time enjoy special opportunities for relationships and celebration? Here are some helpful tips:

1 Break with unhealthy holiday traditions.

There are certain holiday traditions which can be stressful and positively damaging to the health. For instance, many people who don't normally drink will consume alcoholic beverages. Alcohol, even in small amounts, compromises brain blood flow and depletes magnesium, a major anti-stress mineral, as well as vitamin C. A syndrome known as "holiday heart" occurs primarily in weekend and holiday drinkers who eat too much and are stressed. This can cause fatal heart irregularities. Fresh fruit juices with spritzer or sparkling water is a nice replacement for the social drink trap.

2 Avoid stressful substances.

Exhausted, stressed people often turn to "quick fixes" in order to deny the body's cry for rest. Drugs, alcohol, cigarettes, caffeine, sugar, and chocolate stimulate the body's stress responses and actually cause an increase in stress hormones and increased "stress-susceptibility." These substances drain the body of B vitamins and key anti-stress minerals which protect the nervous system. These substances act as muscle and nervous system stimulants, that will, after initial excitement, cause fatigue, tension, and depression. Load up on a variety of fresh fruits that are rich in vitamins and flavonoids, and drink soothing herbal teas for that sweet tooth and overstressed nervous system.

3 Plan a healthy holiday meal.

There is no busier place than an emergency room during the holidays. Americans consume far too much fat, cholesterol, sugar, and animal protein. Overindulgence of these substances during the holidays fills ER's with stroke, angina, and heart attack victims. If you can hardly breath, think, or stay awake after a meal, something is wrong—meals should increase mental clarity, energy, and health. During the holidays they do just the opposite. Over long periods these eating patterns are associated with cancer, dementia, and other degenerative diseases. This year, bless your family and friends with a meal rich in fresh, low fat, and whole grain foods. Try a big garden salad with leaf lettuces and raw veggies and a lemon and olive oil dressing, instead of iceberg lettuce and high cholesterol bleu cheese, for instance. And instead of smothering vegetables in meat fat or butter, use lemon juice, crushed garlic, and vegetable salt—and don't forget to serve plenty of stress-reducing greens. Replace white-flour rolls and dairy butter with satisfying whole grain rolls covered with hummus or Better Butter*. Experiment with meatless main dishes. Make desserts like pumpkin pie sweetened with dates instead of sugar. When visiting, limit your choices to a few favorites. Don't eat everything in sight!

4 Don't graze!

Snacking is the enemy of good health. Grabbing quick snacks adds pounds, does not provide meal satisfaction, and overloads the digestive organs. The result is fatigue, lethargy, and elevated insulin levels. People who snack typically do not eat less at mealtime. Take time to eat plenty of fresh fruits and vegetables, whole grains, beans and legumes at regular mealtimes. This will provide meal satisfaction, vitamins, minerals, and the carbohydrates your body needs for time-released energy and better blood sugar control.

5 Take time for exercise and sleep.

Taking just a 10-minute brisk walk will enhance mood for 1 hour, and reduce tension and fatigue. A snack will do just the opposite. Losing just a few hours of sleep in a week can reduce your body's ability to fight disease by 30%. So, plan bedtime into your family's schedule, and stick to it. Remember that good is the enemy of best. You don't have time for everything—but you must make time for sleep!

6 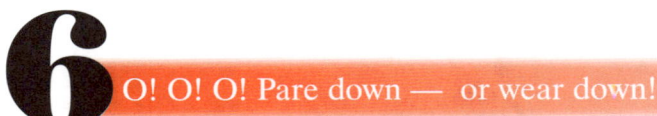 O! O! O! Pare down — or wear down!

Pare down those stress-inducing activities—and determine to cut out— Overeating, Overspending, Overdoing. Plan special moments and activities that don't exhaust you or your budget and are not centered around rich food. Try festive vegetable minestrone, corn crackers, and sesame fingers for a supper instead of hamburgers, pie, and ice cream. Have a warm, fireside gathering with insprational stories instead of a raucous party and television droning in the background.

7
Stay in focus!

Remember accountability to God in the use of time, talents, treasure, and body temple. Being a blessing to others by preserving and promoting healthful activities will boost your own immune system while helping others to be temperate. In this way you will create new and better traditions that leave you and your loved ones healthier, happier, and truly refreshed during the holiday season.

Life seems to be getting more stressful everyday! Pressure at the office, pressures at home, even pressures at the mall and on the road combine to tighten the vice grip of stress upon us. How can we lessen life's added pressures in order to maximize mental, physical, and spiritual health? Are there any simple, effective lifestyle methods available that will turn the vice grip back a few turns—for good? Here are some helpful tips:

Part 1

The Owner's Manual & Ten Natural Doctors

In part 1 we will look at the ultimate handbook of health, and at a group of doctors who make housecalls—at a price anyone can afford!

1. Do We Have an Owner's Manual?

2. Introducing: The Great Physician and His Manual

3. Bible Health and God's Natural Doctors

4. *G* = Gratitude & Benevolence

5. *O* = Obedience

6. *D* = Divine Help

7. *S* = Self control

8. *A* = Air

9. *N* = Nutrition

10. *S* = Sunshine

11. *W* = Water

12. *E* = Exercise

13. *R* = Rest

Do We Have An Owner's Manual?

1

Getting Acquainted with the Owner's Manual

*H*ave you ever purchased a new car? It's amazing how much a man-made conglomeration of metal, plastic, aluminum, wires, dials, gauges, hoses, rubber, airbags, and glass can cost! While cars differ in design, color, size, length, gas mileage, and a host of other factors, there's one thing they all have in common: An owner's manual.

Do We Have An Owner's Manual?

*E*very manufacturer provides an owner's manual. What person would buy a new car—or even a used one—and ignore it? The owner's manual contains very valuable information—advice that could save you thousands of dollars in repair bills in the future, or even the life of the car! It lists what type of oil to use, when to change the hoses, filters, and belts, when to have it serviced, and much, much more. Who would lay down thousands of dollars and ignore the manufacturer's guidelines?

What's More Complex — You or Your Car?

*T*he human body is a much more complex assembly than a car—we have trillions of cells that form tissues, bones, hair, sensory and internal organs, and the complex chemical and hormonal systems that operate them all. Each of your 30 trillion cells perform an average of 10,000 chemical functions every day.

Your body is controlled and coordinated by over 16 billion neurons and 120 trillion "connection boxes" or receptors in a complex system of neuropassageways. But the brain and spinal cord, which orchestrate the whole process, weighs less than 3 pounds!

1 = 1,400?

Imagine. Just one stress reaction produces more than 1,400 known physiological responses! Your heart beats more than 100,000 times daily to move blood 168 million miles around your body. You take about 23,800 breaths a day to bring about 438 cubic feet of air to your lungs. The psalmist David expressed it best when he declared, "I will praise Thee, for I am fearfully and wonderfully made: marvellous are thy works; and that my soul knoweth right well." *Psalm* **139:14**.

Do We Have A Master Designer?

Some people believe that after a spontaneous cosmic explosion, or "big bang," we evolved by *chance* out of a primordial "slime" pool. Such a notion takes a lot of faith to believe! Many scientists now admit that evidence reveals there is a Master Designer, an all-Intelligent, all-Powerful God that created this marvelous human machine and the world it dwells in.

What's the real scoop on the Big Bang theory? God spoke, and BANG—there it was! Read it for yourself.

"By the word of the LORD were the heavens made; and all the host of them by the breath of his mouth...let all the inhabitants of the world stand in awe of him. For he spake, and it was done; he commanded and it stood fast." *Psalm* **33:6-9**.

"In the beginning God created the heaven and the earth." Genesis 1:1

"In the beginning was the Word, and the Word was with God, and the Word was God....All things were made by him; and without him was not any thing made that was made." *John* **1:1, 3**.

Psalm **100:3** tells us that "It is He that hath made us, and not we ourselves."

Where Is Our Owner's Manual?

If Christians are correct, then God as the Designer, must have left us an owner's manual—a step-by-step practical guide to show us how to care for these wonderfully complex machines that He created.

Christians teach that the Bible is God's letter to humanity; a practical guide to finding solutions to the complex problems that confront us in this life. Could the Bible also be God's owner's manual—the Manufacturers Guide to the practical care and maintenance for the complex assemblage of body, mind, emotions, and affections that He created?

"Receive My instruction, and not silver; and knowledge rather than choice gold... Counsel is Mine, and sound wisdom: I am understanding; I have strength." *Proverbs* **8:10, 14**.

Who Created the Physical and Moral Laws That Govern Us?

During this series we will learn that true science, the Bible, and common sense are always in agreement. As science has investigated the incredibly complex human machine, many of its findings have been astounding! And many have validated lifestyle and mental health principles that have been recorded in the Bible for thousands of years! In the upcoming articles we will take a thrilling look at how medical science is validating the simple principles of life and health. And these principles have been handed down to us by a loving Creator who has not left us without an Owner's Manual!.

God is Concerned About Your Health!

Remember, God is interested in every aspect of our lives. He wants you to be healthy, happy, and well-balanced. "My son, attend to my words; incline thine ear unto my sayings. Let them not depart from thine eyes; keep them in the midst of thine heart. For they are life unto those that find them, and health to all their flesh." *Proverbs* **4:20-22**.

It is for this reason that He has ordained protective principles which govern not only our relationship with Him, but also what we eat and drink, how we work and entertain ourselves, organize our schedules, handle stress, and much, much more! Violating the principles which God has laid down to govern our daily lifestyle and activities can be a major cause of disease, stress and depression.

We bring so much disability upon ourselves through ignorance of God's counsel in the Owner's Manual! We are admonished to "ponder the path of thy feet, and let all thy ways be established." *Proverbs* **4:26**. The violation of any of God's laws, whether physical or moral, reaps disaster and ruin. "Can a man take fire in his bosom, and his clothes not be burned?" Prov. 6:27.

The Designer Lifestyle

God is not just sitting in Heaven watching us blunder through life without a care about our welfare! He has a plan for you, and a strong desire to see that plan carried out. That plan is found in *3 John* **2**: "Brethren, I wish above all things that you may prosper and be in health, even as thy soul prospereth."

God has outlined a lifestyle designed to minimize stress, suffering, disease, despair, and disability of every kind! Why? "That thy (God's) way may be known upon the earth, thy saving health among all nations." *Psalm* **67:2**.

He outlines it in all its simplicity and beauty in His Owner's Manual—the Bible. But more than that, He wants to give you the power to implement that plan in your life—TODAY!

You will discover more of His love and special plans for YOU as you read through this section.

Introducing:

The Great Physician and His Manual

Why Look to the Bible for Health Laws?

We learned in lesson 1 that true science, the Bible, and common sense will always be in agreement, because God is the Author of them all! Well, if there is a God, and if the natural laws that govern our beings are His, then it is logical to assume that He wants us to not only learn, but obey those laws.

We have called the Bible God's owner's manual. But why not find health and lifestyle principles in some other book, perhaps more modern and more up-to-date?

God's Owner's Manual Can't be Improved!

It is important to understand that the Bible is entirely different from other books which give good advice. There are three reasons why.

First, in the sacred books of other religions, man is writing his concepts about God. But in the Bible, God talks to us personally about Himself and His plan for us, and that is as great a difference as there is between Heaven and earth! His Word declares, "All Scripture is given by inspiration of God, and is profitable for doctrine, correction, reproof, and instruction in righteousness (right living), that the man of God may be perfect, throughly furnished unto all good works." *2 Timothy* **3:16-17**.

Second, God Himself gives us instruction for living, and commands us to diligently listen to and follow what He has written. "When thou goest, it shall lead thee; when thou sleepest, it shall keep thee; and when thou awakest, it shall talk with thee." *Proverbs* **6:22**.

This instruction is not only given in broad, general principles, but in a personal, specific, caring and loving way. Speaking as a watchful shepherd would over his vulnerable lambs, the Lord declares: "I will instruct thee and teach thee in the way which thou shalt go: I will guide thee with mine eye." *Psalm* **32:8**.

This does not present a picture of a cold, heartless Being who, having made a set of rules, then sits back and watches to see which of the miserable, hairless bipeds He has created can manage to figure them out and follow them! No, a personal God has written a personal Owner's Manual for the subjects of His love and grace.

Third, God's Word has power. One Chinese sage, Mencius wrote this: "Instruction can impart knowledge, but not the power to execute." Here is a vital point! The Bible promises not only instruction, but the power to execute those instructions!

"Now unto Him that is able to do exceeding abundantly above all that we ask or think, aaccording to the power that worketh in us." *Ephesians* **3:20**.

And that power is for you now!

God's Owner's Manual Can't be Improved!

In Old Testament times, when the Jewish people turned away from God to follow their own ways, the prophet Jeremiah rebuked them in despair: "Is there no balm in Gilead; is there no physician there? why then is not the health of the daughter of my people recovered." *Jeremiah* **8:22**

It was because they did not feel their need of a Savior and Guide. Jesus Himself is the Great Physician. *Luke* **5:31-32**. He is also described as the "Wonderful, Counselor" in *Isaiah* **9:6**. He wants to commune with you, heal you, give you instructions for living, and power to obey!

Ever Had to Wait to See the Doctor?

*H*ave you ever had to rush to make a doctor's appointment on time? I think we all know what it is like to experience the mad rush through traffic, the sprint through the parking lot, the squeeze through the crowd in the waiting room to register your name on the appointment list.

You made it on time—but where's the doctor? You hurried, but now you wait—and wait—and wait some more. One hour later you are ushered into a room, interviewed by a nurse (but you wanted the doctor!), followed by a brief but expensive visit by the physician!

The Great Physician is Waiting to See YOU!

*D*id you know that you have a standing appointment with your Physician, Jesus Christ, every day? You don't have to press through crowds or wait in line to visit with Him. He is not looking at His watch when He comes to meet with you. You have His undivided attention—does He have yours?

He says, "Come, let us reason together." He challenges us to think about our relationship to Him, our course of action in life, and to consider the results of unwise lifestyle decisions:

"Can one go upon hot coals, and his feet not be burned?" *Proverbs* **6:28.** "He that diggeth a pit shall fall into it; and whoso breaketh an hedge, a serpent shall bite him." *Ecclesiastes* **10:8**.

What stronger "hedge" of protection can we break than

than the violation of either the moral or physical laws which God has given?

In the next ten sections we will be taking a look at ten of God's natural doctors, which He has given us as a hedge of protection in a sinful world. Oh, by the way, these doctors still make house calls—24 hours a day!

And they're FREE!

 2

Introducing:

The BIG 10

3

Is Anything Going?

We live in a society where "anything goes." If it feels good, do it; if it feels right, it is right; if you want it, take it; if you can't afford it, charge it! But most important, don't think about it—just do it! In many subtle ways this thinking has permeated the philosophy of many societies today, both Christian and non-Christian.

Unfortunately, this philosophy doesn't produce much real happiness. People have more questions than ever. Why the restlessness, unhappiness, chronic disease, social instability, and downright confusion, even in prosperity? Paul addresses this very issue, with a note of irony, to the "anything goes" Corinthians:

"What? know ye not that your body is the temple of the Holy Ghost which is in you, which ye have of God, and ye are not your own? For ye are bought with a price; therefore glorify God in your body, and in your spirit, which are God's." *1 Corinthians 6:19-20*.

God's Owner's Manual Can't be Improved!

He adds: Know ye not that ye are the temple of God, and that the Spirit of God dwelleth in you? If any man defile the temple of God, him shall God destroy; for the temple of God is holy, which temple ye are." He closes with the solemn warning: "Let no man deceive you." *1 Corinthians 3:16-18*.

We're Called to Accountability

*Y*ou are not your own, if you believe the words of Scripture. But many have convinced themselves that God's will is whatever *they* will to do! But you have been purchased with a great price, and God really has a double claim on you and me: We belong to Him by creation and redemption. As a responsible Owner, God wants to alert us to the dangers we are exposed to in a sinful world.

Jesus said: "Take heed to yourselves lest at any time your hearts be overcharged with surfeiting (gluttony) and drunkenness, and cares of this life, and so that day (His second coming) take you unawares." *Luke* **21:34**.

Is Everything Out of Control?

*T*hink about it. Lifestyle diseases alone, such as heart disease, cancer, stroke, dementia, obesity, chronic stress, and diabetes are claiming the lives of 3 out of every 4 adult Americans. Stress-related problems alone cost 43.7 billion per year. Our "hyperdemic" of physical and emotional disease in this nation is a sure marker of a society that is out of control in diet and lifestyle.

Does it matter? Do lifestyle choices affect the morality and spirituality of man, as well as his physical health? Do these choices even affect the course of society?

God has the answer: "Abstain from fleshly lust, which war against the soul." *1 Peter* **2:11**.

"From whence come wars and fightings among you? Come they not hence, even of your lusts that war in your members?" *James* **4:1**.

The sad truth is, for many Americans, disease is not so much a result of chance or even genetics, but rather is the inevitable consequence of violating the laws of nature through unwise lifestyle and dietary choices.

So, Who's In Control?

$\mathcal{G}$od's Word talks about a group of people in the last days "whose god is their belly." *Philippians* **3:19**. Slaves to appetite! If it's there, eat it. If it's not there, search the fridge! If you can't find it, order *take-out*!

All of us know what that feels like—out of control, not able to govern the appetite, passions, emotions, or even reason. We are slaves to bad habits, while vainly seeking answers to life's hard questions, in a hapless pursuit of personal fulfillment.

God knows all about it: "Know ye not, that to whom ye yield yourselves servants to obey, his servants ye are to whom ye obey; whether of sin unto death, or of obedience unto righteousness?" *Romans* **6:16**.

Fortunately, all can find relief from this pitiable state: "If the Son shall set you free, ye shall be *free indeed*." *John* **8:36**. "He is able to subdue *ALL* things unto Himself!" *Phillipians* **3:21**. The question is, who will have dominion over your life, your affections, your conscience, and your daily habits?

So, Who's In Control?

$\mathcal{T}$he story is told of a farmer who found an eaglet and took him home to his barnyard, letting him grow up with his chickens and turkeys. The bird seemed content with his companions, even when he developed a 9 ft. wing span!

One day a naturalist came to visit and was intrigued by the eagle that spent his time with the chickens. He asked the farmer if he could see if the bird had an eagle or a chicken heart! The farmer laughed and said, "He's been in the barnyard too long—he'll never fly like an eagle!"

The naturalist took the bird to the top of the house, and he flew right back into the barnyard. This happened several times. Then he took him far away, to the top of a mountain, and turned his head toward the sun. You guessed it. He caught the vision, gave an eagle's cry, and never returned to the chicken coop. We need to get out of the chicken coop of bad habits and sin—and God can give us the vision to have that mountaintop experience!

Questions? Try GOD'S ANSWER!

*W*e're just like that eagle—bungling through life in the bad habits barnyard—when really we were created to be eagles! But just like that eagle, we need to catch a vision of how special we are to God, and how powerful He is to help us!

"Therefore if any man be in Christ, he is a new creature: old things are passed away; behold, all things are become new. And all things are of God." *2 Corinthians* **5:17-18**.

GOD'S ANSWER is an acronym—each letter stands for a word. In this case, each letter of GOD'S ANSWER stands for a basic health principle, that, if incorporated into the life with the help of God, will not only prevent much of the stress and lifestyle diseases afflicting Americans today, but also work to bring healing and restoration to worried minds, diseased bodies, and broken down immune systems!

God's Answer: 10 FREE Doctors

*F*or the next ten lessons, we are going to visit God's ten free doctors—these are doctors that you can and should be visiting every day.

G = Gratitude   *A* = Air
O = Obedience   *N* = Nutrition
D = Divine Help   *S* = Sunshine
S = Self-control   *W* = Water
                         E = Exercise
                         R = Rest

You'll Be Amazed!

As I stated before, it is a fascinating field in itself to study the many findings of scientific research which validate Biblical health and lifestyle principles. Unlike the "do it and don't think about it" philosophy of today, Christ invites us to investigate and "reason together" with Him regarding the Christian health and lifestyle issues that are vital to our spirituality, happiness, health, and well-being.

As you review with me the medical findings of the past few years and compare them with the "Owner's Manual," you will be amazed!

3

Doctor 1:

The Attitude of Gratitude

G OD'S ANSWER

Attitude: Friend or Foe?

The Bible teaches that there is more to good health than physical habits and good nutrition. A bad attitude can "veto" all the spiritual and physical benefits of an otherwise good lifestyle. Our attitude can be a beneficial friend or relentless foe. Perhaps that is why we are admonished to "let all bitterness, and wrath, and anger, and clamour, and evil speaking, be put away from you, with all malice," as a condition for receiving and maintaining salvation. *Ephesians* **4:31**.

With the aid of the Holy Spirit we are to cultivate gratitude, benevolence (unselfishness, goodwill), kindness, sympathy, joy, optimism, and a contented attitude. God's Word tells us that those who share these traits receive the greater benefit! "But godliness with contentment is great gain." *1 Timothy* **6:6**.

New Evidence: Old Counsel

New medical evidence reveals that, when combined with a wholesome diet, key emotional traits can help promote health, boost the immune system and protect you against a spectrum of diseases ranging from colds to cancer.

Studies show that worry, anxiety, anger, hostility, grief, negativism, fear and mental stress all depress the immune system, especially "T" killer cell activity and its ability to fight viruses, bacteria, and cancer. The evidence is new, but the counsel has been around for centuries: "A merry heart doeth good like a medicine: but a broken spirit drieth the bones." *Proverbs* **17:22**. There is even new evidence linking depression to osteoporosis— "dry bones."

Character, Decision, and Disease

*R*esearchers at the Stanford University School of Medicine and the University of California at San Diego reported that such positive attitudes as:

- *Gratitude*
- *Optimism*
- *Perseverance*
- *Diligence under stress*
- *Absence of malice (benevolence)*

are linked to a better chance of beating disease, and higher survival rates when disease does occur.

The lower stress levels that accompany these traits encourage better memory and learning, because nerve cell expansion is greatly inhibited in the presence of chronic stress. Positive attitudes increase one's learning ability and the ability to handle new challanges and sudden changes. This is a key attribute among centenarians. Senior citizens who volunteer approximately 40 hours a year experience greater longevity than those who do not.

One interesting study showed that helping strangers gave more of an immune boost than helping those we are acquainted with! What a blessed health boon for the person who follows the Bible injunction of gratitude and benevolence, who will "give a portion to seven, and also to eight"! *Ecclesiastes* **11:2**.

In light of this scientific finding, the Bible reminder to "Be not forgetful to entertain strangers" (*Hebrews* **13:2**) takes on entirely new, dynamic proportions as it relates to health!

Wrath-er Cruel?

Conversely, there is a simple statement in the Scriptures that tells us: "Wrath is cruel." ***Proverbs 27:4.*** But the true import of these words is more profound than we may realize. Anger affects more than the person who is the target of this emotion.

As we have mentioned, anger suppresses the immune system. Although there are several factors known to increase the risk of stroke, a new study has also implicated anger and aggression as significant risk factors for sudden stroke.

In addition, people with heart disease double their risk of heart attack when they indulge in outbursts of anger—and the danger lasts for two hours after the episode.

Hostility also increases the risk of atherosclerosis and early death. Stress, depression, guilt, and anger depress the immune system and cause, or exacerbate, a host of diseases. New studies link these traits to proneness to heart disease, memory impairment, dementia and early death.

Stormy Seas and Hostile Harbors?

It is a risky business to harbor anger and ill feelings—even for one day! Your Owner's Manual (the Bible, remember?) counsels us: "Let not the sun go down on your wrath." *Ephesians* **4:26**.

Suppressed anger has some interesting side effects. Attempts to suppress anger, verbalizing negative feelings and adopting a "fighting spirit" in response to stressors are all associated with chronic dyspepsia (indigestion). Research has shown that individuals who direct anxiety and tension inward are more susceptible to early death than those who do not. In fact, pessimism, which is an unpleasant by-product of brooding over real or imagined troubles, has been shown to have an even worse effect on the killer "T" cells of the immune system than depression!

This is why the Lord tells us to come to Him with all that perplexes and annoys. "Casting all your care upon him; for he careth for you." *1Peter* 5:7.

Through prayer, Jesus can truly change our attitudes and help us cope with the bad attitudes of others. "We are troubled on every side, yet not distressed; we are perplexed, but not in despair; persecuted, but not forsaken; cast down, but not destroyed. *2 Cor. 4:8-9*.

You Can Duchenne

If a cheery attitude is so vital to good health, do we need to wait for a good mood to "hit" us before we can smile and receive a benefit? No! Recent psychological research suggests that just *deciding* to have a cheerful countenance can also create a merry heart, and generate amazing changes in the brain itself!

Voluntarily making a certain kind of smile can trigger some of the same physiological responses in the brain that have been associated with positive feelings. This smile, called a "Duchenne Smile" is named after the researcher who studied it.

The "cheeeese" smile given for photographs uses the zygomatic major muscles which surround the mouth. This smile is biochemically unproductive in terms of positive emotion and brain response. But when the orbicularis muscles around the eyes are deliberately flexed as well, it produces the "sincerely happy" smile characteristic of genuinely happy experiences.

Researchers have found that a deliberate decision to smile uactually generated the same positive brain activity in the frontal cortex as a spontaneously happy smile! We can actually cheer ourselves up, as well as someone else, simply by "putting on a happy face." Now, that's easy—and best of all, it's free! Perhaps that's why the Bible says that "God loveth a cheerful giver." *2 Corinthians* **9:7.**

Mood-Changing Strategies

*W*hen a bad mood is looming in the horizon, there are practical steps that can be taken to drive it away!

First, call out to the Lord, and discuss the thing with Him in prayer—find the Bible promises that focus on power for victorious living and God's ultimate justice! This helps to temper the storm and put things in perspective.

Soothing music is a great mood-modifier, and so is a good bout of exercise.

Maybe you are really fatigued, and just need a nap or "time out" to calm down.

Getting involved in a "helping" activity for someone less fortunate, or just focusing on or praying for the needs of others is a good way to redirect "energy" in a positive way.

Most importantly, during those times, we need to set a watch at the door of our mouths and ask the Holy Spirit to help us see and deal with the thing from God's point of view!

You can Duchenne!

REFERENCES

1. Ekman P. Voluntary smiling changes regional brain activity. *Psychological Science* 1993 Sept;4(5):342-345.

2. Commentary: The mind-body connection: emotions and disease. *University of Texas Lifetime Health Letter* 1994 Feb;6(3).

3. Is hostility killing you? *Consumer Reports on Health* 1994 May;6(7).

4. Thayer R. Self-regulation of mood: strategies for changing a bad mood, raising energy, and reducing tension. *Journal of Personality and Social Psychology* 1994;67(5):910-925.

5. Ziegler J. Immune system may benefit from the ability to laugh. *Journal of the National Cancer Institute* 1995 Mar;87(5)Commentary.

6. Scheier M. Person variables and health: personality predispositions and acute psychological states as shared determinants for disease. *Psychosomatic Medicine* 1995 May/Jun;57(3)255-268..

7. Bennett E. Suppression of anger and gastric emptying in patients with functional dyspepsia. *Scandinavian Journal of Gastroenterology* 1992;27:869-874.

8. Mittleman M. Triggering of acute myocardial infarction onset by episodes of anger. *Circulation* 1995;92(7):1720-1725.

9. *Medical Tribune: Family Physician Edition* 1998; 39(13):3.

10. Schier M. Optimism and rehospitalization after coronary artery bypass graft surgery. *Archives of Internal Medicine* 1999;159:829-835.

11. Peterson C. Catastrophizing and untimely death. *Psychological Science* 1998;9:127-130.

2. Lupien S. Stress-induced declarative memory impairment in healthy elderly subjects: relationship to cortisol reactivity. *Jour-*

nal of Clinical Endocrinology & Metabolism 1997 Jul;82(7):2070-5.

13. Segerstrom S. Optimism is associated with mood, coping, and immune changes in response to stress. *Journal of Personality and Social Psychology* 1998 Jun;74(6):1646-55.

14. Silver M. Unraveling the mystery of cognitive changes in old age: correlation of neuropsychological evaluation with neuro-pathological findings in the extreme old. *International Psychogeriatrics* 1998 Mar;10(1):25-41.

Doctor 2:

Obedience

5

G O D'S ANSWER

Health: For Good...Or for God?

People are interested in health for many different reasons. We are living in an era when many individuals vigorously pursue a lifestyle devoted to health for "health's sake." To many, health becomes a god in itself, a reason for living. Their dedication to a healthy lifestyle becomes their "salvation" and security—a substitute for a relationship with God. They strongly believe in obedience to physical laws. But obedience to nature's laws becomes an end in itself—a hapless attempt to escape the reality of aging and mortality—a prospect doomed to failure.

Salvation Without Obedience?

On the other hand, there are a large class of people who believe in the Bible, but believe that the Bible has little to say about how to live life on this earth. They strongly believe in the moral law, but are sure that God does not require dominion or authority over their habits or lifestyle choices.

They do not realize the strong impact of physical habits on the moral and spiritual nature, and do not think that God requires obedience to natural laws that keep the body healthy. Somehow they overlook—or conveniently ignore—the numerous passages in the Bible where God stresses the importance of obedience to natural laws!

Salvation Without Obedience?

*B*oth groups engage in some behaviors or attitudes that bring some health benefits. But there is a vital missing link for both groups. The missing link is that God is not in either philosophy. God requires obedience to both the moral and physical laws He has authored—and we cannot separate them, because God does not separate them:

"And the very God of peace sanctify you wholly: and I pray God your whole spirit and soul and body be preserved blameless unto the coming of the Lord Jesus." *1 Thessalonians* **5:23**.

"Let us cleanse ourselves from all filthiness of the flesh and spirit, perfecting holiness in the fear of God." *2 Corinthians* **7:1**.

The Bible teaches that man needs salvation and cannot have true peace or hope without a living relationship with the Savior. "At that time ye were without Christ...having no hope, and without God in the world." *Ephesians* **2:12**. The Bible also teaches us that before we came to Christ, every faculty was an instrument of our enemy, the devil—for our evil. Now every faculty belongs to God—for our good!

"For as ye have yielded your members servants to uncleanness and to iniquity unto iniquity; even so now yield your members servants to righteousness unto holiness." *Romans* **6:19**.

Salvation Without Obedience?

*W*e are saved by grace—a free gift from God, "not of works, lest any man should boast." *Ephesians* **2:10**. But grace is given for another very important purpose—and that purpose is obedience. "By whom we have received grace..for obedience to the faith among all nations, for His name." *Romans* **1:5**.

Why? "For we are His workmanship, created in Christ Jesus unto good works...that we should walk in them." *Ephesians* **2:10**.

The Bible teaches that true salvation involves more than mental assent to Bible doctrines. "For the kingdom of God is not in word, but in power." *1 Corinthians* **4:20**. Through the grace and power God imparts, He requires obedience to both the moral and lifestyle principles He outlines for His people—obedience is not optional to those who truly love and serve God.

"Know ye not that ye are the temple of God, and that the Spirit of God dwelleth in you? If any man defile the temple of God, him shall God destroy, which temple ye are. Let no man deceive himself." *1 Corinthians* **3:16-18**.

Someone can tell himself or herself all day, every day, that lifestyle decisions don't matter to God, that He isn't concerned with such things. But that won't change the fact that God *is* concerned about it and commands our obedience—"Let no man (or woman) deceive himself (or herself)" on this issue!

Obedience? It's For Our Own Good!

*G*od's command for dominion over our beings is really an expression of His loving desire for our freedom from oppression, unhappiness, disease and untimely death. "And the Lord commanded us to do all these statutes, to fear the Lord our God, for our good always, that He might preserve us alive, as it is at this day." *Deuteronomy* **6:24**.

He wants us to gain the richest benefits in every way, even in this sinful world. His promise to all those who obey is certain: "Blessed shalt thou be when thou comest in, and blessed shalt thou be when thou goest out." *Deuteronomy* **28:6**.

Is He restricting our lifestyle? No! He's giving us the freedom to enjoy life—without worrying about the consequences of our reckless ways!

He merely wants us to be spared needless pain, disability,

and disease that so often attends the violation of Gods laws, both moral and physical.

God clearly reveals this concern in *Exodus* **15:26**:

"*If* thou wilt diligently hearken to the voice of the Lord thy God, and wilt do that which is right in His sight, and wilt give ear to His commandments, and keep all His statutes, I will put none of these diseases upon thee, which I have brought upon the Egyptians: for I am the Lord that healeth thee."

Is Religion Healthy?

Can we expect tangible health and mental benefits for those who adhere to Bible religion? An analysis of 212 peer reviewed studies revealed that 75% of the studies indicated that religious commitment has a beneficial impact on a variety of health conditions, including alcoholism, heart disease, anxiety, and depression.

Adhering to Bible principles of faith, combined with lifestyle, has been associated with

- *50% fewer deaths from coronary disease*
- *56% fewer deaths from emphysema*
- *74% fewer deaths from cirrhosis*
- *53% fewer suicides.*

Patients undergoing heart surgery who were "deeply religious" were more likely than others to be alive 6 months after surgery. Patients without religious commitment were three times more likely to die after the surgery was complete.

Give Me That Old Time Religion!

Sheena Sethi, a psychologist from Stanford University and Martin Seligman, from the University of Pennsylvania, studied 623 members of nine different sects. They concluded that "old time religion" gives its adherents a strong mental health edge over religious liberals and unbelievers.

The highest levels of optimism were linked to fundamentalists who allow religion to influence their daily life—what they eat, wear, and whom they marry.

"What we found was exactly the opposite of what we expected," said Sethi, who suggests more studies of the effects of religion on mental health.

Science is simply verifying what the Bible has said all along: "There is no wisdom nor understanding nor counsel against the Lord." *Proverbs* **21:30**.

We suggest not waiting for more studies before trying it!

REFERENCES

1. Larson D. Religion and mental health: should they work together? Alternative and Complementary Therapies 1996 Mar/Apr:91-98.
2. Matthews D. Healing faith: religious commitment is good for your health. Journal of General Internal Medicine 1995 Apr;4(suppl 10).
3. Parker S. Experts call spirituality an untapped therapy. Internal Medicine News 1996, Jan. 16.

5

Doctor 3:

Divine Power

6

GoD'S ANSWER

Are You Running on Empty?

*W*hen you go to work, or to the shopping center, have you noticed the expression on most people's faces? Americans today have more material goods and conveniences than any generation before them, yet we see more tension, fatigue, sadness and discouragement etched on the faces of people—more than we saw even just a decade ago.

And despite strobe-light tennis shoes, video games galore, closets bulging with designer clothes and the latest toys, and fast food outlets on every corner, children and youth are more stressed and discontented than ever.

It has been said that most people live quiet lives of despair. There seems to be an emptiness in the lives of most people that material things just can't fill. Perhaps the wise man summed it up best when he said: "He that loveth silver shall not be satisfied with silver; nor he that loveth abundance with increase; this is also vanity...All the labour of man is for his mouth, and yet the appetite is not filled." *Ecclesiastes* **5:10; 6:7**.

All Stressed Up...And Nowhere to Blow!

A 1990 Gallup poll revealed that more than 36 percent of Americans live with chronic feelings of loneliness. And according to a recent Princeton University Research Associates survey, at least two-thirds of Americans feel "stressed-out" at least once a week.

Depression, which is often associated with chronic stress, is a major problem in the United States for both young and old. Nearly 15 million Americans will suffer clinical depression each year.

Stress, loneliness and related depression can have some serious health consequences, ranging from higher rates of heart attack, high blood pressure, osteoporosis and cancer, to lowered immune function and resistance to infectious diseases. They can even lead to an increased incidence of dental disease!

Infants of depressed mothers tend to have reduced activity in certain areas of the brain (the left frontal lobe in particular), which can cause academic, social, and attention problems later in life.

Clearly there is a void in the lives of millions—and an urgent need for that void to be filled.

Can Anything...Or Anyone...Fill the Void?

*M*an tries to fill his life with all manner of inventions, but still comes up empty. "Lo, this only have I found, that God hath made man upright; but they have sought out many inventions." *Ecclesiastes* **7:29**. "The way of man is froward and strange.." *Proverbs* **21:8**.

We were made upright, but sin has corrupted us. But thankfully, our Creator and Savior, Jesus Christ, has placed a desire in every human heart for righteousness. "That was the true Light, which lighteth every man that cometh into the world." *John* **1:9**.

There is a void in each one of us that only God can fill. Would you like to have that void filled? When we surrender our lives to Him we can have peace, contentment and even joy in an unstable, inconsistent world. "And the peace of God, which passeth all understanding, shall keep your hearts and minds through Christ Jesus." *Philippians 4:7.*

Faith...That Works!

Those who have totally surrendered their lives to Jesus Christ are the happiest people in the world. Even the scientific literature bears this out. One medical study of elderly Christians stated: "We conclude that faith in God...is strongly associated with life satisfaction."

Later in this series we will see that trust in God, faith, and prayer provide a significant boost to mental as well as physical health. They can also positively influence your chance of recovery should you be stricken with a serious, debilitating, chronic illness.

Someone once said, "He that puts his trust in God is on the highway to health." When you have simple and abiding trust in a Savior who will love you personally, lead you wisely, and supply your needs according to His plan, you have it all. It's just that simple. "Happy (contented) is the man that trusteth in Him (God)." *Psalm 34:8.*

How Can I Get That Trust?

Jesus said, "Come unto Me, all ye that labour, and are heavy laden, and I will give you rest. Take my yoke upon you, and learn of Me, for I am meek, and ye shall find rest (contentment) for your souls. For My yoke is easy, and My burden is light." *Matthew 11:28-30.*

There is no heavier burden than the burden of sin and selfishness. Are you tired of your broken promises, bad habits, and unhappiness? Jesus says, "Come. Give me your burden of sin. I will give you My righteousness—My peace!— in return."

But it doesn't stop there. The Scripture says, "Learn of Me." How do we grow in faith and trust? "So then faith cometh by hearing, and hearing by the Word of God." *Romans* **10:17**.

The Owner's Manual is God's own Book, filled with wisdom, instruction, and power, to all who take the first step— "Come." Won't you give yourself to Him, talk to Him and take time in that Book every day? It's the highway to health. The solution to all that perplexes and annoys. The answer to the great void in every human heart.

REFERENCES

1. Murray M. Lifestyle and dietary factors in depression. *American Journal of Natural Medicine* 1995 Dec;2(10):10-15.
2. Kreisberg R. Cholesterol-lowering and coronary atherosclerosis: good news and bad news. *The American Journal of Medicine* 1996;101:455-458.
3. Kiecolt-Glaser J. Slowing of wound healing by psychological stress. *Lancet* 1995;346:1194-1196.
4. Ibid. A biobehavioral model of cancer stress and disease course. *American Psychologist* 1994 May;49(5):389-404.
5. Restak R. The brain, depression, and the immune system. *Journal of Clinical Psychiatry* 1989 May;50(suppl):5.
6. Monteiro da Silva A. Psychosocial factors and adult onset rapidly progressive priodontitis. *Journal of Clinical Periodontology* 1996 Aug;23(8):789-794.
7. Nidecker A. Depression in moms reduces infant brain activity. *Family Practice News* 1996 Oct.
8. Reyes-Ortiz C. Religious activity improves quality of life for ill elders. *Journal of the American Geriatrics Society* 1996 Sept;44(9):S49.

6

Doctor 4:

Self Control

7

GOD'S ANSWER

This One Won't Make the Headlines!

It is certainly not a phrase we hear on the six-oclock news. It doesn't seem to be a requisite for public office. We don't see much of this teaching in school books, and even the churches don't seem to be making much of a fuss over it.

What Would You Talk About?

If you were called before the President of the United States for a once-in-a-lifetime interview, what would you talk to him about? What would be the most important truths you could impart? What would be the burden of your message?

In the New Testament, we have record of just such an interview. Paul, the great missionary and apostle, was arraigned before the powerful Roman governor, Felix. Felix had the power of our President. Paul was a prisoner whose religious liberty had been violated. But Paul didn't talk about that. He had been subjected to ridicule, torture and false accusations. But he didn't talk about that.

What Was on Paul's Mind?

Felix was curious to know more about this intrepid follower of Christ. He asked Paul to give an account of his religion.

Paul's response was prompt and forthright: "And as he reasoned of righteousness, temperance (self-control), and judgment to come, Felix trembled, and answered, Go thy way for this time; when I have a convenient season, I will call for thee." *Acts* **24:25.**

Incredible! Here, at his only meeting with Felix, Paul felt temperance was important enough to agitate. And his "health nugget" was so powerful, so pointed, it caused Felix to "tremble" and send his prisoner away in order to restore his "comfort zone."

So, What Is It?

Temperance could be defined as "abstaining from that which is harmful, and using wisely that which is good." The dictionary defines temperance as "habitual moderation in the indulgence of a natural appetite or passion."

I like to think of temperance as God having dominion over the entire lifestyle— self control that has its foundation in the power and will of God, not our own weak and vacillating inner resources!.

Is It Just Another New Year's Resolution?

It is a standing joke among Americans about how New Year's resolutions never last past the first few days or possibly weeks of commitment. One pledges never to drink alcohol or smoke again. Another vows never to eat another box of chocolate at midnight. Still another plans to spend less time at the office, and more time with the kids.

But the only resolution that seems to hold, many say, is the resolution "not to make New Year's resolutions." Many approach issues of self-control like New Year's resolutions—and most have exactly the same results—temporary success which will always lead to ultimate defeat and discouragement.

It's Something You Are, Not Something You Do!

aul, in his letter to the Galatians, lists the fruit of the Spirit, which every person who has yielded themselves to Christ will receive. What are they?

"But the fruit of the Spirit is love, joy, peace, long-suffering, gentleness, goodness, faith, meekness, temperance (self-control); against such there is no law." *Galatians* **5:22-23**.

Self-control. Temperance. Only God, through His Holy Spirit, can give you *real* temperance! It's a fruit of heavenly origin.

It's Something You Are, Not Something You Do!

hat's not to say that we should not note the areas of change we need—or even write them down. This has its place. "Ponder the path of thy feet, and let all thy ways be established." *Proverbs* **4:26**.

But many people try to "force" themselves to reform in one area of life or another by sheer will power. They close their eyes, grit their teeth, clench their fists, and exclaim with squinted, determined eyes: "I will no longer eat two bags of potato chips at one sitting," or, "I will no longer waste my time watching soap operas."

But Paul is defining temperance in Galatians, not as an isolated effort in one area of life, but as a divinely implanted principle, or character trait which permeates the whole life. Temperance, then, is not something you do, *it is something you are*. It touches everything—not just the potato chips and soap operas.

"Self"control, which is of heavenly origin, is really "Spirit" control—God working in you "to will and to do of His good pleasure." *Philippians* **2:13**. And His good pleasure is not to see you suffer or go without. Oh no, His good pleasure is your highest good and happiness! *Philippians* **1:9-11**.

You Are Special to God!

*A*s we continue our discussion, we will learn just how important we are to God, and how interested He is in every aspect of our lives. Paul understood this fact when he said: "And every man that striveth for the mastery is temperate in all things."
1 Corinthians **9:25**.

For someone who has grown weary of their own failed self-control, who is tired of being defeated on a daily basis and has finally given the control of his or her life entirely over to God, their motto becomes:

"Whether therefore ye eat, or drink, or whatsoever ye do, do all to the glory of God." *1 Corinthians* **10:31.**

Those "whatsoevers" mentioned in that verse cover a lot of territory! And it's all for our benefit!

God wants to give you the power to include those "whatsoevers" in your life! They make a difference—a big difference that you can feel almost right away! "'Whatsoevers." They're only a prayer away!

7

Doctor 5:

Air

8

GOD'S ANSWER

The Great Brain Robbery

Have you ever noticed that when you sit in a room that is devoid of fresh, circulating air, that you tend to feel groggy, listless, and even a little confused? Your brain is being deprived of an essential element for proper functioning. Without fresh air, proper nerve conduction and transmission cannot take place.

There are other factors which can tend to deprive the brain of adequate stores of oxygen, such as alcohol, caffeine, tobacco, sugar, and a high fat diet. Poor posture and lack of exercise also contribute to the problem. In the long run, chronic brain oxygen deprivation increases the risk of memory deficit, mental decline, and even dementia.

If your "thinking place" seems a little sluggish, perhaps its time to take a personal inventory of lifestyle habits—next to an open window!

Small Organ...BIG Demands!

The brain weighs only about 3 lbs., but utilizes enormous quantities of glucose and oxygen compared to the rest of the body. It consumes 20% of the body's oxygen and 25% of the body's glucose, yet makes up only 2% of the body's weight! The majority of this energy is spent supporting nerve impulse generation and transmission.

The brain never rests, even during deep sleep. In fact, the brain still consumes enormous amounts of energy when someone is under anesthesia. Respiration actually increases during sleep, when so much silent repair and rejuvenation takes place. For this reason, it is important to keep windows cracked a bit at night so fresh, vitalizing air is available for your brain and all its hard work!

Systemic Super Highway

Not just the brain, but every organ of the body is dependent on fresh air for optimum functioning. In one sense, your blood is a complex oxygen-transporting superhighway. Red blood cells are oxygen-hungry, and when we take deep inspirations of fresh, pure air, the red blood cells rush their precious store of oxygen and nutrients to the body tissues (provided you've had enough water to keep the blood flowing freely!).

Oxygen is essential to tissue health, both externally and internally. In the absence of oxygen, cell death begins to take place. And cells that are deprived of oxygen are the most subject to malignant change—cancer!

The Pollution Problem

Air pollution is consistently associated with increased death rates from certain diseases and increased incidence of asthma, lung damage and, surprisingly, death from cardiovascular disease. It is thought that the peripheral airways become inflamed, and the blood also coagulates, blocking vital air passages and aggravating existing heart conditions.

Not only are smog, cigarette smoke, and other environmental pollutants annoying and stressful, they are also a threat to health. It is estimated that passive cigarette smoke (breathing a smoker's smoke) causes 5,000 lung cancer deaths each year!

Indoor air quality is also affected when combustible heat is used (wood stove, kerosene, etc.) Fresh air ventilation is essential. It is also important to keep the home as free as possible from dust and dirt, since metalic pollutants collect on dust, and can be a potential health threat to city dwellers in particular.

Nitty Gritty in the City

An imperceptible mist of toxic chemicals in the air we breath exposes those living in urban areas to an elevated risk of cancer. Nationally, the Environmental Defense Fund estimates that 360 of every million Americans develop cancer as a result of these air toxics, many of which are unfamiliar to the general public.

"The numbers show that cars, trucks and small businesses tend to be responsible for much more of the nation's air toxicity than is generally recognized," said David Roe, attorney for the New York-based Environmental Defense Fund. "Up to now, lack of information has meant lack of attention to some of the biggest causes of toxic air."

Although environmental officials have long targeted air pollution, such as summertime smog, now officials are looking at a less well understood part of the problem: the poisoning that occurs from exposure to 148 different chemicals produced by motor vehicles, industry smokestacks and businesses. States don't regularly test for most of these air toxics, and scientists are unsure of all their effects.

Coughing Cars

Motor vehicles account for 60 percent of the cancer and other health risks from air toxics across the country. Only one of the top five hazardous chemicals—a banned dry cleaning fluid called carbon tetrachloride—is not found in tailpipe exhaust. Almost 6 million people in Massachusetts alone and 220 million people nationally live in neighborhoods where the lifetime risk of cancer is at least 100 times the goal spelled out in the federal Clean Air Act.

For New England, all those air toxins translate into roughly 4,500 cancers among current residents, led by the 2,200 cancers in Massachusetts and 1,400 in Connecticut, according to reports.

Is it unreasonable to suggest that it may be time to consider where you live in relation to your body's need for daily fresh, pure, air? If you need to beat a path to a new environment, remember this promise: "In all thy ways acknowledge Him, and He shall direct thy paths." *Proverbs* **3:6.**

The Breath of Life

*W*hen God formed man out of the dust of the earth, the Bible says that He "breathed into his nostrils the breath of life, and man became a living soul." *Genesis* **2:7.**

A new, living, vitalized being awoke to health, strength, and life. Our Creator desires us to have a relationship and connection with Him that is as intimate, fresh, and life-giving as that first vivifying breath that Adam, the first man, received from God. In fact, it is as essential to our happiness, welfare, and salvation as breath is to life itself!

So, go out and get some clean, fresh air every day. How much? Talk 2 20-minute walks for the best results. Also, when you're feeling a bit tired, go outside, or open up a window, and breath in that free air!

"In Him we live, and move, and have our being." *Acts* **17:28.** What is more important to life and health than the quality of the air we breath? And what is more essential to the quality of the life we live than a vital, living connection with our Creator?

REFERENCES

1. Blaylock R. Excitotoxins: The Taste That Kills. Health Press, Santa Fe, NM. 1997.

2. Griffin D. Dieting, Victory From the Jaws of Defeat. Review Graphics, Hagerstown MD. 1994.

3. Griffin V. Calamity in a Cup: Caffeine and its Calamitous Cousins. Review Graphics, Hagerstown MD. 1996.

4. Kuruoglu C; Arikan Z, et al. Single photon emission computerized tomography in chronic alcoholism. British Journal of Psychiatry 1996 Sept;169(3):348-354.

5. Rourke S; Dupont R; et al. Reduction in cortical IMP-SPET tracer uptake with recent cigarette consumption in a young group of healthy males. European Journal of Nuclear Medicine 1997 Apr;24(4):422-427.

6. United States Sports Academy (Sport Supplement) Winter 1995.

7. Lemus R; Abdelghani A; et al. Health risks from exposure to metals in household dusts. Review of Environmental Health 1996 Oct/Dec;11(4):179-189.

8. Setiani O. Indoor air quality and ventilation strategies in the use of combustion space heating appliances in housing. Hiroshima Journal of Medical Science 1994 Dec;43(4):163-167.

9. Peters A; Doring A; et al. Increased plasma viscosity during an air pollution episode: a link to mortality? Lancet 1997 May;349(9065):1582-1587.

8

Doctor 6:

Nutrition

9

GOD'S ANSWER

The Stern Creditor

When we overextend our credit, payment comes due with interest. Stuffing the bill in the drawer doesn't make it go away, unfortunately.

The same is true with our health. Nature is a stern creditor—what we sow in disobedience to her laws, we reap in unnecessary pain, disability, disease, expense and even death. We can only ignore those laws for so long—and then comes the grim payment: the sacrifice of health, happiness, even life itself!

"Be not deceived; God is not mocked: for whatsoever a man soweth, that shall he also reap." *Galatians* **6:7.**

If new diagnostic paramaters that are being suggested for four major illnesses—diabetes, high blood pressure, high cholesterol, and overweight—were adopted today, 75% of the US adult population would be considered diseased! As a nation, we spend in excess of 700 billion on hospital care, doctors, and pills. This constitues 47% of corporate profits, and 11% of the Gross National Product! In both human and economic terms, lifestyle diseases have become a national public health crisis.

Our Account is Overdue!

Let's face it. The American diet and lifestyle is catching up with us. Every 30 seconds another American is diagnosed with cancer. Every 55 seconds an American dies of cancer. This year, 180,200 women will learn they have breast cancer, and an estimated 44,190 will die of the disease. Since 1990, about 10 million new cancer cases have been diagnosed. Each year, approximately 560,000 people will die of the disease, or about 1,500 each day. That means that 1 out of every 4 deaths in the U.S. is due to cancer.

According to Dr. Michael McGinnis, a former official of Health and Human Services, more than 85% of cancer cases in this country are caused by two factors: smoking and diet. The cost: $104 billion per year. The second leading cause of male cancer deaths is prostate cancer,with 165,000 new cases and 41,800 deaths each year. According to researchers at Harvard Medical School, the risk is highest for those who consume beef, pork, processed meat, bacon, and hot dogs.

We're Paying the Price — With Interest!

Cancer isn't the only lifestyle disease that is taking its toll—with interest—on the American family.

Heart disease causes 50% of the deaths in the United States. Every 25 seconds someone suffers a heart attack, and every 45 seconds, someone dies of heart disease.

According to Dr. Scott Grundy, a heart disease researcher at the University of Texas, it is our high fat diets, particularly saturated fat and cholesterol, that cause the majority of heart disease in this country. The American Medical Association has stated that 97% of coronary occlusions (plaque blockages in the arteries) could be prevented by a vegetarian diet.

We lost 56,000 American soldiers during the 10-year Vietnam War. Protestors were on the news daily! We lose 60,000 Americans every six weeks to heart disease—and no one says a word!

Past Due — A Look at the Facts

*D*id you know that a new diabetic is diagnosed every 50 seconds, and costs Americans 100 billion dollars a year? The death rate from diabetes has risen by 30% since 1980. An estimated 135 million people worldwide, and 16 million Americans, have diabetes.

Other diseases which are often related to lifestyle include stroke, osteoporosis, arthritis, and numerous forms of senility. According to Dr. McGinnis, lifestyle diseases such as the ones we have discussed cause more deaths each year than homicides, suicides, auto accidents, and war casualties—*combined*!

It's SAD!

*T*hat's right. It's the *S*tandard *A*merican *D*iet (SAD) that is a major culprit! Too much sugar, animal fat and animal protein, and too little fiber, fresh fruits, whole grains, and vegetables! (Remember—fiber is found only in plant foods).

The Designer Diet Advantage

*G*od has some wonderful pills for what ails us—and they are not expensive or nasty-tasting! We call it ***The Designer Diet***— and it's bursting with wonderful advantages!

The scientific literature these days is "blooming" with one exciting discovery after another about the benefits of a diet based on plant foods, such as whole grains, vegetables, beans, fruits, and nuts.

According to Dr. John Potter, the director of the University of Minnesota's Cancer Prevention Research Unit, plant foods contain powerful "phytochemicals" which not only prevent cancer, but also fight it.

Fighting with Phytochemicals

It has been shown that high plant food consumption lowers the risk of breast cancer; carrots and leafy green vegetables lower lung cancer rates; and for colon cancer, the cruciferous vegetables (broccoli, cabbage, cauliflower, potatoes, and carrots) are helpful.

For preventing cancers of the larynx, throat, mouth, and esophagus, fruit has consistently been found to be important. For stomach cancer prevention, try leaf lettuce and onions. Yellow, orange, or red vegetables, which are high in carotenoids, have been shown to help combat cancers of the mouth, throat, lung, stomach, and bladder.

No need to try and memorize the list—just enjoy them all, lightly steamed or raw, and in a good variety each day!

Blossoming With Benefits

Not only cancer, but all degenerative diseases (like the ones we have discussed) are dramatically reduced on a plant-based diet. One study published by the American Dietetics Association discussed the reversal of even severe coronary artery disease without the use of lipid-lowering drugs by using a combination of a vegetarian diet, stress management, and exercise.

Vegetable meals centered around baked or steamed potatoes, brown rice, beans, or pasta fill you up—not out—and are heavy on satisfaction, low in fat, and balanced in protein.

Saving — Money, Health, and Life!

Satan is a robber and a thief. "The thief cometh not, but for to steal, and to kill, and to destroy." *John* 10:10. He wants to steal your health, rob you of vitality, and destroy your usefulness on this earth. But Christ came to give us life, and a more abundant one at that! "I am come that they might have life, and that they might have it more abundantly." *John* **10:10** .

God's original, plant-based diet is still the best. *Genesis* **1:29.** Science is proving it, and common sense tells us it is so.

REFERENCES

1. Cancer Facts and Figures, 1997. American Cancer Society.
2. Journal of the National Cancer Institute 1993;35:1571.
3. Diehl, Hans. To Your Health. Lifestyle Medicine Institute, Loma Linda CA 92354. 1990.
4. Journal of the American Medical Association 1961;176(9):806-807.
5. Nutrition Action, April 1994.
6. Journal of Environmental Pathology, Toxicology, and Oncology 1990 May/Jun;10(3).
7. ADA Reports 1993(11):1317-1319.

 9

Doctor 7: Sunshine

10

GOD'S ANSWER

Sunshine's Getting Some "Heat"

Most of you are probably familiar with some of the "bad press"—some of the heat—that sunshine is getting these days. It is true that chronic overexposure to the sun's ultraviolet rays is associated with problems like premature skin aging, skin cancer, immune-suppression, and cataracts. However, recent studies indicate that high circulating levels of antioxidant vitamins C and E have been found to be protective against skin malignancy, wrinkling, photosensitivity reactions, and immune-suppression.

Vitamin C is found in green vegetables, berries, citrus fruits, kiwi, cantaloupe, pineapple, tomatoes, sweet peppers, and a host of other fresh vegetables and fruits (Apples, bananas, and pears are low—so enjoy a variety)!

Excellent sources of vitamin E include whole grains, dark green leafy vegetables, nuts, seeds, wheat germ, legumes, unsaturated plant oils, asparagus, and peas.

Depletors of these substances include refined sugar, caffeine, alcohol, birth-control pills, and stress. In addition to a healthy diet, daily exposure to sunshine is critical to human health and well-being. In fact, the healing benefits of sunshine are so great, that the Lord alludes to the sun in reference to His own divine healing power:

"But unto you that fear my name shall the Sun of righteousness arise with healing in His wings." *Malachi* **4:2**.

Sunshine and the "Sunny Personality"

*W*hen we think of a sunny personality, we think of someone who is cheerful, energetic, and a quick-thinker. Exposure to sunshine promotes all these qualities! It is known that exposure to light helps to set and maintain your internal "body clock" (circadian rhythm), which is essential for regulating hormones, sleep patterns, mood, and appetite.

Exposure to full spectrum bright light can improve alertness as well as cognitive function (mental ability). Exposure to daylight can greatly reduce symptoms of "jet lag," and has been used successfully in the treatment of various types of depression, including the "winter blues" and its associated fatigue. Bright light has also been used to treat the temporary depression many women suffer during certain phases of their monthly cycle.

Our society's pattern of late-night activities combined with sleeping during the beneficial, early-morning hours of sunlight are contrary to good principles of mental and physical health.

So, who's supposed to be up at night? The truth is, God made the beasts of the forest to keep those kind of hours! Truly! Listen: "Thou makest darkness, and it is night: wherein all the beasts of the forest do creep forth." *Psalm* **104:20**.

When we keep late hours, not only do we suffer physically, but spiritually as well! Why? Because we also miss our morning appointment with the Great Physician on that type of schedule. "I love them that love Me; and those that seek me early shall find me." *Proverbs* **8:17**.

Don't Shun Shine!

*C*asual exposure to sunlight is the major source of vitamin D for most people. Vitamin D3 is formed in the skin and synthesized by the liver to the form (actually a hormone) used by the system for a variety of essential functions. One of vitamin D's jobs is to stimulate intestinal calcium absorption. It is also essential to the calcium metabolism necessary for strong bones.

Sunscreen can decrease the incidence of skin cancer by up to 30%. However, sunscreens contain titanium dioxide, which can accumulate in the skin and may be carcinogenic. Using too much sunscreen, as well as lack of outdoor activity in the sun, is associated with increased risk of osteoporosis, osteomalacia, and bone fracture.

Synthesis of vitamin D through casual exposure to sunlight can alleviate rheumatoid and psoriatic arthritis, type I diabetes, hypertension, arrhythmias, seizure disorders, and eczema.   It also helps prevent a number of cancers, such as prostate, colon, breast, and leukemia. Check with your physician, because certain diseases are aggravated by exposure to sunlight.

If you're considering passive sungathering by the picture window, consider this: sitting behind a glass window eliminates 95% of the ultraviolet radiation, so opening windows is the best way to receive the sun's benefits when indoors. However, overexposure to ultraviolet radiation by artificial methods such as tanning beds significantly increases the risk of skin cancer and other radiation-related problems.

Sunshine — A Bonny Blessing!

It is known that exposure to sunlight has a cholesterol-lowering effect. Sunlight is also able to speed up the body's circulation which enhances the elimination of toxins. It also increases the number of white blood cells, which helps to defend the body against invading germs. And don't forget that sunlight promotes wound healing and kills many bacteria after short exposure.

As early as 1915 one scientific paper reported that exposure to sunlight had a calming, pain-killing effect on arthritis

sufferers. A quote from that article's conclusion is very enlightening:

"[Sun treatments] apply not only to cases suffering from
chronic pain, especially in the bones or joints, or from nervous
hyper-irritability, or both. Sunshine, when properly used, has
both a powerful analgesic and a sedative action...In a word, sunshine is a simple, cheap, and efficient analgesic-sedative, of which
more extensive use can be made with correspondingly gratifying
results."

And, even older than that quote, thousands of years ago, a
wise man said under the inspiration of God: "Truly the light is
sweet, and a pleasant thing it is for the eyes to behold the sun."
Ecclesiastes **11:7**.

How much sun do you need each day? That will vary
depending upon the day of time you are out and about and where
you live. Check with your local health care providers to find out
what's best in your area.

Will you commit today to adjust your lifestyle to accommo-
date this essential, free doctor, sent from Heaven? It can be very
enlightening!

REFERENCES

1. Partonen T. Effects of light on mood. Annals of Medicine 1993 Aug;25(4):301-302.

2. Kraft M; Martin R. Chronobiology and chronotherapy in medicine. Disease-a Month Series 1995 Aug;41(8):501-575.

3. Grimes D; Hindle E. Sunlight, cholesterol and coronary heart disease. Quarterly Journal of Medicine 1996 Aug;89(8):579-89.

4. Holick M. Noncalcemic actions of 1,25-dihydrooxyvitamin D3 and clinical applications. Bone 1995 Aug;17(2 Suppl):107S-111S.

5. Zabaluyeva A. The mechanism of adaptogenic effect of ultra-violet. Vesta Akad Med Nauk 1975;3(23).

6. Bryant J. Sunshine: its neglected analgesic-sedative action. Boston Medical and Surgical Journal 1915 Oct;173(16):583-585.

7. Skin and Allergy News, Feb. 1997.

8. Eberlein-Konig B. American Academy of Dermatology 1998 Jan;38(1):45-48.

9. Moseley H. A hazard assessment of artificial tanning units. Photodermatology, Photoimmunology & Photomedicine. 1998 April;14(2):79-87.

10

Doctor 8:

G O D' S   A N S W E R

...And Not A Drop to Drink?!

How much water do Americans drink every day? Well, have you ever had the opportunity to visit Niagara Falls when it is in full flow, and watch the giant cataracts of water surge over the gigantic horseshoe precipice? If you watch for just 30 seconds, you will see 33 million gallons thunder over those falls! But that's not how much water Americans drink each day—that's how much coffee they drink!

So, Where's the Water?

Well, if you check with the Beverage Marketing Corporation, you will discover that the average American consumes 537 cans of soda pop every year. In the South, each person stacks up 663 cans of soda per year!

So, where's the water? Perhaps we should pay a visit to those Americans who are more health conscious. Many well-meaning parents are switching from soda pop to fruit juice as the beverage of choice for their toddlers and children. Children under the age of five consume an average of nine gallons of juice annually. Children under the age of 12 consume more juice than any other age group. They are getting anywhere from 25 to 60 percent of their total daily energy intake from juice alone!

Is there water anywhere?

Water, Water — Anywhere?

*W*ater. It covers more than 70 percent of the earth's surface and fills a large percentage of the air we breathe. It accounts for 60 to 70 percent of our body weight. We play in it, wash in it, relax in it, and float on it. But most of us aren't drinking it!

Next to air, water is the most important ingredient in the recipe for a healthy life. Remember—flavored, caffeinated, or sugary drinks do not take the place of Adam's Ale—which was the beverage of choice for God's first man—water!

Water — Wet and Wonderful!

*S*ome of the ingredients in many drinks can actually cause more frequent urination and subsequent dehydration. When you are dehydrated your body is stressed in a number of ways. Dehydration can cause or aggravate fatigue and irritability, and can cause mental confusion and intellectual decline.

Dehydration can make it harder to think, as well as make it harder for your body to excrete toxins and salts. As a result, the body tends to become bloated.

According to the American Dietetic Association, many Americans are dehydrated. Dehydration of as little as 2 percent loss of body weight can reduce your mental and physical abilities.

New research indicates that reduced water consumption can increase the risk of urinary stone disease because the lack of water increases the contamination levels in the urine, thus overworking the kidneys. It can also cause cancers of the breast, colon and urinary tract, and can also lead to immune-suppression, which increases disease potential. It can also be a factor in childhood and adolescent obesity, infections, hormonal disturbances, mitral valve abnormalities, and altered salivary gland function.

Did You Drink Your 2,500 Gallons of Water Today?

If you had to drink all the water your body uses for its different functions, you'd have to drink 2,500 gallons each day! Fortunately, your body re-uses all but a small amount—but that small amount, you need!

Your kidneys filter 400 gallons of blood every day, yet only about 5 1/2 glasses of water from that blood are voided as urine. Another two glasses are exhaled in breathing, while two more are lost through normal perspiration, and about 1/2 cup by way of the bowels.

Five Cheers For Water!

You need about 8 glasses of water per day. Why? There are five important reasons: 1) Water is basic to balanced nutrition. It helps in the digestive process to break, soften, and transport food. The blood, which is 90% water, transports nutrients. 2) Water controls body temperature—through perspiration. 3) Water is a lubricant. In the same way that oil prevents friction between machinery parts, water prevents friction between the body's joints and muscles. 4) Water minimizes dehydration. 5) Water reduces stress on the circulatory system. It enables your blood to carry life and energy-giving nutrients to the body's cells.

The Clear Benefits

Drinking plenty of water reduces the risk of bladder cancer, because water dilutes urine and increases the frequency of urination. This, in turn, can reduce the contact between cancer causing toxins in urine and the cells of the bladder.

Interestingly, drinking mineral-rich hard water may help prevent heart attacks, according to recent research. A Swedish study of women ages 50 to 69 found that those who lived in towns with *hard* water, which contained high levels of magnesium and calcium, were 30 percent less likely to die of a heart attack than those who drank the softest water, which contains lower levels of the mineral.

Spring water, which is rich in these nutrients, may also be protective against osteoporosis. Conversely, water softeners work by exchanging the calcium and magnesium ions in the water with sodium or potassium ions. Depending on the hardness of the inflow water the treated water can end up containing significant amounts of sodium or potassium. Patients with kidney disease, diabetes or hypertension should be warned against drinking water treated in potassium-based water softeners.

Bottled water will vary in mineral content. Currently, there are no national guidelines governing bottled water, so beware:The bottled water you purchase could have been taken from the tap behind the store!

New research is linking chlorinated water with an increased risk of bladder and colon cancer. A good water distiller may be a good option for those who live where the water quality is less than desirable.

A Timely Tip

Try having a glass of water about 45 minutes before breakfast, instead of coffee. It will charge your digestive system so your stomach will be ready for breakfast! Then, instead of drinking with your meals, which dilutes digestive juices and causes indigestion, try having your water between meals.

You will not go to the table thirsty, and will be able to eat the right amounts of food, and relieve your poor stomach of the extra work that snacks create! We will talk more about that later. By the way—how can you know if you're properly hydrated?

Simple! Your urine should be pale, but not clear. Now that's a test that anyone can perform — and it's FREE!

If you wait to drink water until you're thirsty, you're already dehydrated! So, drink those eight glasses of water all through the day, not just at one time. And if you have children, don't wait for them to ask for water, give them water to drink throughout the day to avoid dehydration in them, especially if they are outside playing.

Are You Thirsty?

*J*esus tells us, "Ho, every one that thirsteth, come ye to the waters." *Isaiah 55:1*. When we see how vital water is to life and health, is it any wonder that Jesus refers to Himself and the precious gospel invitation as "the Water of life"? Listen.

"And the Spirit and the Bride say, Come. And let him that heareth say, Come. And let him that is athirst come. And whosoever will, let him take the water of life freely." *Revelation 22:17.*

We all need plenty of water—both physically and spiritually. Will you come? Will you drink?

REFERENCES

1. Cardiovascular News, April 1986, p.4.
2. Beverage Marketing Corporation, 1989.
3. Clydesdale F, Kolasa K, Ikeda J. All you want to know about fruit juice. Nutrition Today March/April 1994.
4. Continuing survey of food intakes by individuals. Human Nutrition Information Service, USDA. Springfield, VA; National Technical Information Service, 1989-90.

5. Smith M, Lifshitz F. Excess fruit juice consumption as a contributing factor in nonorganic failure to thrive. Pediatrics 1994 Mar;93(3):438-443.

6. Simenson B. Drinking Water. Poinsetta 1995;35(4).

7. Rubenowitz E. Magnesium and calcium in drinking water and death from acute myocardial infarction in women. Epidemiology 1999;10(1):31-36.

8. Zheng W. The association of drinking water source and chlorination by-products with cancer incidence among postmenopausal women in Iowa: a prospective cohort study. American Journal of Public Health 1997;87(7):1168-76.

9. Graves, John W. Hyperkalemia due to a potassium-based water softener. New England Journal of Medicine 1998 Dec;339:1790-91.

10. Garzon, Philippe and Eisenberg, Mark J. Variation in the mineral content of commercially available bottled waters: implications for health and disease. American Journal of Medicine 1998 Aug;105:125-30.

11

Doctor 9:

Exercise 12

GOD'S ANSWER

The Perpetual Sit-in

Remember the sit-in demonstrations in the 1960s and 70s? Well, many Americans today are engaged in perpetual *sit-ins*. Really! According to a recent study of nearly 10,000 people, 54 percent said they did little or nothing during their leisure time.

There are an estimated 250,000 deaths each year directly attributable to lack of exercise, and for this reason the Center for Disease Control and the American College of Sports Medicine recommend that Americans engage in at least 39 minutes of exercise daily (I suppose you could throw in an extra minute for good measure).

Like Father, Like Son?

Children are also becoming alarmingly sedentary. Ideally, children in grades 1 through 12 should get at least a daily 30-minute physical education class, but only 36 percent do, according to the Presidents Council on Physical Fitness and Sports. That is one reason why 40 percent of children as young as 5 already exhibit at least one heart disease risk factor such as obesity, diabetes, or elevated cholesterol.

Alarmingly, a recent report from the American Heart Association revealed that the more risk factors a person has for heart disease, the greater the risk of developing memory and learning impairments. Each risk factor carries with it a 23% increased risk of mental impairment!

Conversely, numerous studies show that exercise actually boosts the ability of both young and old to pay attention and learn. Why? Because exercise tends to enhance memory, concentration, cognition, creativity, and word fluency.

Down in the Dumps

Apparently all this immobility isn't making us very happy, either, and may be contributing to the rising levels of stress, tension, and anxiety that Americans are experiencing.

A new survey of 1,000 adults found that depression, anxiety, and psychological problems actually impair physical and social functioning and overall quality of life more than do common medical disorders such as arthritis and diabetes. Nearly 15 million Americans suffer clinical depression each year.

Stress and Depression

Depression is often associated with chronic stress. Aside from dietary practices that promote stress, such as nicotine, caffeine, and refined sugar consumption, lack of exercise is a major lifestyle stressor that promotes depression, tension, and anxiety.

A major study of 8,000 adults revealed that the less active a person was, the more depressed they were likely to be. Regular exercise significantly boosted mood, regardless of the level of depression the individual suffered at the beginning of the study.

The Bible says in *Proverbs* **19:15** that "slothfulness casteth into a deep sleep, and an idle soul shall suffer hunger."

Although the Scripture obviously has broader significance, one of the meanings for the word "sleep" is "drooping in spirit," "faint" or "dull"—which describes exactly how we feel when we don't get exercise!

Exercise Can Really Go to Your Head!

*D*id you know that regular daily exercise not only increases overall health and muscle tone, but also mental sharpness, mood, concentration, and self-esteem? One interesting study showed that just a 10-minute brisk walk will yield one hour of increased energy and reduced tension, whereas a sugar snack will ultimately result in fatigue and tension.

The Link Lesson

*T*he following true story took place in the 1930's. A discouraged, despondent man came to see Dr. Harry Link, a famous doctor in New York City. The despondent man had lost his job. He felt like nobody loved him anymore. He wanted to commit suicide to end his troubles.

Dr. Link explained that he had been too sedentary, having exercised only his mind while neglecting his body. "I will give you a program of manual work," he said, "and soon you will be feeling better."

"I don't like manual work," said the man. "I don't want to work. I want to commit suicide."

Dr. Link did his best to persuade the man to accept a program of work, but it was no use, and at last in exasperation he said, "All right then, commit suicide. But if you do, why not do something out of the ordinary, something heroic, and get into the headlines when you die."

The man liked the idea. "What do you suggest, Doctor?" he asked. The doctor said, "I have never heard of a man running himself to death. If you want to get into the headlines, run around the block until you drop dead, and every newspaper will have it on the front page."

"That's what I'm going to do," said the man, and off he went to make the news.

He went home, wrote his letter of farewell, then started running. He ran and he ran, but he couldn't drop dead. He got so tired he said, "I'll have to finish it tomorrow night." He went back home and slept better than he had for a long time.

The next night he ran again, around and around; but he couldn't drop dead, and—you've guessed it—he didn't drop dead at all! He literally ran himself back to health and strength!

The Finish Line

*N*ow, we are not suggesting such a drastic program! But the good news is that you can make a decision about your health, your lifestyle, which will promote not only physical wellness by reducing the risk and progression of heart disease, stroke, osteoporosis, kidney disease, diabetes, and cancer, but also will improve mental health.

What is the best form of exercise? For alleviating stress and maximizing pleasure try vigorous but not violent, cooperative but not competitive, activities. Brisk walking, hiking, bicycling, swimming, canoeing, chores like splitting wood, gardening, jumping on a trampoline, stair-climbing, stationary exercise machines—all provide good, non-jarring activity.

With the help of God, will you choose to make moderate exercise-at least 20 minutes twice a day—a God-ordained priority in your life?

Good! You can start right now!

REFERENCES

1. Crespo C, Keteyian S, Heath G, et al. Leisure-time activity among U.S. adults. Results from the Third National Health and Nutrition Examination Survey. Archives of Internal Medicine 1996 Jan;156(1):93-98.

2. Brink S. Smart Moves: 1995 Health Guide. U.S. News and World Report, Inc.

3. Spitzer R, Kroenke K, Linzer M, et al. Health-related quality of life in primary care patients with mental disorders. Journal of the American Medical Association 1995 Nov;274(19):1511-1517.

4. Camacho T, et al. Physical activity and depression: evidence from the Alameda County Study. American Journal of Epidemiology 1991;134(2):220-231.

5. Weyerer S, Kupfer B. Physical exercise and psychological health. Sports Medicine 1994;17(2):108-116.

6. Thayer R. Energy, tiredness, and tension effects of a sugar snack versus moderate exercise.

7. Hare E. Make God First. Washington D.C. Review and Herald Publishing Co., 1964.

8. American Heart Association Report, March 1999; Abstract #492.

9. Steinberg H. Exercise enhances creativity independently of mood. British Journal of Sports Medicine 1997;31(3):240-45.

Doctor 10:

Best

13

GOD'S ANSWER

Sleepier Than Ever!

Americans are suffering from daytime sleepiness so pervasive that it interferes with their daily activities, according to experts at the National Sleep Foundation. According to their surveys, 40% of adults say that they are so sleepy during the day that it interferes with their daily activities.

For example, drowsy driving causes 100,000 crashes in the U.S. each year. Sixty percent of children under the age of 18 complain of being tired during the day, with 15% falling asleep at school on a regular basis. Surprisingly, 62% of Americans experience problems falling asleep several nights a week, with smokers and alcohol users experiencing the highest frequency of sleep-related problems.

Burning on Both Ends?

Is getting to bed on time on your list of important things to do each day? "Burning the midnight oil" may be burning you out—in more ways than one!

Michael Irwin, a psychiatrist at the San Diego Veterans Affairs Medical Center, and his team, studied 23 healthy men, age 22 to 61, who spent 4 nights in a sleep laboratory. He found that even modest levels of sleep deprivation resulted in a 30 percent drop in immune function. Returning to normal sleep patterns restored immunities. God made the beasts to go out after dark—not man! "Thou makest darkness, and it is night: wherein all the beasts of the forest do creep forth." *Psalm* **104:20**.

Early to Bed, Early to Rise...

*I*s it true that early-to-bed, early-to-rise, makes a man healthy, wealthy, and wise? Even though this saying is not in the Bible, there is a similar truth laid out by our Creator:

"The sun ariseth, (the wild beasts) gather themselves together, and lay them down in their dens. Man goeth forth unto his work and to his labour until the evening." *Psalm* **104:22-23**.

Science confirms this simple truth about man's proper bedtime being soon after sunset.

Dr. Thomas Weir, head of the clinical psychobiology branch of the National Institute of Mental Health, is conducting some interesting studies to see if people who follow the "early-to-bed, early-to-rise" maxim are actually gaining health benefits. So far, his studies have shown that sleeping in a "dusk-to-dawn" pattern, as opposed to late bedtime and late rising, actually causes an increase in the brain's production of melatonin.

Melatonin is a hormone produced in the pineal gland that is implicated in the regulation of sleep, mood, puberty, and ovarian cycles. Melatonin insufficiency may be involved in such disorders as chronic fatigue, insomnia and jet lag, lethargy and fatigue in night workers, depression, and even suicide.

Sealed Instructions

*W*e read in the book of Job: "When deep sleep falleth upon men, in slumberings upon the bed; then He openeth the ears of men, and sealeth their instructions." *Job* **33:15-16**.

It is in deep sleep, primarily in the hours before midnight, that information learned during the day is transferred from the hippocampus area of the brain (short-term memory bank), to the permanent storage area of the neocortex.

Research suggests that deep, uninterrupted sleep is when the majority of memory storage takes place in the brain. In a study published in Science, researchers reported that deep sleep is critically important to the learning process, and that people tend to absorb knowledge about new skills while sleeping.

In the words of the researchers, "We and others have found that an improvement in perceptual performance occurs neither during or immediately after practice of a procedure, but rather eight to 10 hours after a training session has ended."

Sleep Time — Valued Time!

Many people not only go to bed late, they also get up early, catching naps in order to "keep going." But according to some researchers, fragmented sleep may be worse than a bout of no sleep at all, in terms of the affect on motor skills, mood, and cognitive ability.

According to a 1990 National Commission for Sleep Disorders Research report, Americans, on average, get 20% less sleep than their counterparts did a century ago.

The different phases of sleep which occur during the night restore the relationship between the nervous system and muscles, glands, immune and other body systems, as well as maintaining learning, reasoning, and emotional balance.

Remember the Fabulous Four?

Don't cheat yourself out of sleep. There are four essentials to establishing good sleep habits.

First, *Quantity*. The average person needs eight to nine

hours of sleep daily. This is essential for proper immune function, tissue repair, and nervous system and hormone balance. Children and teenagers need more.

Second, *Regularity*. Having a set bedtime and rising, as well as set times for eating, exercise, study and work, helps your body to establish regular biorhythms, which reduces cancer risk and normalizes hormone metabolism.

Third, *Timing*. As mentioned before, an early-to-bed pattern of sleeping enhances learning, mood, overall health, and childhood development.

Fourth, *Quality*. Ever sleep a long time and wake up tired? There are a number of factors that can interfere with quality sleep. Eating late, sugary foods, lack of regular exercise, smoking, and the use of caffeinated beverages or drugs can seriously impair the quality of sleep. Certain prescription drugs, including sleeping pills and anti-depressants, can cause sleep problems.

Stress, television, harsh music and bright lights at night can also reset the body's inner clock to late-night wakefulness and diminish quality sleep. Anger and guilt can destroy peaceful sleep.

Someone once said, "A clear conscience makes a soft pillow." Hanging onto grudges and anger robs us of inner peace that is essential to sound sleep. Perhaps that is why the Bible tells us not to let the sun go down on our wrath, but as far as possible, "be at peace among yourselves." *I Thessalonians* **5:13**.

Sleep: It Should Be a Top Priority!

*Y*our Creator and Savior understands your need of sleep, and He will help you plan it into your lifestyle. Indeed, we now know from science that if you do not make proper sleep a top priority, you will pay a price!

In this troubled and perplexing world, our Savior is interested in our sleep habits: "It is vain for you to sit up late...He giveth His beloved sleep." *Psalm* **127:2**.

It was Jesus who, pressed with cares and an urgent mission, told his weary disciples, "Come ye yourselves apart...and rest awhile." *Mark* **6:31**.

Jesus invites all of us who are weary of sin to come to Him for rest from our sinful ways. He wants us to find spiritual rest from our heavy burden of sin, perplexity, and sorrow. He also invites us to plan refreshing, restoring physical rest into our lives. With His help, we can achieve both essentials—spiritual and physical rest!.

REFERENCES

1. Wilson M. Reactivation of hippocampal ensemble memories during sleep. Science 1994 Jul;265(5172):676-679; 603-604.
2. Irwin M. Partial sleep deprivation reduces natural killer cell activity in humans. Psychosomatic Medicine 1994;56:493-498.
3. Cox News Service, Nov. 3, 1994
4. Dorland's Illustrated Medical Dictionary. 28th edition, 1994. W.B. Saunders Co., Philadelphia, PA.
5. Harvard Women's Health Watch, March 1994.
6. Internal Medicine News 1996 Aug;29(16)55; April;29(8)11.
7. Boivin D. Dose-response relationships for resetting of human circadian clock by light. Nature 1996 Feb;379(6565):540-542.
8. Totterdell P. Associations of sleep with everyday mood, minor symptoms and social interaction experience. Sleep 1994;17(5):466-475.
9. National Sleep Foundation Survey, Spring, 1999.

13

ℒ ifestyle Matters!

In part 2 we'll discover simple, effective lifestyle choices we can make that will greatly reduce overall stress and help us to better cope with the stresses we can't avoid!

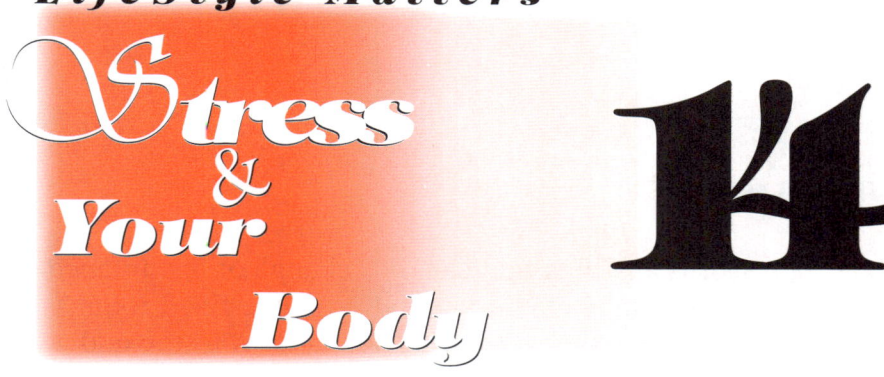

Stress & Your Body

14

Stress: It's A Part of Life

I don't think anyone would argue the fact that stress is a part of life—a big part for most people. As was mentioned earlier, two-thirds of Americans say they feel "stressed-out" at least once a week.

Most people associate being "stressed-out" with external factors over which they have no control. The cranky boss, the crashed computer, the finances, the leaky faucet—all can be unavoidable stressors. As a matter of fact, sometimes life seems to be a virtual sea of stress.

What Is Stress, Anyway?

Stress is a well-known, often used, but often ill-defined term. It has different meanings to different people. Living organisms survive by maintaining homeostasis, or dynamic equilibrium.

A technical definition of "stress" is a state of disharmony, disequilibrium, or threatened homeostasis. Perhaps a more practical definition would be "the sum total of our responses to the various forces impinging on our lives. These forces can be physical, emotional, chemical, spiritual or symbolic in nature. Stress is the sum total of your responses to the demand for extra body functions.

What Is A Stressor?

A stressor is anything that causes a change or disturbance in body function. It can be environmental (a smoke-filled room that makes you cough), physical (a brick falling on your toe and breaking it), chemical (alcohol ingestion which causes dizziness or nausea), spiritual (your conscience telling you not to steal), emotional (someone yells at you), or symbolic (the sight of a tombstone reminds you of a departed friend).

Let's Get Specific

*B*ut there's more to the stress story. A stressor can be specific or non-specific, local or general. For instance, a bee sting is a local, specific stressor to a certain area of the body. A fever is a general stress response to an infection.

An example of a nonspecific stressor would be the effect of a high fat diet on two different people. After years of too much fat in the diet, one person might develop diabetes, while another may have a heart attack. The stressor was the same—too much fat. But the response varied according to the individual constitution and genetic makeup of the individual, as well as several other factors.

The stress response will also vary with the magnitude, length, and timing of the stressful event. But your constitution, environment and nutritional status are all factors.

When You're Stressed

*T*he initial response to stress has been called an "alarm reaction." A typical stress reaction results in a series of more than 1,400 known physiochemical reactions. We can all identify with the queasy stomach, rapid heart beat, shallow breathing, sweating, agitation, dry mouth, etc.

Other, more subtle signs of stress include excessive talking, perfectionism, memory problems, procrastination, fatigue, insomnia, volatile emotions, poor job performance, and depression.

A little stress is good—it enhances memory and prepares the body for physical or mental emergencies. But continued exposure to stress can result in exhaustion, disease, shock, dementia or even death.

Are You Unnecessarily Stressed?

Stress is capable of exerting its influence upon the metabolism and function of virtually every system of the body, including nerves, muscles, organs, glands, and vessels. We also know that stress is able to alter your body's nutrtient needs. How?

Chronic stress increases the need for foods rich in vitamin A, B, C, E, zinc and magnesium, for instance. Junk food exacerbates the problem by causing depletion of the very nutrients needed to service the body's increased demands due to stress. This state of depletion stimulates the body to produce more stress hormones, thus causing a vicious "stress-depletion" cycle that can adversely affect your health!

Lifestyle Stressors

Increasingly, science is revealing an amazing number of "lifestyle stressors," which, unlike the unhappy and uncontrollable type we all must face, are not only identifiable but also controllable! In addition, science is also revealing some amazingly simple ways to "handle" the uncontrollable stressors in such a way as to minimize emotional and physical pain as well as disease.

Interestingly, these are also Biblical principles. Many of us are ignorantly bringing unnecessary stress into our lives and dealing inappropriately with the stressors that are unavoidable.

As mentioned earlier, when your body is stressed, disease is often the result. In the following series, we will explore simple ways to reduce or eliminate controllable stressors, as well as build emotional and physical coping power to manage the stressful events that are unavoidable and potentially debilitating.

It is God's will "that every one of you should know how to possess his vessel in sanctification and honour." *I Thessalonians* **4:4**. In the following pages, we will learn that when we obey the natural laws that govern our beings, not only is God honored, but improved health of body and mind is sure to follow.

REFERENCES

1. Chrousos G. Mechanisms of Physical and Emotional Stress. New York, NY: Plenum Press; 1988.
2. Baldwin B. Stress. Journal of Health and Healing. 18(3):54-58.
3. Selye H. The Stress of Life. New York, NY: McGraw-Hill Books, 1956.
4. Nutrition and Stress. Nutrition News, October 1986.

14

LifeStyle Matters

Up In Smoke

15

Those Old Ads Wouldn't Fool Anyone Today

Back in the 1950s, cigarette ads were different. One claimed that "more doctors recommend Lucky Strike" because they were easier on the lungs. Camel cigarettes were touted to be the brand that more doctors smoked than any other.

Today, people have changed. Advertisements have changed. Times have changed. But cigarettes *have not* changed. Why do people smoke when we have so much knowledge as to their harmful effects? It seems to defy logic. How can we understand the phenomenon of smoking? Why do people smoke, when they know it is killing them? There are several possible reasons.

Smoking's Not Addictive?

Scientists are just beginning to understand that there are several mechanisms of addiction in operation when a person smokes. The major addicting component of cigarettes is nicotine. Nicotine belongs to a class of alkaloids that includes cocaine, morphine and strychnine. One recent study revealed how even tiny amounts of nicotine turn on chemical "switches" in the brain which speed up and intensify the flow of glutamate, a powerful brain neurohormone. The result is the magnification of brain signals and short-term heightened perceptions. On the downside, excess glutamate flow in the brain may be associated with such neurodegenerative diseases as Alzheimer's and Parkinson's.

A Legal Narcotic?

Nicotine also imitates the action of acetylcholine, a powerful neurotransmitter. The result is muscle, heart, nerve, and brain stimulation. But it also stimulates dopamine transmission in a specific area of the brain (mesolimbic system in the nucleus acumbens), which is recognized as a critical target of drugs of abuse.

Nicotine has similar addictive properties and chemical action as cocaine and heroin. Perhaps that is why the addiction profile for cigarette smokers is about the same as heroin addicts— only about 3-5% are able to quit unaided.

Smoking Their Blues Away?

Studies are beginning to show that those who are susceptible to foul moods, stress, loneliness, boredom and restlessness (about 40 million Americans) were more likely to be smokers! Depression is a double curse because it seems to drive many people to start smoking, and then makes it harder to quit.

Interestingly, even though nicotine manipulates brain chemistry, it has not been shown to enhance mood until a high level of tolerance to the drug is developed. But smoking is a stressful and depressing activity in itself. A recent analysis showed that within six months of quitting, stress levels of ex-smokers had dropped by 50%!

Legacy of Death and Disease

Worldwide smoking is killing about 3 million people each

year. That is about six people every minute. Smoking dramatically increases blood pressure in the user, and significantly increases the risk for cancer, stroke, heart disease, cataracts, psoriasis and lumbar disc disease.

Those who are exposed to passive smoke not only increase their risk of lung cancer, but almost double their risk of coronary heart disease. The babies of smoking mothers may suffer serious birth weight deficits. New data has revealed that the offspring of fathers who smoke for five years or more have a 70 percent greater risk of developing cancer (lymphoma) and almost three times the risk of developing brain tumors. This is due to smoking-induced damage to the sperm's DNA.

Packing A Punch During Pregnancy

Early studies have linked maternal smoking with attention deficit hyperactivity disorder, while recent data reveals that learning disorders and aggressive antisocial behavior are associated with maternal smoking during pregnancy. Babies exposed to cigarette smoke are at increased risk for sudden infant death, middle ear infection, and respiratory illnesses.

Young men who smoke increase their risk of infertility and increase the risk of having children with mental impairment because of genetic damage to their sperm.

Is There Any Good News?

Now that we understand how insidious and destructive smoking is, let's consider the good news. The good news is that you can decide not to smoke. "I've made that decision a hundred times," you may be thinking. But how do I really make it "stick?"

First of all, remember that "with men it is impossible, but not with God: for with God all things are possible." *Mark* **10:27**.

You can ask Him now to take away your desire for smoking and to put a hatred in your heart for it. Remember, "He is able even to subdue all things unto Himself"— even your strong desire to smoke. *Philippians* **3:21**.

Can prayer be an aid to stop smoking? Absolutely—and science validates the conclusion. A recent study conducted at John Hopkins University revealed that when a person prays and asks God for help, he or she is three times more likely to succeed in kicking the smoking habit!

But why should that surprise us? Shouldn't we expect this? These lifestyle issues become very serious when we consider them from God's point of view. Paul showed his understanding of God's requirement for physical as well as moral purity:

"But I keep under my body, and bring it into subjection: lest that by any means, when I have preached to others, I myself should be a castaway." *I Corinthians* **9:27**. Why not take God at His Word today, and ask Him to help you stop smoking—for good! You are valuable to Him!

Tips For Quitting

Throw away the cigarettes and avoid old smoking "places."

• Instead of focusing on what you have to give up, load yourself with benefits from Nature's Storehouse so you can feel great every day.

• Try leaving off caffeine and sugar, and replace these unhealthy stimulants with plenty of pure water and lots of fresh fruits and vegetables (especially greens) every day.

• Get at least 30 minutes exercise in the fresh air and sunshine every day, and be sure to go to bed early so your body can repair and be well-rested.

• When craving a cigarette, take a cool shower when possible, and have some calming herb tea like chamomile.

　• Pray! Pray! Pray! Dart a prayer to Heaven, and repeat the promise in *Romans* **8:37**: "Nay, in all these things we are more than conquerors through Him that loved us."

　• In addition to your Heavenly Friend, line up a friend on earth that you can call and talk to if you are feeling tempted to pick up that pack again. Gather strength and courage from him or her during your conversation. It really helps!

REFERENCES

1. Pontieri F. Effects of nicotine on the nucleus accumbens and similarity to those of addictive drugs. Nature 1996;382:206-207, 255-257.

2. McGehee D. Nicotine enhancement of fast excitatory synaptic transmission in CNS by presynaptic receptors. Science 1995 Sept;269(5231):1692-1696.

3. Blaylock, R. Excitotoxins: The Taste That Kills. Health Press, Santa Fe, NM. 1997.

4. Foulds J. The role of nicotine in tobacco smoking: implications for tobacco control policy. Journal of the Royal Society of Health 1995 Aug;11f5(4):225-230.

5. Cohen S. Perceived stress, quitting smoking, and smoking relapse. Health Psychologist 1990;9(4):466-478.

6. Kawachi I. A prospective study of passive smoking and coronary heart disease. Circulation 1997 May;95(10):2374-2379.

7. Wakschlag L. Maternal smoking during pregnancy and the risk of conduct disorder in boys. Archives of General Psychiatry 1997 Jul;54(7):670-676.

8. Mure K. Genotoxic potentials of lifestyles assessed by urinary mutagenicity. Medical Journal of Osaka University 1994

Sept;43(1-4):9-15.

9. Owen M. Relation of infant feeding practices, cigarette smoke exposure and group child care to the onset and duration of otitis media with effusion in the first two years of life. Journal of Pediatrics 1993;123:702-711.

10. Cui J. Effects of passive smoking on respiratory illness from birth to age eighteen months. Journal of Pediatrics 1993;123:553-558.

11. Manninen P. Incidence and risk factors of low-back pain in middle-aged farmers. Occupational Medicine 1995 Jun;45(3):141-146.

12. Christen W. A prospective study of cigarette smoking and risk of cataract in men. Journal of the American Medical Association 1992 Aug;268(8):989-993.

13. Baughman R. Psoriasis and Cigarettes: another nail in the coffin. Archives of Dermatology 1993 Oct;129:1329.

14. Voorhees C. Heart, body, and soul: impact of church-based smoking cessation interventions on readiness to quit. Preventative Medicine 1996 May/Jun;25(3):277-285.

LifeStyle Matters

Alcohol 16

Some Sobering Statistics

No one would disagree that alcohol is the number-one drug problem in North America. Alcohol contributes to 100,000 deaths annually, making it the third leading cause of preventable death in the US, after tobacco and diet.

In 1992, more than 7 percent of the population 18 years and older—nearly 13.8 million Americans—had problems with drinking. About 43% of the adult population—76 million people—have been exposed to alcoholism in their family. Nearly 50 percent of highway accidents and 50 percent of the incidents of domestic and job violence are estimated to be alcohol-related. In the US, alcohol is implicated in 50 percent of homicides, 33 percent of suicides, 50 percent of rapes, 72 percent of assaults, 70 percent of robberies, and 50 percent of child-abuse cases.

Youth On A Binge

Approximately 10 million Americans under the age of 21 had at least one drink last month; of these, 4.4 million were "binge" drinkers. Eighty-one percent of high school seniors have used alcohol, with the first usage occurring at age 13.

Thirty-percent of children in grades four through six report that their classmates have pressured them "a lot" to drink beer, and 80% of teenagers don't know that a can of beer has the same amount of alcohol as a shot of whiskey or a glass of wine. Approximately 8% of the nation's eighth graders, 21% of tenth graders, and 33% of twelfth graders report that they have been drunk during the last month. Forty percent of college students have "binged" on alcohol during the past two weeks.

The "Grain" Brain Drain

Not every drinker is a criminal. Many people in our society use alcoholic beverages to *unwind*. A glass of wine or two seems to act as a mild anesthetic—a harmless way to relieve the stress and tension of living, right?

What social drinkers do not understand is that the alcohol and the acetaldehyde it produces wreak destruction in the brain. Protein synthesis is diminished, and the smaller cells in the frontal cortex (the judgement area of the brain) are gradually damaged or destroyed.

Just two drinks a day is known to produce irreversible nerve-cell damage. World-renowned neurologist, Dr. Cyril Courville, studied the data from 40,000 brain specimens and confirmed that the most common cause of brain atrophy (shrinkage or weakening) is alcohol.

One of the little-known injuries of alcohol is that it causes clustering of red blood cells, which block tiny blood capillaries. The result? Blood flow is reduced to the brain and muscles, which causes impaired muscle coordination, mental acuity, judgement and eventual muscle and brain wasting.

The French Correction

For years now, the media has touted reports that moderate use of wine (2-3 glasses per day) lowers coronary heart disease risk, and the French have been used as an example. What the news reporters failed to reveal is that French men are three times as likely to die of esophageal cancer, and that both men and women are twice as likely to die of stomach cancer. Stomach and esophageal cancer care both tied to alcohol use.

The French mortality rate from cirrhosis of the liver and chronic liver disease is twice as high as for Americans. They also have higher suicide and accident rates, 50% of which are alcohol-related.

In reality, wine's heart benefits are weak at best. Recent studies have shown that the French have lower milk and butterfat consumption and higher vegetable oil, and fruit and vegetable consumption than countries with higher heart disease rates. All of those factors tend to lower heart disease risk.

Although wine consumption slightly elevates HDL cholesterol, it is now known that it is not the HDL value alone that is important, but the ratio of HDL to LDL that is significant, which is achieved only through a healthy lifestyle. (Pesticide ingestion also raises HDL, but is anyone actively encouraging us to use it for this benefit? The risks far outweigh the weak advantage!)

While some reports indicate that it would actually take up to 6 drinks of wine a day to receive a slight benefit, the newest research from Britain reports "no evidence" that drinking red wine in *any amount* provides protection against heart disease.

A Wee Bit Too Much?

Alcohol affects virtually every organ system in the body, even in small amounts. As little as 1 1/2 ounces a day can lead to cirrhosis of the liver. Small amounts of alcohol over time can compromise the immune system, create vitamin and mineral deficiencies, and increase hypertension by raising blood fats and blood pressure.

Just one glass a day generates destructive free radicals, destroys significant amounts of vitamin C and antioxidants, and may also destroy vitamin E and selenium. Alcohol irritates the stomach, causing marked increases in gastric ulcers and bleeding. It slows digestion and blood circulation, and can cause digestive disorders. It is now known that cancer of the oral cavity, pharynx, larynx, esophagus, stomach, large bowel, pancreas, thyroid, and breast are more prevalent in alcohol users.

A Cluster of Benefits

The Bible says that "the new wine is found in the cluster...destroy it not; for a blessing is in it." *Isaiah* **65:8**. This is so true!

Pure grape juice contains resveratrol, which acts as an anticoagulant and cholesterol-lowering agent. Grape juice is also an excellent tonic for the stomach and is a healing agent for a number of stomach disorders. Grape juice is also rich in antioxidants that fight free radical damage and cancer.

A Cluster of Council

The Bible has sound council for all who would tamper with alcoholic beverages. There is no contradicting message: "Wine is a mocker, strong drink is raging: and whosoever is deceived thereby is not wise...Look not thou upon the wine when it is red, when it giveth his colour in the cup; when it moveth itself aright. At the last it biteth like a serpent, and stingeth like an adder. *Proverbs* **20:1; 23:31-32**.

Perhaps William Shakespeare summed up this Bible truth best: "Oh, that men should put an enemy in their mouths, to steal away their brains!"

REFERENCES

1. Facts About Alcohol. US. Dept. of Health and Human Services 1981(Pub. #ADM. 80-31).

2. Alcohol and Health; Sixth Special Report to the U.S. Congress 1987(Pub. # ADM 87-1519).

3. Alcohol Health and Research World 1985 Sum;9(4):16-62; 1986 Spring;10(3).

4. Alcoholism and Alcohol-related problems. National Council on Alcohol and Drug Dependence, 1997.

5. Youth and Alcohol: an Overview. Ibid.

6. Journal of Health and Healing 1995;18(3).

7. Diet and Nutrition Letter 1992;9(12).

8. Artaud-Wild S. Differences in coronary mortality can be explained by differences in cholesterol and saturated fat intakes in 40 countries but not in France and Finland. Circulation 1993 Dec;90(6):3118-3119.

9. Shaper A. Alcohol, the heart, and health. American Journal of Public Health 1993 Jun;83(6):799-801.

10. Lecomte E. Effect of alcohol consumption on blood antioxidant nutrients and oxidative stress indicators. American Journal of Clinical Nutrition 1994 Aug;60(2):255-261.

11. Nutrition and Cancer, Etiology and Treatment. Raven Press, 1981.

12. Kafer E. Disruptive effects of ethyl alcohol on the mitotic chromosome segregation in diploid and haploid strains of Aspergillus nidulans. Mutation Research 1984;135:53-75.

16

LifeStyle Matters

Caffeine 17

There's Trouble Brewing

Coffee. It has trouble brewing in American pots. Americans drink 33 million gallons of coffee daily, the equivalent of 30 seconds of full flow of Niagara Falls! That's about 28 gallons per person every year—and that's just from coffee and doesn't include the caffeine in tea, cola, chocolate, and many drug medications.

A Nervous Nation

Nine out of ten North Americans use caffeine daily, with world consumption exceeding 4 million tons per year. It has been called the world's most widely used psychoactive drug. The average American consumes 280 mg.of caffeine every day. By conservative estimate, 30% of adult Americans consume more than 500 mg. a day. More than 80% of adults consume what the American Psychiatric Association terms "behaviorally active" doses.

Caffeine: "Rushing" Roulette

Caffeine is a non-amine stimulant, as is cocaine and nicotine, and is part of a larger group of drugs related to amphetamines called analeptics. Coffee and its calamitous cousins, tea, cola and chocolate, are really chemical relatives. Each contains toxic alkaloid chemicals known as methylated xanthines, which include caffeine, theobromine and theophyline.

Caffeine is a chemical stressor. It contains no nutrients, and draws on the body's emergency reserves of energy by creating a *chemical* emergency. But like any credit card purchase, money borrowed comes due with interest! Remember: stress causes physiological change, whether that stress is of an emotional, physical or chemical nature.

We are marvelously adapted to handle temporary bouts of stress, but what happens to us when stress becomes prolonged? The result is disease, disability, dementia or even death.

Big Charge For A Little Rush

Most people drink coffee because they feel they need a "lift" and want to perform their work more efficiently. What actually happens is that there is about a 30% decrease in brain blood flow with as little as 250 mg., and a significant increase in stress and anxiety levels.

Caffeine has been shown to have a detrimental effect on delicate motor performance and has a negative affect on free-recall. Prolonged use can permanently impair memory and create a surplus of stress hormones in the brain (cortisol in particular), which can promote long-term depression.

Caffeine users are three times more likely to interpret an event as stressful, and respond impulsively to stressful situations. Caffeine users are more likely to experience elevated levels of hostility, anxiety, depression, fatigue and anxiety. Do any of us need more of these things?

Are the Perks Worth the Price?

Just one cup of coffee a day is associated with increased

risk of stomach, kidney, lung, rectal, and esophageal cancer. Two cups a day doubles the risk of fatal bladder cancer, raises colon cancer risk by 250% and increases the risk of ovarian and pancreatic cancer.

Vitamin deficiencies and poor iron absorption are also associated with caffeine use, especially tea. One to five cups of coffee a day increases heart attack risk by 60%, while 6 or more cups increase the risk 250%. Just two cups a day can raise blood pressure by 20%.

Caffeine also stresses the pancreas and compounds diabetes by raising blood sugar levels and serum fatty acids, which can lead to functional hypoglycemia. It is also associated with calcium loss from the bones. A child drinking a 12-ounce soda gets the equivalent amount of caffeine intake, on a body weight basis, of an adult who drinks 4 cups of instant coffee.

Is Decaff "De" Answer?

*H*ardly. Even decaffeinated coffee has a number of potentially harmful chemical components, such as irritating caffeols and other alkaloid substances. During roasting the coffee bean undergoes a chemical transformation that creates 700 volatile substances, including acetaldehyde, ammonia, carbon disulfide, acetic acid, and notrosamines. Sound yummy?

De-Stress Your Life!

*C*affeine not only causes disease, it also creates emotional stress, while aggravating existing stress! Coffee does not help you cope—it adds to life's bundle of problems. What are some healthy alternatives? Postum and Roma both are delicious, coffee-like beverages that do not contain caffeine. They are available at your health food store or the grocery store.

How about a nice herbal tea on a cold winter night? And if you need a "lift," try a big, sparkling glass of water and a brisk jaunt up a flight of stairs! Many times we're droopy because we are dehydrated and physically sluggish from lack of exercise.

Sleep deprivation is also a big reason for an overtaxed stress system, and consequent fatigue. Most important, remember that only the Lord can deliver you from the strong bondage of bad habits. "Thy God hath commanded thy strength...the God of Israel is He that giveth strength and power unto his people." *Psalm* **68:28, 35**. Jesus Christ alone can lift you out of the bondage of caffeine and keep you free. "He is able to keep that which I have committed unto him against that day." *2 Timothy* **1:12**.

REFERENCES

1. Cardiovascular News, April 1986, p.4.
2. Robeson B. A closer look at the deadly effects of caffeine. The Nutritional Consultant 1984/May.
3. Glass R. Caffeine dependence. What are the implications? Journal of the American Medical Association 1994 Oct;272(13):1065-1066.
4. Greden J. Coffee, tea and you. The Sciences 1979;7:6-11.
5. Strain E. Caffeine dependence syndrome. Evidence from case histories and experimental evaluations. Journal of the American Medical Association 1994 Oct;272(13):1043-1048.
6. American Medical News, October 10, 1994, p. 23.
7. Akers R. Drugs, Alcohol, and Society. Belmont, CA. Wadsworth Pub, 1992.
8. Griffin V. Calamity in a Cup. Silver Springs, MD: Review and Herald Pub., 1995.

LifeStyle Matters

Sugar 18

Sugar: The Sweet Stressor!

$\mathcal{A}$s we have discussed, a "stressor" is anything that disturbs homeostasis, whether it is physical, mental, chemical, or spiritual. Is it possible that the refined sugar consumption of Americans is contributing to the rising toll of disease, depression, chronic fatigue, tension, insomnia and anxiety that plague so many millions?

Sweeter As The Days Go By?

$\mathcal{S}$ugar consumption in the United States rose from approximately 35 pounds per person in 1880 to about 100 pounds in 1970. It is estimated that today's sugar consumption hovers somewhere around 35-40 teaspoons per person per day—that's 110 to 115 pounds per person per year!

While some reports indicate that white refined sugar consumption is down, the drop is largely due to an increased use of high fructose corn syrup, a concentrated sweetener processed from cornstarch. U.S. Department of Agriculture figures show a 250% increase in high fructose corn syrup consumption over the last 15 years.

About 70% of the sugars we consume are hidden in obvious places like soda, cookies, cakes, pastries, candy, donuts and ice cream. But hey are also unsuspected guests in a majority of processed and refined foods such as gravies, sauces, peanut butter, bouillon cubes, seasoning mixes, ketchup, mayonnaise, salad dressing, canned fruits and vegetables, processed cheese spreads, stuffing and bread mixes, sweet pickles, fruit yogurt, cereals, frozen juices, etc.

Juicy Juniors

Today, sugar accounts for about 20 percent of the calories we consume each day. Two hundred years ago, it accounted for less than one percent. We mentioned earlier that the average American consumes a mind-boggling 537 cans of soda pop each year, with the amount hovering at 643 for Southerners.

Many well-meaning parents are switching from soda pop to fruit juices as the beverage of choice for their toddlers and children. Children under the age of five consume an average of nine gallons of juice annually. The calories from juice are almost entirely simple carbohydrates, and the mineral content, with the exception of potassium, is very low.

Juice provides calories in the form of sugar but does not contain the fat, protein, complex carbohydrates, fiber, vitamins and minerals essential for proper growth and nutrition. One study found that children consuming 12-30 ounces of juice per day were getting up to 60% of their daily calories from juice alone! Is it any wonder that only 1% of US children meet the United States government dietary guidelines?

How Sweet It Isn't

All that sugar doesn't seem to be making us sweeter as a nation. It may be contributing to mood swings, fatigue and a host of diseases. Some researchers believe that sugar represents the "basic addiction" that precedes all others—and it can be one of the hardest to kick.

Sweet foods affect brain chemistry—but there's a down side to that quick lift. Research from Yale University showed that children who were given sugar on an empty stomach released large amounts of adrenaline, which resulted in shakiness, anxiety, excitement and concentration problems.

Significant relationships have been found between destructive, aggressive and restless behaviors in hyperactive children and refined sugar intake. Other studies have shown that high sugar intake is associated with lowered intelligence and achievement scores of children aged 5 to 16.

Sugar has been shown to have an adverse effect on energy, tiredness and tension. On the other hand, one study revealed that people suffering from major depression showed significantly reduced depression levels on all measures when abstaining from sugar and caffeine.

The Sour Side of Sweets

Excess sugar depletes vitamins and minerals, especially the B vitamins. This depletion can cause nervous system reactivity, irritability and anxiety. In other words, you increase your vulnerability to stressful events by taking in too many sweets and refined foods. Remember—sugar and fat are buddies. When a food is high in sugar, it is often also high in fat and low in fiber and nutritional value.

Too much sugar is implicated in premature puberty and aging, cataracts, headaches, tooth decay, bowel cancer, irritable bowel syndrome, breast cancer, lowered immune function, ulcers, and hypoglycemia.

As pointed out earlier, high fructose corn syrup consumption has gone up 250% in the last 15 years, and is implicated in chromium loss, as well as damage to the heart and pancreas.

Sweeten Up — Naturally!

*R*efined sugar is a lifestyle stressor worthy of careful monitoring. How can you dramatically reduce refined sugar intake? It's not difficult! Just remember that most processed foods contain sugar in one form or another. So cook dry beans rather than using canned beans. Start using fresh or frozen vegetables rather than canned products. Rather than buying packaged gravies and sauces, make your own. They taste great!

As you increase your intake of whole grains, beans, vegetables and fresh fruit, the need to snack can be eliminated because these foods are high in fiber, which increases satisfaction and delays gastric emptying.

Breakfast Bonanza!

*U*nrefined, whole grain hot cereals as opposed to instant, pre-sweetened cereals, are a nutritious alternative for breakfast. Millet, rice, rolled oats, barley grits, and multi-grain cereals can be sweetened with bananas, chopped dates, raisins, or little honey or rice syrup for a tasty breakfast treat.

By the way, pure honey has been shown to have healing properties that are absent in other sugars. Honey is sweeter than sugar and raises blood levels higher, but less is required to sweeten food.

Artificial sweeteners are not recommended due to potential side effects, some of them quite serious. Time-released energy, better mood and a more even temper are just a few of the rewards for shifting our focus from "fast food frenzy" to "fabulous, fresh, and fiber-filled!"

As we come closer to the "Designer Diet" given to our first parents in Eden, we may experience satisfaction instead of hunger, energy instead of fatigue, and health instead of chronic sickness and disease. How can we not thank our Creator, Jesus Christ, "Who satisfieth thy mouth with good things, so that thy youth is renewed like the eagles." *Psalms* **103:5**.

REFERENCES

1. Boucher F, Binnette A. Living Well With Stress. Psychological Guidance and Consultation Service, University of Montreal. 1989.
2. Basic Care Bulletin #13. Medical Training Institute of America. Box 3113 Oak Brook, IL 60522.
3. Clydesdale F, Kolasa K, Ikeda J. All you want to know about fruit juice. Nutrition Today March/April 1994.
4. Continuing survey of food intakes by individuals. Human Nutrition Information Service, USDA. Springfield, VA; National Technical Information Service, 1989-90.
Smith M, Lifshitz F. Excess fruit juice consumption as a contributing factor in nonorganic failure to thrive. Pediatrics 1994 Mar;93(3):438-443.
5. Demas A. Low fat school lunch programs—achieving acceptance. Summit on Cholesterol and Coronary Disease, Sept. 4-5, 1997.
6. Suguna L, Chandrakasan G. Influence of honey on collagen metabolism during wound healing in rats. Journal of Clinical Biochemical Nutrition 1992;13:7-12.
7. Science News, Sept. 25, 1993.
8. Phelps J, Nourse A. The Hidden Addiction and How to Get Free. Boston MA: Little Brown and Co. 1986.
9. Jones T, Borg W. Enhanced adrenomedullary response and

increased susceptibility to neuroglycopenia: mechanisms underlying the adverse effects of sugar ingestion in healthy children. Journal of Pediatrics 1995 Feb;126(2):171-177.

* This reference list is partial due to the extensive information presented. Publication of data with full referencing and additional information is pending.

Digestion: A Churning Question

During our lifetime, approximately 90,000 pounds of food and 55,000 quarts of fluids are processed by our digestive systems. Fortunately, we have internal machinery custom designed by our Creator for maximum efficiency and endurance. Unfortunately, about 25% of Americans have some kind of digestive complaint or disorder.

People talk about having "cast iron" stomachs, and we often treat our digestive organs like an old iron furnace. But in reality our digestive machinery is complex and very delicate.

Chewing the Facts...

When the stomach is deranged through improper nutrition or bad eating habits, virtually any other organ in the body can be adversely affected. For instance, a long-term observation was performed to determine the prevalence of gastrointestinal disorders in 1,500 patients with different forms of bronchial asthma.

Researchers discovered that 48% of the patients had different gastroenterological complaints, most of which began with simple indigestion. Interestingly, gastrointestinal disorders, and especially indigestion, were associated with food allergies.

The Indigestion Question

Indigestion can be caused by frequent eating, overeating, eating too fast, eating highly salted or spiced foods, as well as eating large amounts of foods high in concentrated fat, sugar or protein. Eating too quickly has been associated with a rapid rise in blood sugar, while eating more slowly results in more stable blood sugar levels—a very important point for diabetics!

According to Dr. Thomas Brunoski of the Institute of Human Nutrition of Columbia Medical School, aspirin and other anti-inflammatory drugs are a leading cause of stomach inflammation and ulcers. Also at the top of the gastritis and ulcer-causing list are tobacco, coffee, sugar and alcohol. Even aspartame (Nutri-Sweet) can cause stomach upset.

New research shows that chronic indigestion and ulcers are a significant cause of depression and personality disorders.

Stomachs In A Stew

Stomach cancer is on the rise in the United States, and researchers are beginning to point to possible dietary and lifestyle factors as possible causes.

In one hospital study, stomach cancer and gastritis patients were more likely to be smokers and have higher saturated fat and cholesterol intake. Recent studies have linked esophageal cancer (cancer of the throat) and pickled vegetable consumption. Other factors found to increase throat cancer risk were highly salted foods, alcohol intake, tea consumption, smoking, low vegetable and fruit consumption, and drinking soups and drinks at a very hot temperature.

It is already known that eating black pepper increases stomach cancer risk. Now new research on capsaicin, or red hot pepper, brings some new "heat" to this topic.

A study conducted in Mexico City revealed that red pepper

consumers were at high risk for gastric cancer compared to non-consumers. Conversely, high fruit and vegetable consumption is associated with lower incidence of digestive cancer.

Better Never Than Late

*S*nacking and late-night eating can really set off some gastrointestinal fireworks. Eating between meals can delay gastric emptying for hours, causing indigestion and fatigue. A high-fiber diet eliminates the need for snacking with most people.

Numerous studies have linked late-night eating with increased cancer rates, as well as higher serum cholesterol levels and LDL, and a higher LDL:HDL ratio than daytime eaters. It has been suggested that night time food intake may be associated with metabolic disturbances in lipid (fat) metabolism, and may lead to ischemic heart disease.

Night time eating may also reset the body clock to establish an "owl," or late, pattern of sleeping rather than a "lark," or early pattern of bedtime and sleeping. Researchers have found that going to be early is associated with numerous health benefits.

Late-night eating can also result in gastroesophageal reflux, a condition where gastric acid back-flows into the throat. This occurs when a person lies down or reclines after a meal. Such reflux can cause sore throat, wheezing, coughing and hoarseness.

Clearly, going to bed with a stomach full of food is a sure-fire way to "fire up" your digestive organs.

Taming Troubled Tummies

*O*ur loving Creator designed His children to be on a schedule—He loves order, not confusion. And even our very body rhythms respond to an orderly schedule. The wise King Solomon tells us in *Ecclesiastes* **10:17**:

"Blessed art thou, O land, when...thy princes eat in due season (at the proper times), for strength, and not for drunkenness."

Meal type, timing and quality all affect health, well-being and even society itself!   Stomachs are less likely to be upset on a program of regular meals at a set time.

Studies with pilots show that high salt and protein foods like meat, cheese, and chips tend to upset the stomach, while starchy foods like bread, cereal, and potatoes tend to have a calming effect.

We have seen that high consumption of fresh fruits and vegetables are beneficial and eliminate the need for snacking. Some wonderful curatives for upset stomachs include raw cabbage juice, charcoal tablets, ginger tea, DGL, aloe, slippery elm, mint tea, catnip tea and plantain bananas.

Frozen bananas whizzed in a blender have been reported in the literature to have a healing effect on gastroenteritis (irritation of the stomach lining and intestine). They also put a big smile on your face!

REFERENCES

1. Lemki L. A new tendency in speleotherapy. Allergy 1996;5(suppl):55.

2. Doctor's Forum, 1996. Keat's Publishing.

3. Zhang S. Smoking, dietary fat, fiber and vitamins influence the progression of chronic gastritis to distal gastric cancer: a case-control study. Gastroenterology 1995 April;108(4 suppl): abstract 515.

4. Cheng K. Pickled vegetables in the aetiology of oesophageal cancer in Hong Kong Chinese. Lancet 1992;339(8805):1314-1318.

5. Vecchia C. Tea consumption and cancer risk. Nutrition and Cancer 1992;17(1):27-31.

6. Lopez-Carillo L. Chili pepper consumption and gastric cancer in Mexico: a case-control study. American Journal of Epidemiology 1994 Feb;139(3):263-271.

7. Jess P. The personality patterns in patients with duodenal ulcer and ulcer-like dyspepsia and their relationship to the course of the diseases. Journal of Internal Medicine 1994;235(6):589-594.

8. Lennernas M. Nocturnal eating and serum cholesterol of three-shift workers. Scandinavian Journal of Work Environment Health 1994;20:401-406.

9. Medical Tribune News Service, June 1997.

10. Cortlandt Forum 1992 Aug;5(8).

11. Environmental Nutrition, Feb. 1996.

LifeStyle Matters

Tense and Tired

*M*any people think of sleep as a necessary evil, or an inconvenient nuisance at best. For them, sleep interrupts the steady stream of activities and projects that seem more "productive" than lying unconscious and uninvolved with the world.

We learned in our earlier discussion on rest (see Chapter 13) that the average American gets 20% less sleep than his or her counterpart did a century ago. Perhaps one reason is that so many of us live with disruptive, irregular schedules, eating patterns, work hours and constant interruptions. This tends to result in late hours, sleepless nights and fitful sleeping.

"For a dream cometh through a multitude of business...and much study is a weariness of the flesh." *Ecclesiastes* **5:3; 12:12**.

The United States of Insomnia

*A*mericans consume about 600 tons of sleeping pills a year— second only to aspirin. But sleeping pills often complicate and further disrupt an already poor quality of sleep.

An eight-year study of insomniacs revealed that there were three major factors contributing to chronic problems with sleeplessness: Depression, poor physical health and low levels of physical activity. Researchers concluded, however, that physical, not mental, ill-health was a greater risk factor for insomnia.

Lifestyle is a major determinant of both physical and mental health, and proper sleep is part of a healthy lifestyle. Basically, lifestyle affects sleep patterns, and sleep affects overall health and mood. Trying to correct poor sleep habits without considering lifestyle factors is a losing proposition.

We discussed earlier that some lifestyle factors that contribute to insomnia are lack of exercise, eating late at night, diets high in sugar, the use of caffeine or alcohol, stress, bright lights at night and certain drugs. Another major factor that causes sleep disruption, simply put, is a frenzied, irregular schedule!

Rhythm and Reason

The wise King Solomon wrote these inspired words: "To everything there is a season, and a time to every purpose under the heaven." *Ecclesiastes* **3:1**.

Our very physiology speaks to the grand order in which the Lord not only created and runs our external world, but also our internal machinery. Studies in chronobiology (body cycles) reveal that we have various "circadian," "circa," or "biological" rhythms which fluctuate according to time or day/night cycles.

The importance of circadian rhythms has been dramatized by giving deadly drugs to animals at different. Most of those treated at one time of day died. But when the same drug and dose were given to different animals at another time, most survived. The only variable? Daily circadian rhythm fluctuations.

Because of daily fluctuations in body metabolism, hormones and temperature, same-calorie meals taken at different times will affect weight-gain. In one study subjects were fed one daily meal, either at breakfast or dinner. The dinner-only subjects tended to gain weight, while breakfast-only subjects lost weight.

Circadian Cycles

*C*ircadian rhythms alter body temperature, heart rate, blood pressure, cortisol levels (cortisol is a stress hormone that peaks in the morning and declines throughout the day), adrenaline and norepinephrine levels, to name just a few.

Body temperature and metabolism begin to decline in the early evening in preparation for rest. God has ordained it: "The sun ariseth...man goeth forth unto his work and to his labour until the evening." *Psalm* **104:22, 23**.

We have 28-day cycles, 7-day cycles, and many more that depend on lifestyle and regularity for proper functioning. God designed that we should have periods of planned rest, not only daily, but once a week on the seventh day. (See: Exodus 20:8-11.) Our very physiology demands that we cooperate!

Keep that Sleep!

*S*taying up late at night can "desynchronize," or unbalance, the circadian rhythms that govern sleep and other body functions. Studies with shift-working nurses have indicated disruption of temperature and heart rate, increased fatigue and drowsiness, and decreased cognitive function because of the disruption of their normal circadian rhythms.

A number of studies indicate that mood is directly associated with circadian wake/sleep cycles. As we accumulate a "sleep debt" during the week, mood, motivation, attention, alertness, short-term memory, ability to complete routines, task performance and physical performance are all negatively effected.

Lark or Owl?

*W*e discovered in the section on rest that an early-to-bed

pattern of sleep as opposed to a "night owl" pattern is more productive in terms of mood, learning, and body restoration.

Studies with depressed patients suggest that early bedtime patterns result in more "dense" sleep, less depression, and better mental acuity, memory and performance.

Seize Those ZZZZZ's!

*D*on't short-change yourself by shortening your sleep. Remember: Quality, timing, regularity and quantity are all essential to maintaining healthy body cycles. It is also essential to have set times for rising, eating, exercise, study, work, worship and recreation. Your body was designed to be on a schedule.

Here's an important bit of advice—if you don't pare down, you'll wear down. Don't be a slave to chaos—ask God to restore order, sleep, and sanity to your life! "And the work of righteousness shall be peace; and the effect of righteousness quietness and assurance forever." *Isaiah* **32:17**.

REFERENCES

1. Morgan K. Risk factors for late-life insomnia in a representative general practice sample. British Journal of General Practice 1997 Mar;47(416):166-169.
2. Halberg G. Chronobiology and nutrition. Contemporary Nutrition 1983;8(9).
3. Gupta S. Desynchronization of circadian rhythms in a group of shift working nurses: effects of pattern of shift rotation. Journal of Human Ergology 1994 Dec;23(2):121-31.
4. Giam G. Effects of sleep deprivation with reference to military operations. Annals of the Acadamy of Medicine, Singapore 1997 Jan;26(1):88-93.
5. Riemann D. Advanced vs. normal sleep timing: effects on depressed mood after response to sleep deprivation in patients with major depressive disorder. Journal of Affective Disorder 1996 Apr;37(2-3):121-8.

LifeStyle Matters

Exercise II

21

Sitting Statistics

We discussed in our previous section on exercise that many Americans are guilty of staging perpetual sit-ins. A study of 10,000 adults revealed that 54 percent were sedentary during leisure time. This dearth of exercise causes an estimated 250,000 deaths each year and is a complicating factor in many other disorders!

Immobile Youth

Children are alarmingly sedentary, with only 36% even getting a 30-minute physical education class at school. Teens are becoming increasingly obese and diabetic. Before 1992, new cases of adolescent diabetes ran at about 4 percent per year. By 1994 that figure jumped to 16 percent—a 300% increase! That increase paralleled an increase in children's weights.

Sadly, it has been shown that even transient (temporary) obesity in adolescence may have a permanent impact on adult susceptibility to diabetes and other metabolic disorders.

Leisure hours that used to be spent doing chores, gardening, climbing trees, hiking and swimming are now often spent in front of the TV, playing video games, cruising in cars or surfing the

Internet. In spite of all these easy activities, children and youth
are more stressed and unhappy than ever before.

Life's Ups and Downs

*I*nactivity is strongly linked to higher levels of depression,
anxiety, stress, hostility, confusion and fatigue. A new survey of
1,000 adults found that depression, anxiety and psychological
problems actually impair physical and social functioning and
overall quality of life more than do common medical disorders
like arthritis and diabetes.

Regular exercise has consistently been shown to increase
overall health and immune function, and to reduce stress, tension
and fatigue. It also boosts mood, mental clarity, concentration,
self-esteem and even creativity!

Women at either end of the age spectrum benefit from
exercise. Exercise reduces postpartum depression in new mothers, and can prevent or relieve depression, sleeplessness, hot
flushes and mood swings in menopausal women. Weight-bearing
exercise like walking reduces a woman's risk of osteoporosis.

A single bout of exercise for anyone has been shown to
significantly reduce tension, depression, anger and confusion in
people of all ages, both male and female.

Vigorous...Not Violent

*W*hat is the best form of exercise? For alleviating stress
and maximizing pleasure, try vigorous but not violent, cooperative
but not competitive, activities. Brisk walking is being promoted as
one of the best forms of exercise for the majority of adults.

Hiking, bicycling, swimming, canoeing, gardening, jumping
on a trampoline, and even strenuous chores like splitting wood—
all have a rejuvenating effect on body and mind. Stationary

exercise machines or even climbing a good flight of stairs can provide healthy indoor exercise in bad weather.

Intensity and Immunity

A moderate dose of endurance exercise is beneficial to the immune system, bone density, heart health and life span. However, more intense and stressful exercise has been shown to have an adverse effect. There is growing evidence that over-exercise and violent exercise stresses the body by reducing its resistance to viral infections and overall cancer risk.

Violent exercise also increases the risk for high impact injuries, such as shin splints, sprains, and fractures. High impact aerobics are associated not only with bone, muscle and tendon injuries, but also permanent hearing impairment due to the loud, jarring music often associated with it.

Competition: Does Anyone Win?

*T*hose who engage in organized competitive sports may experience a stress condition known as *pre-competitive anxiety* while preparing for an event, as well as experiencing physical and emotional competitive anxiety during the game.

High levels of competition are linked to high levels of stress and an increased incidence of depression. In fact, some forms of sports and games such as karate and ice hockey, are associated with elevated systolic blood pressure, anger, and hostility.

Children involved in organized competitive games tend to have higher levels of stress and anxiety and often have to deal with highly stressed coaches and / or parents.

An interesting study reported in a sports medicine journal reported that children who engage in high contact sports such as football, develop moral standards more slowly, are more aggressive off the playing field and are less mature in their "moral reasoning." Remember, we are talking about organized competitive sports and activities, not a friendly family game of ball, tag or hide-and-seek.

Cooperation vs Competition

*M*any studies have shown that children placed in cooperative rather than organized, competitive physical exercise settings have higher levels of self-efficacy and achievement than those who compete. Cooperative games have consistently been shown to result in better cooperation during free play time, while competitive games result in increased aggression during unstructured play time.

Cooperative problem-solving increases intrinsic motivation (inner drive), develops more rapid problem-solving, positive interaction and higher belief in success.

Some examples of cooperative physical activities include hiking, seesawing, canoeing, a bicycle trip, building a tree house, working on a building project, gardening, etc.

Don't Blast the Brethren

*T*he values promoted in competitive sports are best depicted in the language used by sports writers and announcers—Team A is out to beat, blast, crash, crunch, trounce, trample, stomp, pound, pulverize, and otherwise demolish, demoralize and denigrate Team B.

Just for fun? Then why the high dollars, drugs, flared tempers and fights in the grandstands? At the "unprofessional" level we too often see hostility, aggression, tears, name-calling and depression. Science bears out what our eyes see and the Bible teaches. The Bible says that all our activities should cultivate Christian courtesy and cooperation, because "All ye are breth-ren." *Matthew* **23:8**. "Let nothing be done through strife or vainglory; but in lowliness of mind let each esteem other better than themselves. Look not every man on his own things, but every man also on the things of others." *Philippians* **2:3-4**.

These virtues can be very compatible with the energy, zeal and fun of outdoor activities, when conducted in the right way. They are also more beneficial!

REFERENCES

1. Unger J. Sedentary lifestyle as a risk factor for self-reported poor physical and mental health. American Journal of Health Promotion 1995;10(1):15-17.
2. Brink S. Smart Moves: 1995 Health Guide. U.S. News and World Report, Inc.
3. Pinhashamiel O. Increased incidence of non-insulin dependent diabetes mellitus among adolescents. Journal of Pediatrics 1996 May;128:608-615.
4. Ibid, (commentary) pp. 591-592.
5. Spitzer R. Health-related quality of life in primary care pa-tients with mental disorders. Journal of the American Medical Association 1995 Nov;274(19):1511-1517.
6. Murray M. Lifestyle and dietary factors in depression. Ameri-can Journal of Natural Medicine 1995 Dec;2(10):10-15.
7. Unger J. Sedentary lifestyle as a risk factor for self-reported poor physical and mental health. American Journal of Health Promotion 1995;10(1):15-17.
8. Camacho T. Physical activity and depression: evidence from the Alameda County Study. American Journal of Epidemiology 1991;134(2):220-231.

9. Young R. The acute effects of exercise on mood state. Journal of Psychosomatic Research 1996;40(2):123-141.

10. Thayer R. Energy, tiredness, and tension effects of a sugar snack versus moderate exercise. Journal of Personality and Social Psychology 1987 Jan;52(1):119-125.

This reference list is partial due to the extensive information presented. Publication of data with full referencing and additional information is pending.

21

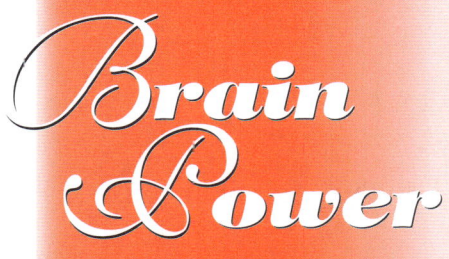

How "Plastic" Is Your Brain?

*Y*ou may be asking yourself: "Do I really want a plastic brain?" The answer is a resounding "Yes!" An emphatic, "Absolutely!"

Plasticity refers to the brain's general ability to adapt to different demands, stimuli or environments. Carl Cotman, a neuroscientist from California who recently organized a "brain plasticity" symposium, reported that the number of brain cells a person has is fixed, but the number of connections between brain cells may be quite flexible and may be increased.

High levels of mental stimulation build more connections between brain cells. In other words, plasticity can play a large part in how your nervous system responds to new information and stress.

Do You Have Connections?

*H*aving more nerve connections means that more information can be processed and sudden mental challenges and stresses can be more efficiently and appropriately handled!

In addition, aerobic fitness increases the density of capillaries in the brain—which means increased blood flow and greater protection against loss of brain cells. I don't know about you, but that sounds very good to me!

Use It...Or Lose It!

*W*hen it comes to the brain, it's safe to say that "use it or lose it" definitely applies. *Using it* refers to plenty of daily physical exercise, which stimulates capillary production. It also means having daily mental challenges, which will encourage new nerve cell connections.

Studies suggest that physical and mental stimulation actually stimulate special genes in the brain to "switch on" and produce denser, more fibrous nerves and additional capillary support systems! The deterioration seen in aging brains today is more likely due to disease processes rather than the aging process itself.

According to recent research, new brain nerve synapses and support systems can be generated well into old age. "There is no doubt that the brain has the ability to grow these connections back again by using healthy nerve cells," Cotman says.

Losing Plastic...Or Gaining Credit?

*T*here are a number of lifestyle factors that can decrease brain plasticity resulting in poor memory, decreased ability to learn new information, inability to appropriately handle stress and increased depression.

Chronic stress (fear, anxiety, hostility, negativism, etc.) also affects brain plasticity. It can actually ruin the delicate nerves in the hippocampus area of the brain, an important memory center. When those nerves are destroyed or damaged, it could lead to long term depression. These nerves also balance and regulate important hormonal levels.

Abused children and war veterans who have experienced

post-traumatic stress disorder have been shown to have actual shrinkage of the hippocampal area of the brain ranging anywhere from 12- 26%.

Animal studies have shown that stress inhibits actual nerve granule generation (neuron production) in a specialized area of this same portion of the brain. Nerve granulation only takes place during low stress times, and without it, it is difficult to learn and store new information, especially conditioned learning responses which require memory storage.

Lifestyle and Learning

$\mathcal{I}$t's important to remember that chemical stressors can produce the same type of damage. Such dietary stressors include caffeine, large amounts of sugar, and excitotoxic food additives such as MSG, aspartame and hydrolyzed vegetable protein (found in soy sauces, chicken-like and beef-like seasonings, etc.).

Too much dietary fat is known to decrease the oxygen supply to the brain, and is associated with increased neurodegenerative diseases like Alzheimer's. Tobacco and alcohol also decrease brain blood flow and cause cell destruction.

There are also non-dietary stressors that affect brain plasticity. Amazingly, viewing television for just four hours a day has been found to be a factor in the development of dementia (senility). Listening to harsh music (rock and rap are two examples) is also destructive to brain health because of the stress reaction it produces.

Let's Promote Plastic

$\mathcal{T}$here are numerous dietary and lifestyle practices which promote brain plasticity, which means enhanced learning and memory capabilities, better ability to deal with stress and new situations, and less risk of stress or diet-related dementia.

Eating a diet rich in whole grains, beans, fresh fruits and vegetables (with raw fruit and veggie intake daily) provides the brain with antioxidants that fight the free radical destruction which causes cell death. The rich supply of vitamins and minerals are essential to brain hormone regulation, enzyme activity, and proper nerve cell reactivity and health.

A proper plant-based diet will be naturally lower in fat, so blood oxygenation will be superior. Drinking plenty of water keeps the nutrient flow at optimum levels and exercise will enhance circulation and promote brain capillary growth.

Increase Your "Word" Power!

Finally, one of the most exciting ways to increase brain plasticity is to study God's Word, the Bible, and memorize Scripture passages. Daily Bible study and memorization increases plasticity, which increases the power of your mind. Such activities also increase our capacity for knowing Christ, the Source of all strength and victory.

Such a lifestyle will give us the ability to live above the power of degrading habits and sinful attitudes by engrafting right principles into our hearts. These truths are enunciated throughout the Word of God and summarized in these words:

"My son, attend to my words; incline thine ear unto my sayings. Let them not depart from thine eyes; keep them in the midst of thine heart. For they are life unto those that find them, and health to all their flesh...Ponder the path of thy feet, and let all thy ways be established [in Bible principles]." *Proverbs* **4:20-23, 26.**

REFERENCES

1. Cotman C. Adaptive versus pathological plasticity. Possible contributions to age-related dementia. Advances in Neurology 1993;59:34-35.

2. Bridges R. Gliotoxic actions of excitatory amino acids. Neuropharmacology 1992 Sep;31(9):899-907.

3. USA Today, 11/30/93.

4. Sapolsky R. Why stress is bad for your brain. Science 1996 Aug;273:749-750.

5. Gould P. Clinical and biochemical manifestations of depression. New England Journal of Medicine Aug;319(7):413-419.

6. Gould E. Neurogenesis in the dentate gyrus of the adult tree shrew is regulated by psychosocial stress and NMDA receptor activation. Journal of Neuroscience 1997 Apr;17(7):2492-2498.

7. Aronson M. Does excessive television viewing contribute to the development of dementia? Medical Hyphothesis 1993;41:465-466.

22

Fast and Frenzied

*A*s the pace of American life becomes more frenzied, "fresh" is out, and "fast" is in. But our health is floundering as a result. It is no secret that the typical American fare is far too high in fat and protein and loaded with sugar. It's also high in refined, processed carbohydrates and salt, but low in fiber, complex carbohydrates, and fresh fruits and vegetables. As mentioned earlier, Nature is a stern creditor, and what we sow in disobedience to her laws, we will reap in disability, disease and possibly death.

"Be not deceived: God is not mocked: for whatsoever a man soweth, that shall he also reap." *Galatians* **6:7**.

Have You "Herd" What We're Eating?

*A*ccording to the World Health Organization, we are eating a diet totally unknown to our species one hundred years ago. Seventy-five percent of our protein and energy intake used to come from plant sources. Now it comes from animal sources.

As Americans come to rely heavily on meat and dairy products as the principle staple of diet instead of beans, brown rice, potatoes, pasta, or other complex carbohydrate foods, disease rates have risen proportionately. In his or her lifetime, the average American will make his stomach the graveyard for:

- *15 cows*
- *24 hogs*
- *12 sheep*
- *900 chickens*
- *1,000 pounds of fish and fowl*
- *26,250 pounds of dairy products!*

"Herding" Up Trouble

*O*ur standard diet is loaded with saturated animal fat and cholesterol. Chronic disease caused by poor lifestyle, such as cancer, diabetes, heart disease and stroke kills 70% of Americans who die each year. According to Dr. Gio Gori of the National Cancer Institute, "The dietary factors responsible for cancer are primarily fat and meat intake."

About one-third of the 560,000 cancer deaths this year are estimated to be directly due to diet. Fifty million children have elevated cholesterol, with as many as 70% already exhibiting fatty streaks in their arteries, which could become plaques later in life.

We consume an average of 135 pounds of fat every year per person, which totals 1 ton every 15 years and 4 tons in 60 years! One-half million men and close to 1 million women die yearly of heart disease.

There are an estimated 16 million diabetics in this country, and it is now well-established that a high-fat diet is the principle cause of adult-onset diabetes. Diabetes is a complicating factor in many other diseases. It is estimated that in 1993 about 400,000 deaths from all causes occurred in people with diabetes.

Meat and dairy product consumption, loaded with animal fat and cholesterol, are taking a terrible toll on human health. Remember—even a lean meat like fish or turkey has cholesterol levels as high as beef, and a number of studies now implicate animal protein as a causative factor in the lifestyle diseases that were once thought only to be associated with fat intake.

The High Cost of Eating Meat

*D*ietary factors and tobacco constitute the largest factors in calculating the highest demand for medical services. Direct health care costs attributable just to meat-eating are estimated to be as high as $8.5 billion for hypertension, $9.5 billion for heart disease, $16.5 billion for cancer, $17.1 billion for diabetes, $2.4 billion for gall bladder disease, $1.9 billion for obesity-related musculoskeletal disorders, and $5.5 billion for food-borne illnesses.

The total direct medical costs (not counting lost work time and productivity, etc.) are estimated at approximately $61.4 billion per year. The average cost of just one hospital stay for a heart attack is $50,000. An angioplasty costs $10,000, and there is usually more than one. In 1996, $150 billion was spent on heart disease in this country!

How Now Brown Cow?

*N*o discussion of dietary habits would be complete without mention of the unhealthy animals and conditions which characterize much of the large-scale meat and dairy agribusinesses today.

One hundred thousand "downer cows" (cows who fall down and can't get up) die and are rendered (ground up) each year in this country, only to wind up in the feed of other animals, often of the same species.

Dead carcasses of diseased cows, chicken, sheep, pigs and road kills, often filled with cancer, are rendered and fed to other animals to increase the feed's protein content. Eating that contaminated feed puts the animals— and those who consume them once they're slaughtered—at increased risk for cancer, bacterial or viral infections, or deadly prion diseases.

Unhealthy Hitchhikers

The government estimates that food-borne disease sickens up to 33 million people per year, killing up to 9,000. Bacterial and viral contamination of animal products has reached horrific proportions, with listeria, shagella, salmonella, polio, leukemia and other bugs often being unwelcome hitchhikers on these foods.

Pasteurization of milk does not eliminate potentially harmful bacterial or viral fragments. According to US Government guidelines, grade A milk can contain 750,000 lymphocytes (pus cells!) per cc. (about 8 drops)—and still be sold to consumers!

A 1988 FDA survey of milk samples from grocery stores in 10 cities found that 73% of the samples contained pesticide residues. A General Accounting Office report indicated that the FDA tests for just four of the 82 drugs that are commonly used in dairy cows. And many drugs, including sulfamethazine, are used illegally by farmers to treat sick cows.

Even the lowly fish has become a questionable dietary mainstay, as they are becoming increasingly contaminated with mercury, pesticides, deadly bacteria and tumors. This is largely due to industrial dumping and animal farm sewage spillage into the waterways.

A Predicted Predicament

The Lord predicted this world's predicament in *Isaiah* **24:4-6**: "The earth mourneth and fadeth away, the world languisheth and fadeth away...The earth also is defiled under the inhabitants thereof; because they have transgressed the laws...Therefore hath the curse devoured the earth."

There is no denying that the greed and gluttony of man has brought a terrible curse of disease upon the animal creation and the human race. Fortunately, we have the promise in *Genesis* **8:22** that "while the earth remaineth, seedtime and harvest...shall not cease."

God created the perfect man and woman with a perfect diet of plant foods (*Genesis* **1:29**), and it will be the fabulous fare of the redeemed (*Revelation* **22:2**) in heaven. Perhaps those who are ripening for Heaven should consider the warning and invitation given to those who are living in these last days! "Whether therefore ye eat, or drink, or whatsoever ye do, do all to the glory of God." *1 Corinthians* **10:31**.

REFERENCES

1. Nation's Restaurant News, 1994.
2. Oski F. Don't Drink Your Milk. Mollica Press, Syracuse, NY 1989.
3. Klapper M. Simply Vegan. Gentle World, Inc. Umatilla Fla 1987.
4. Proceedings, Summit on Cholesterol & Coronary Disease, Sept. 4-5, 1997, Lake Buena Vista, Fla.
5. Cancer Facts and Figures, 1997. American Cancer Society.
6. Diehl H. To Your Health. Lifestyle Medicine Institute, Loma Linda CA 1990.
7. Diabetes Statistics, 1997. National Institute of Diabetes and Digestive and Kidney Diseases.
8. Barnard N. The medical costs attributable to meat consumption. Preventive Medicine 1995;24:646-655.
9. Griffin V. Moooove Over Milk. Review and Herald, Hagerstown MD 1997.

23

LifeStyle Matters

Television & Music

24

Serenity...Or Insanity?

As we have been studying various Christian lifestyle issues, we begin to see some interesting contrasts. The principles of living that are taught in the Bible tend to promote strength rather than sickness, order rather than chaos, genuine pleasure rather than artificial stimulation, and soundness of mind rather than depression and mood swings.

God's prescription for leisure time is no different—He offers serenity instead of insanity, joy instead of jitters. "These things have I spoken unto you, that My joy might remain in you, and that your joy might be full." *John* **15:11**.

Biblical counsel on how to live is so critical to health, happiness and salvation that we are admonished: "Receive My instruction, and not silver; and knowledge rather than choice gold." Prov. 8:10.

Recreation...Or Entertainment?

The kind of cooperative and exhilarating exercise mentioned in the last discussion yields unbounded mental, physical, and spiritual benefits. A trip to the park, zoo, or museum—hobbies, crafts, reading, volunteer work, a picnic, building project, even chores—these kinds of recreational activities have a positive impact on the stress system, immune system and mood. They promote a healthy appetite, sound sleep, a sense of well-being and relieve tension.

That's recreation—but much of today's entertainment has far different effects. Unfortunately, the above-mentioned activities pale in comparison to America's major pastime: watching television. Television—is it a harmless outlet for the harried, or an entertainment trap that ensnares and destroys?

TV AIDs: The Automatic Income Reducer!

Television and movies seem to be a major pastime of both young and old. It is estimated that 99% of American households own at least one television. The average person spends more than 7 hours a day watching TV—2,555 hours per year. Motivational speaker and author Zig Ziglar calls TV "the automatic income reducer" because of the non-productive, wasted time spent there!

The average child watches 31 hours of TV every week, which is 5,000 hours by the time they enter the first grade, and 19,000 hours by the time they finish high school. By the age of 16, a typical young person will have viewed 200,000 acts of violence, and seen 31 incidents of sex, violence and profanity per programming hour.

Eighty percent of all television scenes depicting sexual relations occur outside of marriage. By the age of 18, the average child will have viewed 50,000 murders or attempted murders. By age 21, he or she will have seen 90,000 incidents of drinking alcoholic beverages, and 100,000 beer commercials.

TV: Gradual Brain Drain

According to a study conducted at Yale University,

children who watch a lot of television are more aggressive than non-viewers, show decreased reading ability, lower levels of imagination, short attention spans and higher levels of restlessness and hyperactivity.

Watching violent television produces biological effects in the body. These effects include cardiovascular stress, suppression of the immune system, and elevated levels of three different stress hormones, especially cortisol. Elevated cortisol levels are associated with neural damage to the hippocampus area of the brain, and are implicated in poor memory, senility and chronic depression.

One study of 1,100 television-viewing children showed that watching "reality-based" programs for as little as two hours a day increased the incidence of aggression, stealing, bullying, temper-tantrums, and impulsiveness. These characteristics increased over time.

Now For the Real News

An interesting study from London, England, showed that watching just 14 minutes of negative news significantly impacted anxiety and sadness levels in viewers. In addition, they were more likely to evaluate their own life problems in a catastrophic or disproportionately negative way, compared with non-viewers. Reading printed newspaper accounts, however, did not produce the same effect.

Music, Mind and Mood

Certain types of music also seem to reduce stress and enhance brain function. A study conducted by the Center for the Neurobiology of Learning and Memory at the University of California has confirmed that soothing Mozart sonatas and similar complex, highly structured music seem to stimulate cognitive and neural pathways, resulting in IQ scores as much as 10 points higher in test subjects.

Conversely, the harsh rhythms of rock and jazz interfere with abstract reasoning and can actually destroy delicate brain nerves. Researchers from Pennsylvania State University reported that students who listen to the most rock have the highest levels of anxiety, depression, and "sensation-seeking."

Heavy metal and rap music is associated with increased incidence of behavior problems, drug and alcohol use, sexual activity, low grades and criminal arrests. When young David played his harp for the moody King Saul, he was "refreshed, and was well, and the evil spirit departed from him." *1 Samuel* **16:23**.

Rhythm and Reason

*T*he Bible says: "The hearing ear, and the seeing eye, the Lord hath made even both of them." *Proverbs* **20:12**. We are accountable to God for the use of our sensory organs as well as our time. And right use brings blessings! God's television and magazine guide can't be beat!

You will find it in *Psalm* **101**. It is not only worth reviewing—it's worth living!

REFERENCES

1. Monroe R. Television's invasion of the sanctuary of the home. Home School Digest, Fall 1994.
2. Medical Tribune, March 27, 1995.
3. Report, American Psychiatric Association. Dr. Nuchanart Venbrux, Pennsylvania State University, May 24, 1993.
4. Johnston W. The psychological impact of negative TV news

bulletins; the catastrophizing of personal worries (report) Mental Medicine Update 1995;4(1).

5. The New Physician, April 1994.

6. USA Today, April 12, 1994.

7. Aronson M. Does excessive television viewing contribute to the development of dementia? Medical Hypothesis 1993;41:465-466.

8. Black D. Television violence and children. British Medical Journal 1995;310(letter):273-274.

9. Medical Tribune 1995 April;36(8).

10. Valkenburg P. Influence of TV on daydreaming and creative imagination: a review of research. Psychological Bulletin 1994 Sep;116(2):316-339.

11. Rauscher F. Music and spatial task performance. Nature 1993 Dec;365(6447):611; 366(6455):520.

12. Stratton V. Affective impact of music vs. lyrics. Empirical Studies of the Arts 1994;12(2):173-184.

This reference list is partial due to the extensive amount of information presented. For a complete reference list, send a self-addressed, stamped envelope to the address on the order page of this publication.

24

Excitotoxins

What are excitotoxins? Excitotoxins are a class of commonly used flavor enhancers that overstimulate the brain and are implicated in such diseases as Alzheimer's, Parkinson's, Attention Deficit Disorder, Attention Deficit Hyperactivity Disorder, memory and cognitive decline, as well as a host of other hormonal and neurological problems.

Russell Blaylock, MD, a neurosurgeon in Jackson, Mississippi, has done extensive research into the effects of excitotoxins on the human brain. What he has found is most shocking.

Since 1945, our usage of excitotoxins has doubled every 10 years. Excitotoxins are now added to many processed foods, fast foods, diet foods and frozen foods. It has been demonstrated that excitotoxins actually destroy nerve cells in the brain and in the retina of the eye.

If possible, excitotoxins should be avoided, especially by young children and older adults. Human beings are more sensitive to excitotoxins than any other primate, with children and the elderly being the most susceptible to these damaging, sometimes deadly agents. *There are more than 70 used in processed foods, including many vegetarian foods and seasonings.*

What are the names of some of these agents? When you read labels—the two most common names to look for are MSG (monosodium glutamate) and aspartame (Nutra-sweet). But just because a label says something is "MSG-Free," doesn't necessarily mean that it is excitotoxin-free Look for these names on your labels when you shop--so you won't drop!

Additives that always have excitotoxins

- Monosodium glutamate
- Hydrolyzed vegetable protein
- Hydrolyzed protein
- Hydrolyzed plant protein
- Plant protein extract

- Sodium casseinate
- Calcium casseinate
- Yeast extract
- Textured protein
- Autolyzed yeast
- Hydrolyzed oat flour

Additives that may have excitotoxins

- Malt extract
- Malt flavouring
- Boullion
- Broth
- Stock
- Flavoring
- Natural flavoring
- Natural beef or chicken flavor
- Seasonings
- Spices

Check your labels. If the ingredients listed include *any* of the above items, that product may pose hazards to your brain, and overall physical and mental health. Basically, the closer to home-made you can keep your food, the better off you will be.

This is a very serious matter—not a far-fetched scare tactic. The scientific validation of the problem is extensive and compelling.

Your brain health and your ability to think, memorize, learn and recall may be at risk.

For more information on excitotoxins, we strongly recommend the book by Russell Blaylock, MD, *Excitotoxins: The Taste That Kills***. You can also purchase a video interview with Dr. Blaylock, also called** *Excitotoxins: The Taste That Kills***.**
Call 1-800-453-8732 for more information.

Nutritional Analysis

An item appearing in red is an analysis of the food that a particular recipe would be replacing in your diet. These entries are given so you can see the comparison of the nutritional values of recipes in this cookbook when compared to what you may have eaten in the past. You'll be amazed!

Breakfasts

Breakfasts	Calories	Protein (G)	Carbs (G)	Fiber (G)	Fat (total) (G)	Fat (sat.) (G)	Fat (mono) (G)	Fat (poly) (G)	Cholesterol (Mg)	Vitamin A (RE)	Niacin (Mg)	Vitamin B6 (Mg)	Vit B12 (Mcg)	Folacin (Mcg)	Vitamin C (Mg)	Vitamin E (Mg)	Calcium (Mg)	Copper (Mg)	Iron (Mg)	Magnsn. (Mg)	Potassium (Mg)	Selenium (Mcg)	Sodium (Mg)	Zinc (Mg)
Almds Ahoy Gr, 1/2 C	232	7	29	5	10.9	2.79	3.97	3.40	0	2.21	0.89	0.17		25.1	0.10	2.80	45.8	0.31	1.88	85.4	293	11	132	1.35
App. Apple Crsp,2/3C	173	2	31	3	5.22	1.08	1.93	1.77	0	3.08	0.53	0.11		8.25	3.15	1.14	17.9	0.13	0.90	26.7	260	6.25	34.9	0.51
Apple Crsp, reg, piece	146	1	25	1	5.32	1.04	2.27	1.69	0	2.74	0.41	0.01			3.68	1.08	20.4	0.08	0.77	11.8	112	2.57	65.7	0.90
Appl'Oat Delight, pc	176	5	25	4	7.58	2.44	2.65	1.71	0	5.22	0.37	0.10		8.52	1.84	0.50	20.3	0.25	1.42	45.6	286	6.26	99.7	0.94
Belgian Best Wfl, 2pc	191	7	32	5	4.83	0.62	1.21	2.58	0	10.1	1.16	0.15		28.6	0.12	1.90	24.5	0.25	1.84	73.5	242	9.46	209	1.49
Boxed Waffle, 2 pc	410	14	54	2	16	5.40	5.80	3.00	118	2	1.80	0.06		0.48	0	4.40	358	0.12	2.40	28	292	27.4	1030	1.03
Blue Blaze Tpng.1/2C	71	1	18	2	0	0	0	0	0	6.34	0.36	0.05		4.46	1.10	22.4	6.19	0.04	0.19		64.7	0.60	4.98	0.09
Blueberry Buckle, svg	444	10	74	9	14.4	2.56	6.85	3.88	0	6.61	3.06	0.23		76.4	12.1	4.37	43.5	0.36	3.01	99.2	363	32.8	365	1.99
Breakfast Pizza, 1	421	17	43	9	22.4	3.44	8.50	8.96	0	76.8	61.7	10.1		132	2.29	3.12	223	0.10	7.20	192	852	31.5	897	5.07
Chsy Tfu Scrmbl,1/2C	312	11	11	6	25.4	3.54	8.73	11.6	41	19.1	3.12	2.39		125	13.6	3.87	164	0.78	7.68	237	409	23.1	556	5.56
Crmy Cshw Milk, 1C	207	4	23	3	12.1	4.68	5.21	1.57	0	0.91	0.10	0		15.4	0.15	1.63	19.6	0.49	1.47	70.2	152	11.4	438	1.41
E-Z Almond Milk,1C	106	4	3	2	9.53	0.90	6.19	2	0	0.57	0.02	0		6.96	0.11	3.67	49.7	0.21	0.67	53.9	137	0.75	8.88	0.63
Festve Frt Tpng. 1/2C	70	0	18	2	0	0	0	0	0	3.15	0.37	0.05		11.7	43.3	0.14	12.3	0.04	0.54	9.87	102	1.35	3.55	0.11
Good Erth Crl, 1/2 C	210	7	34	5	7.62	0.85	2.65	3.52	0	5.33	0.76	0.15		27.1	0.50	2.38	29.5	0.25	2.15	72.3	272	11.3	171	1.69
Golden Waffles, 2 pc	161	7	28	4	2.83	0.48	0.82	1.17	0	5.28	0.60	0.07		22.9	0	0.92	29.4	0.23	1.73	68.5	232	9.34	220	1.23
Healthy Hashers, 1C	136	4	31	2	0	0	0	0	0	1.27	20.5	3.61		37.8	19.8	0.08	11.1	0.34	0.75	39.7	569	3.19	43.7	0.72
Holiday Grnola, 1/2C	199	6	30	5	6.70	1.30	2.13	3.62	0	0.33	0.10	0.23		13.6	0.68	2.77	22.1	0.20	1.63	62.1	175	10.2	54.6	1.43
Incredible Crepes, 1	147	7	13	2	8.41	0.87	3.85	3.15	0	6.44	0.37	0.05		14.6	0.17	2.77	69.9	0.21	3.74	81.4	128	5.07	85	1.05
Mrng Millet Milk, 1C	148	5	13	3	9.56	0.93	6.08	2.10	0	1	0.05	0.13		16.4	0.13	3.85	53.8	0.28	0.86	67.5	150	0.87	274	0.85
Nty Crisp Waffles,2pc	242	8	40	5	6.48	0.81	1.71	3.38	0	7.66	0.62	0.10		19.3	0.27	1.14	31.3	0.24	2.10	79.3	194	12	221	1.56
Nty Crnch Grnla,1/2C	247	5	39	5	12	4.67	2.02	4.56	0	43.5	0.65	0.16		16.3	1.53	1.39	35	0.34	1.99	54	411	6	103	1.02
Peechy Keen Crsp, pc	177	3	32	4	5.42	1.13	2.07	1.86	0	49.7	1.43	0.10		12.3	25.4	1.97	17.2	0.16	0.77	30.3	268	7.55	32.5	0.60
Pimple Crm Pdng, svg	245	4	43	2	8.03	1.57	3.81	2.14	0	3.06	0.86	0.19		35.6	15	34.6	10.9	0.87	0.92	88.2	302	4.66	218	1.05
Quick Crps or Pnck.1	107	3	20	3	2.33	0.23	1.10	0.75	0	0.90	0.93	0.06		9.20	0.04	0.83	10.9	0.87	1.43	61.8	88.2	13.1	62	0.68
Regal Rice Pdng, svg	203	3	43	3	3.19	1.36	1.05	0.52	0	3.94	1.35	0.27		15.4	8.90	0.77	22.9	0.24	0.99	52.5	306	10.7	141	0.71
Tofu Super Scr, 1/2 C	97	8	10	2	3.83	0.53	0.80	2.06	0	8.43	1.35	0.27		62.4	4.55	2.62	103	0.40	5.21	120	282	5.46	213	1.38
Scrambled Eggs, 1/2C	187	14	1	0	13.2	3.97	7.56	1.72	650	91.9	15.8	1.34	79	0	0.24	1.13	68	0.07	2.48	16	165	8.89	346	2.02
Trpcl Dlight Milk, 1C	189	3	27	2	9.14	1.80	5.35	1.55	0	3.08	0.53	0.11		18.3	7.79	1.50	25.7	0.52	1.46	64.4	215	5.16	388	1.25
Viva La Frnch Tst, 1	186	7	29	4	6.03	1.32	2.74	1.64	0	0.66	1.76	0.15		32	0.02	1.03	161	0.32	1.99	66.0	179	25.1	388	1.23

Breakfasts / Breads / Dressings

Item	Calories	Protein (G)	Carbs (G)	Fiber (G)	Fat (total) (G)	Fat (Sat.) (G)	Fat (mono) (G)	Fat (poly) (G)	Cholesterol (Mg)	Vitamin A (RE)	Niacin (Mg)	Vitamin B6 (Mg)	Vit B12 (Mcg)	Folacin (Mcg)	Vitamin C (Mg)	Vitamin E (Mg)	Calcium (Mg)	Copper (Mg)	Iron (Mg)	Magnsm. (Mg)	Potassium (Mg)	Selenium (Mcg)	Sodium (Mg)	Zinc (Mg)
Well Dne Waffles,2pc	129	5	20	3	3.53	0.48	0.88	1.85	0	3.26	0.65	0.11	0	24.8	0.08	1.21	20.4	0.19	1.34	52.9	179	8.90	93.4	1.30
Wheat Trt Ht Crl,1/2C	97	2	21	4	1.50	1.17	0.09	0.09	0	0.64	1.02	0.08	0	6.12	0.03	0.23	13.1	0.11	0.57	30.4	155	3.92	219	0.37
Breads																								
Basic Muffin, 1	154	5	29	4	2.90	0.24	1.41	0.93	0	0.01	2.60	0.12	0	50.5	0.03	1.41	13.9	0.17	1.61	45.4	148	25.7	181	0.99
Corn Crackers, 1 each	50	2	7	1	2.27	0.48	1.05	0.56	0	3.05	3.83	0.66	0.50	19.7	0.08	0.57	7.08	0.10	0.49	20.9	62	3.12	403	0.59
Country Corn Mfn, 1																								
Delicious Cornbrd,pc	207	5	45	5	1.73	0.28	0.47	0.75	0	11.2	2.19	0.13	0.06	15.3	0.18	1.26	61.2	0.12	1.79	46.6	145	14.7	340	0.89
NiceNLght Roll, 1	198	6	37	5	3.72	0.31	1.83	1.19	0	0.01	3.00	0.13	0	33.8	0.03	1.73	18.7	0.19	2.06	50.6	174	31.5	236	1.09
Holiday Stuffing, 1C	285	8	32	5	15	1.85	6.18	5.71	0	8.12	176	29.8	0.03	50	1.80	1.09	120	0.58	4.35	117	246	1.39	768	1.32
Pumpernickel Plse, sl	60	2	13	1.16	0.23	0.03	0	0	0.81	0.03	0	20.2	0	20.2	0	0.27	10.5	0.09	0.82	9.26	28.9	6.12	156	0.21
Dressings / Spreads																								
Better Butter, 1 Tb	26	1	3	1	1.41	1.13	0.08	0.06		1.43	2.92	0.50	0.40	0.30	13	0.17	2.47	0.02	0.20	6.95	35.5	2.07	109	0.26
Gldn Sld Dressing,1T	73	0	3	0	6.79	0.92	4.97	0.57	0.14	30.8	5.29	0.01	2.42	4.79	0.89	9.13		0.08	0.40	13.0	25	0.23	78.2	0.08
Hearty Hummus,1/3C	88	4	9	2.53	4.45	0.60	1.57	1.96	0	1.26	0.53	0.16	0	54	2.06	0.42	25	0.21	1.18	37.4	120	4.06	183	1.13
Kwick Kntry Ktch,1T	54	1	6	1	3.51	0.48	2.50	0.34		35	0.48	0.08	0.08	4.21	7.02	0.62	7.48	0.09	0.46	8.11	141	0.20	188	0.13
Marvi Whp Mayo,1T	57	2	1	0	5.51	0.75	3.53	0.94	8.13	1.79	1.21	0.22	0.17	8.52	23.2	1.27	0.05	1.14	0.07	22.1	35.8	0.81	91	0.24
Mayonnaise, reg, 1T																								
Miracle Mustard,1T	7	1	0	0	0	0	0	0		2.26	0.03	0.01	0.04	1.06	1.51	0	8	2.50	0.02	0.07	4.69	0.48	78	0.02
Pineapprict Jam,1T	27	0	7	1	0	0	0	0		33.7	0.22	0.05	0	0.16	0	0.38	5.50	0.05	0.37	5.22	109	0.29	0.69	0.07
Sun Seed Dress, 1 T	47	2	4	1	3.08	0.33	0.59	2.02	0	0.35	0.41	0.09	0	16.5	1.22	1.24	8.97	0.13	0.48	26.2	52.4	4.34	89.6	0.40
Sny Salad Dress, 1 T	35	1	2	0	2.96	0.31	0.56	1.95	0	1.28	0.28	0.10	0	14.6	0.39	0.21	10.6	0.11	0.46	22	50	4.32	67	0.32
Superior Sr Crm,1T	87	2	8	1	5.47	1.08	3.17	0.95	0	0.15	7.25	1.27	0	10.4	2.96	0.98	12.4	0.30	0.89	40.6	88.3	5.01	198	0.77
Tahini Tang Dress,1T	68	2	4	1	5.66	0.80	2.13	2.48	0	0.75	0.58	0.88	0	10.9	1.97	0.15	16.5	0.17	0.58	36.3	55.6	4.32	183	1.06
That's Itln Dress, 1T	48	1	2	0	5.50	0.53	1.91	1.85	0	0.35	0.24	0.09	0	13.1	2.04	1.29	8.43	0.10	0.38	19.1	44.3	3.76	77.0	0.28
The Bst! Bn Spd,1/2C	181	7	16	6	10.9	1.45	6.41	2.45	0	15.2	2.72	0.51	0.30	79.6	4.52	2.57	69.5	0.26	3.22	68.8	297	5.33	198	0.96
V. La Frnch Dress,1T	23	0	3	0	1.79	0.24	1.26	0.18	0	26.3	0.35	0.05	0	2.95	5.68	0.36	5.17	0.69	0.34	5.98	104	0.11	74.3	0.10

ENTREES

ENTREES	Calories	Protein (G)	Carbs (G)	Fiber (G)	Fat (total) (G)	Fat (sat.) (G)	Fat (mono) (G)	Fat (poly) (G)	Cholesterol (Mg)	Vitamin A (RE)	Niacin (Mg)	Vitamin B6 (Mg)	Vit B12 (Mcg)	Folacin (Mcg)	Vitamin C (Mg)	Vitamin E (Mg)	Calcium (Mg)	Copper (Mg)	Iron (Mg)	Magnsm. (Mg)	Potassium (Mg)	Selenium (Mcg)	Sodium (Mg)	Zinc (Mg)
B-B-Q Tofu Rib, each	72	5.31	7	1.78	3.52	.49	.93	1.8		45.9	6.3	1.12	.80	36.5	7.9	2	64.4	.26	3.22	62.5	284	5.4	231	.93
Rib, Pork, equal wght	520	38	0		39.7	15.4	18.6	4.60	158		7.17	.46	1.41	5.25	0	.50	61.4	.19	2.42	31.5	419	46	122	6
Better Burger, each	79.5	3.26	11.6	2.45	.31	.54	1.42			2.00	1.65	.27	.15	17.5	.77	.77	27.5	.14	1.34	37.2	89.1	2.62	85.1	.52
Burger Delight,1/3C	114	3.57	17.2	4.54	4.48	1	2.75			33.3	2.13	.30	.12	21.4	.71	.71	31.5	.24	1.02	45.2	250	6	13.9	.58
Beef, grnd, equal wt	240	20	0		17.2	6.75	7.52	.65	74.3		4.80	.23	2.43	7.82	0	.52	8.80	.07	2.02	16.6	242	21.5	68.4	4.30
Carrib. Curry, 1 1/4 C	298	12.8	49.7	7.9	6.19	.96	2.38	2.32		26.2	2.81	.35	0	90.3	18.4	3.71	98	.38	5.08	159	409	24.5	14.7	1.97
CousCous, 1 cup	171	5.95	26.2	3.83	5.23	.69	3.37	.60		709	176	29.9	1.42	76.7	6.50	.77	63	.48	3.21	86.6	275	19.8	440	1.27
Crnch. Ndl Cass, 3/4C	160	5.10	25.2	2.02	4.49	.77	2.09	1.31		42	76.6	12.8	.01	35	3.61	.48	29.8	.41	2.99	66.1	105	16.4	297	1.67
Chicken Ndl, eq. wght	157	9.43	11.1	.52	7.72	2.19	3.04	1.67	44.2	55.7	1.84	.07	.23	4.03	35	5.74	11.1	.08	1.01	15.9	90.5	12.3	257	.92
Fies. Mexicana, 1 ea	463	15.2	13.5	24.9	15.9	4.13	0			132	101	17.2	.77	241	31.3	5.74	177	.68	7.43	157	877	16.8	1108	2.09
Garb. Sp. Psta, 1 1/2C	356	13.1	64.5	8.02	5.82	.76	2.9	1.32		213	6.49	.42	.06	127	30	2.20	59	.53	4.72	80	776	35.5	42.9	1.67
Gard. Gm. Qche, 1pc	182	8.99	14.4	3.76	11.2	1.19	5.80	3.32		208	133	22.8	1.33	91.5	6.42	4.13	129	.49	5.52	143	302	13.3	466	1.72
Qche Lorraine, 1 pc	600	13.0	.54		48	23.2	17.8	4.10	285	19	1.2	.15	.17	17	5.5		211	.140	1.4	23	283	15	653	1.95
Gdn. Lntl Patty, 1 ea	60	3.50	10.9	2.22	.55	.09	.14	.22		136	37	6.35	.01	41	7.9	.36	72	.22	1.58	36.1	199	2.76	143	.59
Grk St. Veggil, 1 serv.	226	9	36	11	6.33	2.18	2.74			1070	2.41	.31	0	133	50.1	15.9	21.9	.35	3.41	63	672	11	833	1.19
Heyl Stacks, 1 each	664	21	58	17	43.5	6.05	20.0	14.7		117	15.9	2.72	1.79	230	36	5.6	280	1.07	8.40	246	918	27.2	967	5.76
Leb. Len. Loaf, 2/3 C	203	11	24	6	8.93	1.06	3.47	3.77		65.3	8.14	1.40	.89	164	13.3	2.67	67.5	.44	3.94	76.5	604	10.5	505	2.26
Mac&Chse Plse, 3/4 C	239	9	32	4	9.68	1.71	4.77	2.44		30.6	13.1	2.09	1.60	69.9	11.4	1.11	26.4	.48	2.57	73.1	219	9.67	328	2.37
Mac&Chse,reg, 1 ser.	322	13	30	.90	16.5	7.35	5.55	2.70	33.0	9.75	1.35	.04	.22	7.73	.75	2.64	272	.07	1.35	27.6	180	22.5	815	.900
Mexic-Enchilada, 1 ea	196	9	29	4	6.77	2.10	2.90			146	126	21.3	.02	48	11.4	3.15	140	.614	6.94	142	473	8.98	469	1.32
Mock Salm. Lf, 1 serv	151	5	27	5	3.73	1.44	1.27			83	3.31	.39	.15	30	23.1	2.32	58.3	.16	1.52	54.2	407	3.75	24.3	.710
Not-Cotta Fill., 2 Tb	53	4	2	.8	3.48	.566	1.18	1.51	.119	7.47	.151	.19	0	10	2.32	1.83	58.3	.16	2.87	57.6	86.5	1.48	157	.56
Ricotta Cheese, 2 Tb	53.5	3	.94	0	3.99	2.55	1.11	.119	15.5	2	.032	.013	.104	1.75	0	.199	63.6	.010	.117	3.50	32.1	.56	25.9	.356
Oh Boy! Oat Bg, 1 ea	112	4	13	2.22	5.51	2.03	2.36	.77	1.30	23.5	4.04	1.33	48.7	2.34	.48	20.8	.19	1.06	34.4	192	7.12	235	.996	
Hamburger Patty 1 ea	257	12	30	.31	9.5	3.63	5.09	.77	37.0	7.6	3.84	.124	.822	17.3	.204	122	145	2.29	19.8	145	26.5	460	2.13	
Perfect Patty, 1 each	93.3	3.98	11.5	2.29	3.98	.45	.91	2.28		3.78	5.09	.90	.68	34.8	.53	.91	20.6	.15	1.02	38.5	129	8.49	7.09	.86
Pizza, reg, 1/2 10 inch	519	24.4	76	4.20	14.1	6.19	4.22	2.20	82.5	7.46	6.12	.07	.07	70.2	2.75	.82	359	.615	3.48	63.9	367	36.3	1193	2.66
Pizzaz Pizza, 1 pita	414	16.3	54	8.52	17.6	6.15	7.62	0	70.6	28.3	4.33	3.35	152	25.0	1.44	119	.700	4.15	138	594	40.1	598	4.63	
Rice Pecan Lf, 2/3 C	187	4.22	23	2.71	9.43	.90	5.57	2.38		5.97	6.12	.67	.96	32.8	1.43	.95	39.8	.24	1.12	51.6	153	14.4	398	1.47

ENTREES

Item	Calories	Protein (G)	Carbs (G)	Fiber (G)	Fat (total) (G)	Fat (sat.) (G)	Fat (mono) (G)	Fat (poly) (G)	Cholesterol (Mg)	Vitamin A (RE)	Niacin (Mg)	Vitamin B6 (Mg)	Vit B12 (Mcg)	Folacin (Mcg)	Vitamin C (Mg)	Vitamin E (Mg)	Calcium (Mg)	Copper (Mg)	Iron (Mg)	Magnsm. (Mg)	Potassium (Mg)	Selenium (Mcg)	Sodium (Mg)	Zinc (Mg)
Sloppy Joes, 1 each	394	13	65	13	11.8	1.28	2.68	6.76	0	77.5	11.7	1.64	1.03	86	14.3	1.93	87.3	.68	3.63	247	653	46.5	334	2.27
Soy Great Patty, 1 ea.	59	4.78	7	1.73	2.02	.29	.46	1.01	0	.86	54.9	9.46	.805	38.8	.32	1.27	33.8	.210	1.74	44.8	149	4.24	232	.78
Egg Foo Yng patty, 1	130	9	4	1		2.10	3.10	2.50	182	95	.95	.13	0	22.0	3		28	0	.85	12.0	143	0	188	.81
Soy-egg Salad, 3/4 C	269	15	7	3.09	22	3.05	11.8	5.90	182	21.6	127	21.9	.56	56.8	3.58	7.72	221	.66	11.0	232	348	4.86	806	1.90
Egg Salad, reg, 3/4 C	328	14.1	2	.02	29.1	6.26	9.90	10.1	472	.118	.136	.21	.15	75.4	8.73	9.08	70.4	.18		16	158	30.1	321	1.68
Spinach-ini Ts, 1 serv	179	9.06	29	3.87	3.53	.70	.93	1.58	0	1.72	.21	.15				2.18	262	.30	3.59	122	339	16.4	353	1.48
Stfd Bell Pepr, 1/2 ea	137	5.38	23	4.63	4.03	.47	1.33	1.82	0	48.9	55.3	9.44	1.82	77.1	36.7	1.16	38	.34	1.70	62	324	13.3	227	1.35
Stfd B. Pepr, reg, 1/2	108	5.20	8	.72	6.25	2.63	2.62	.32	0	14.4	1.48	.11	.58	6.95	41.4	.46	7.40	.07	1.16	11.5	113	6.10	105	1.29
Tant. Tofu Roll, 1 pc	182	9.66	16	3.25	10.2	.96	4.42	3.99	0	6.96	8.74	1.40	1.09	51.7	.15	4.31	90.3	.221	4.90	101	198	14.5	187	1.46
Tasty Tofu Rib, 1 ser.	43	3.74	.93	.59	3.09	.442	.84	1.60	0	3.90	32.9	5.65	.005	9.09	.04	1.80	54.4	.06	2.79	58.8	58.4	.68	85.7	.422
Bkd Chick., same wgt	93	14	0	0		3.62	.10	1.30	.83	43.5	7.66	4.46	.23	.16	2.79	.29	7.31	.033	.16	12.2	118	10	41.8	1.02
Tasty Tofu Ntbl, 2 ea	78	4.57	5	1.22	5.15	.56	1.16	3.05	0	6.60	5.86	1.02	.80	34.6	.411	1.07	42.5	.16	4.71	39.7	107	3.93	233	.72
Tater Ntbl, 2 ea	134	3.96	14	2.14	7.85	.761	1.79	4.82	0	3.34	6.45	1.15	.80	40.9	5.18	.60	30.9	.30	1.03	36.2	262	4.83	347	.83
Meatbl w/sce, apr.wt	39	1.82	4	.28	1.50	.39	.72	.25	0	33.7	2.05	.36	2.14	.77	.37	8.11	.08	.505	26.3	37.5	1.38	169	.344
Tender Glut. stk, 1	136	10	22	3	1.17	0.09	0.17	0.31	0	13	12.4	0.25	13.5	55.9	0.11	13.2	13.2	0.05	26.3		138	6.06	95.4	0.97
Vegetarian Steak, 1	160	12	4	0	11				0	8.40	0.84	2.20	0	0	0		67	0	2	0	340	0	530	0.62
Terrfc Tofu Patty, 1 ea	61	3.01	5	1	3.52	.52	1.94	.78	0	6	25.7	4.40	.70	30.2	1.07	34.6	34.2	.11	1.55	34.2	92.8	4.08	83.3	.54
Tofu Croquettes, 1 ea	48	2	4	1	2.90	0.38	1.22	1.11	0	2	0.35	0.25	13.5	13.5	0.09	26.1	26.1	0.09	1.26	25.3	83.1	1.57	98.4	0.33
Wht Grm Patty, 1 ea	114	4.94	10	2.37	6.98	.71	1.52	4.22	0	2.19	29.5	5.14	.602	49.9	1.57	22.3	22.3	.28	1.29	54.2	192	9	120	1.63
Wndrfl Wlnt Tmb, 1	94	3	9	.89	5.79	.706	1.47	3.31	0	1.68	2.27	.37	.32	18	.614	89.5	89.5	.13	.64	17.8	84.2	4.45	208	.408
Zucchini Tfu Yng, 1	93	4	4	1	7.26	0.90	3.13	2.84	0	9.59	0.07	0	15.1	2.56	1.74	48.2	48.2	0.15	2.05	46.4	128	2.13	172	0.46

Soups & Beans

Soups & Beans	Calories	Protein (G)	Carbs (G)	Fiber (G)	Fat (total) (G)	Fat (sat.) (G)	Fat (mono) (G)	Fat (poly) (G)	Cholesterol (G)	Vitamin A (RE)	Niacin (RE)	Vitamin B6 (Mg)	Vit. B12 (Mg)	Folacin (Mcg)	Vitamin C (Mg)	Vitamin E (Mg)	Calcium (Mg)	Copper (Mg)	Iron (Mg)	Magnsm. (Mg)	Potassium (Mg)	Selenium (Mcg)	Sodium (Mg)	Zinc (Mg)
AyeAye N.B. Ch., 1 C	233	13	35	11	6.11	1.22	3.18	1.18	30.8	172	29.6	1.02	202	10	2.10		122	.963	5.47	159	558	8.69	417	2.49
Bountfl Bkd Bn, 3/4C	185	8	38	13	.619	.136	.055	.287	28.9	1.70	.383	.062	77.9	8.39	3.03		49.9	.493	3.83	82.2	841	8.73	98.4	1.17
Chw Dn Chli Bn, 3/4C	109	6	20	8	.932	.118	.179	.446	31.4	1.61	.313	.125	114	13.4	.480		42.9	.220	2.13	46	415	5.18	10.9	.808
Corn Chowder, 3/4 C	104	4	17	3	3.41	1.81	.684		7.30	95.6	16.4	.739	50.8	6.39	.648		29.1	.429	1.73	69.6	280	4.04	234	1.06
Crm Soup, reg, 3/4 C	111	4	13	.255	4.84	2.82	1.30	.420	16.5	50.3	.481	.067	.372	6.90	.900		125	.097	.405	12.7	242	1.65	795	.506
Crm of Spin. Sp, 1 C	32	1	7	1	.118	.005	.042	0	122	67.6	11.6	.010	39	8.44	.456		36.7	.237	1.27	45.1	207	.880	186	.330
Crm of Crp Ch, 3/4 C	97	3	14	2	4.12	2.35	.721	0	7.07	62.4	10.7	.009	24	10.5	.774		29.7	.450	1.53	64.4	288	3.59	161	.814
Crmy Tom-ew Sp, 1C	155	5	21	3	7.87	1.55	4.55	1.35	100	4.85	0.85	0.48	63.7	32.8	1.63		31.3	0.59	2.16	66.1	521	5.63	21.9	1.41
Tm. soup w/milk, 1 C	160	6	22	0.5	6	2.90	1.60	1.10	73	1.52	0.16	0.45	20.9	68.4	0.11		159	0.27	1.81	22	450	8.49	932	0.29
Crock-it Brly Stw, 1 C	81	4	17	3	.362	0.04	0.16			427	1.15	0.18	0	40	10	0.34	30	0.19	1.30	29.7	313	4.67	15.8	0.62
Frijoles Príctos, 2/3 C	285	10	31	13	14.3	10.1	1.41	0	26.6	128	22	0.57	217	9.46	2.36		102	0.60	4.96	115	642	8.86	329	1.49
Luscious Lntl Sp, 1 C	172	10	27	5	3.38	0.47	2.20	0.46	474	1.61	0.31	0	154	12.4	1.06		37.2	0.39	3.46	49	542	4.34	22.3	1.39
Mexi-Beans, 1 C	185	10	31	13	2.92	0.40	1.56	0.47	72	9.03	1.62	1.14	220	13.8	1.10		77.0	0.35	3.58	71.2	710	10.3	12.1	1.73
Old Eng. N.B Ch, 1 C	156	9	10		0.65	0.16	0.56	0.28	189	0.69	0.22	0	154	11.8	1.20		89.7	0.31	2.79	64.7	465	3.68	7.33	1.15
Clam Chowder, 1 C	163	9	17	1	6.60	2.26	1.08		22	4	1.03	0.13	10.3	11	3.50	0.11	187	0.14	1.48	23	300	16.5	992	1.30
Persian Lntl Stw, 1 C	264	20	47	10	0.87	0.12	0.13	0.38	373	127	21.9	0.20	308	24.7	1.10		79.6	0.97	7.75	132	891	8.67	339	2.79
Beef & Veg. Stw, 1 C	220	15	3	3	11	4.50	4.40	0.50	569	4.70	0.28	1.60	37	17	2.15		29	0.19	2.90	40	613	15.2	292	5.29
Potato Supr. Sp: Sp, 1 C	83	2	12	1.50	3.41	2.08	0.50	0	7.50	16.4	2.83	0.57	29.5	3.90	0.60		19.5	0.22	0.83	29.8	219	3.93	196	0.70
Suddenly...Sp, 1 C	73	2	13	3	1.63	0.22	1.07	0.20	108	16.5	2.85	0	154	10.4	0.47		26.9	0.21	1.15	27.2	270	1.03	68.1	0.36
Vegetable Beef Sp,1C	79	6	10	0.81	1.90	0.85	0.80	0.11	5	189	1.03	0.08	0.32	10.6	2.40	0	17	0.14	1.11	6	173	0	956	2
Tofu Gumbo Sp, 1 C	103	5.50	9	3	6.29	1.02	1.84		296	70.7	12	0.54	41.3	7.91	1.85		67.4	0.31	2.92	77.4	272	3.23	471	0.91
Tomato Rce Sp, 3/4 C	64	1	7	1.50	3.73	2.55	0.42	0	62	31.6	5.39	0.01	21.1	16.3	0.92		41.9	0.20	1.11	29.8	267	1.88	99	0.31
Reg. Tom. Sp, 3/4 C	90	2	16	1	2.04	0.39	1.01	1.50	56.6	0.80	0.06	0	10.2	11.1	0		17.3	0.10	0.59	3.75	247	0	611	0.39
VryVeg. Chowd, 3/4 C	96	3	15	3	3.41	0.66	1.88	0.60	534	78.9	13.6	0.61	48.1	23.7	0.75		39.2	0.43	1.70	65.6	355	4.08	201	0.10
Cheese Soup, 3/4 C	233	8	16	0	15.8	9.98	4.45	0.44	164	0.60	0.04	5.77	0				213	0.19	1.12	6	231	0	1440	0.97
Vry Veg-mato Sp, 1C	53	2	12	2.09	0.18	0.23	0.06	0.03	396	83.2	14.3	0.01	19.3	19.7	0.24		34.4	0.33	1.49	52.3	335	1.60	225	0.42
Veget. Veg. Soup, 1 C	70	2	12	2	1.93	0.29	0.73	0	301	0.92	0.06	0	10.6	1.00	0		21	0.22	1.08	7	209	0	823	0.46
Where H.Y.B? St, 1C	171	9	32	7	1.20	0.15	0.19	0.54	33.5	52.4	8.83	0.01	112	13.5	0.79		59.3	0.41	3.59	66	420	11.7	203	1.22

Desserts

Desserts	Calories	Protein (G)	Carbs (G)	Fiber (G)	Fat (total) (G)	Fat (Sat.) (G)	Fat (mono) (G)	Fat (poly) (G)	Cholesterol (Mg)	Vitamin A (RE)	Niacin (Mg)	Vitamin B6 (Mg)	Vit B12 (Mcg)	Folacin (Mcg)	Vitamin C (Mg)	Vitamin E (Mg)	Calcium (Mg)	Copper (Mg)	Iron (Mg)	Magnsm. (Mg)	Potassium (Mg)	Selenium (Mcg)	Sodium (Mg)	Zinc (Mg)
Banana Dt Nt Ck, slice	312	4.5	42	4	15.7	1.23	6.79	6.75	0	4.40	1.89	0.36		69	4.27	2.90	25.6	0.32	1.58	47.3	362	10.5	360	0.75
Bluebry Chscake, slice	325	9	57	6	10.1	1.81	3.39	4.21	0	18.1	0.97	0.32		30.9	16.5	4.93	97.4	0.34	4.86	111	429	4.97	231	1.18
Cheesecake, reg, slice	300	6	38	0	14.3	8.90	0	1.10	30	110	0.60	0.05	0.03	7	1	0	181	0.06	0.36	22	241	0	366	0.43
Brazil Nut Cookie, 1	108	2	10	1	7.21	1.64	2.95	2.22	0	0.61	0.16	0.03	0	2.85	1.12		13.5	0.12	0.50	21.9	61.3	59	81	0.46
Caramel Corn, 1 C	202	6	19	3	12.8	1.51	6.63	4	0	1	2.80	0.07	0	22.1	2.61		23.2	0.25	1	61.3	183	2.41	73.5	0.83
Carob Cake, slice	290	3	40	3	15.2	4.17	5.44	4.71	0	0.77	0.99	0.11	0	13.5	2.23		19.1	0.20	1.03	33.7	142	12.6	6.02	0.69
Carob Nut Brwnie, 1	240	3	37	3	11.4	0.97	4.33	5.54	0	1.77	0.63	0.19	0.05	13.4	1.13		75.3	0.20	0.94	26.8	136	3.87	14.8	0.50
Choc. Nut Brwnie, 1	284	4	33	1	18.8	4.19	8.37	3.59	53.8	0	0.90	0.11	0.13	12	0.03	1.50	26.9	0.27	1.20	33.5	105	8.97	153	0.93
Carob PB Icing, 1 Tb	41	1	5	1	2.74	0.26	1.77	0.57	0	0.20	0.23	0.01	0	3.86	0.92		17.2	0.58	0.24	15.8	66.7	0.33	30.7	0.16
Cocont Blst Frst, 2 Tb	37.4	0	4	1	2.36	2.09	0.10	0.03	0	0	0.03	0.01	0	0.70	0		1.69	0.03	0.15	3.54	21.9	1.39	35.3	0.08
Date Apple Cky, 1	42	1	7	1	1.45	0.56	0.27	0.51	0	0.94	0.13	0.02	0	2.95	0.11		5.22	0.05	0.30	11	52.9	1.73	22.1	0.21
Date Nut Cake, slice	307	5	44	5	15	1.35	4.23	8.59	0	5.15	1.68	0.22	0	32.3	1.42		38.5	0.43	1.44	58.5	404	7.86	138	0.87
Drmy Crm Whip, 1 T	72	2	7	0	4.49	0.35	2.31	1.57	0	1.58	0.06	0.01	0	3.59	1.45		20	0.04	1.04	19.2	26.8	0.34	14.6	0.16
Festve Crnbry Mld, svg	78	1	10	2	4.25	0.39	0.96	2.64	0	7.30	0.17	0.07	0	13	0.55		19.4	0.13	0.28	15.9	121	0.86	2.18	0.24
5th Ave Crb Pie, slice	232	4	37	5	10.4	2.08	4.92	2.79	10.9	2.32	0.81	0.12		15.8	32.6	1.75	116	0.07	1.56	54	315	5.92	192	1.01
Choc. Cream Pie, slice	226	5	31	3	9.16	3.30	3.60	1.78	0	2.91	0.34	0.28		8	0.36	1.86	20.5	0.17	1.27	39.4	161	6.42	311	0.54
Great Grnola Bar, 1	201	4	27	3	9.42	0.78	4.44	3.57	0	17.8	0.34	0.06	0	10	0.38		29.3	0.11	1.52	45.3	163	7.28	62.3	0.76
Granola Bar, reg, 1	213	5	31	2	9.22	1.93	2.85	3.69	0	1.68	0.34	0.03	0	0.43	1.86		20.5	0.35	2.09	51.6	166	8.22	143	0.94
Haystack Cookies, 1	79	1	8	1	5.04	2.58	0.95	1.24	0	0.55	0.50	0.05	0	5.09	0.24		6.26	0.09	0.35	14.5	84	2.81	29	0.26
Lemn Chiffon Pie, pc	282	4	44	2	11.9	1.67	5.44	4.04	0	3.93	0.42	0.11	0	25.8	2.89		44.8	0.19	2.09	51.6	225	4.06	125	0.68
Lemon Merengue, pc	355	5	53	2	14.3	3.50	6.20	3.67	137	3	0.83	0.05	0.33	13	0.97		25	0.08	1.40	70	250	9	395	0.51
Lemon Sauce, 2 Tb	23	0	6	0	0	0	0	0	0	0.01	0.01	0	0	4.20	0.97		4.40	0.02	0.01	3.29	70	9	45.7	0.03
Lemon Velvet Pie, pc	237	3	47	3	6.45	1.26	2.56	2.15	0	8.68	0.50	0.12	0	22.2	1.22		32.4	0.18	1.06	35.7	250	4.15	58.6	0.58
Nut Sandies, 1	95	2	9	1	6.06	1.12	2.53	2.09	1	0.61	0.16	0.02	0	2.72	0.95		13.8	0.13	0.48	22.3	59.2	65	18.4	0.46
Nty Crb Fdge Balls, 1	126	3	10	1	10.1	2.19	3.60	3.89	0	0.35	0.16	0.02	0	6.28	0.92		31.8	0.23	0.72	43.1	104	45.9	45.2	1.04
Chocolate Nt Fdge, 1	114	1	19	2	4.99	2.25	1.42	1.30	13	0.11	0.03	0.04		3.62	0.12	0.72	22	0.08	0.30	15	124	13.8	47.9	0.25
Oatmeal Raisin Cky, 1	86	1	11	1	4.52	0.36	2.04	1.84	0	0.80	0.19	0.03	0.01	4.20	0.81		13.3	0.17	0.44	13.8	60.8	2.90	42.4	0.26
Peanut Butter Cky, 1	117	2	15	1	6.11	0.81	3.15	1.79	0	0.13	1.17	0.04	0	8.21	1.16		4.96	0.10	0.41	16.9	70.5	3.87	41.9	0.32
Pneaple Tfu Chsck, pc	339	10	46	4	16.2	3.40	4.84	7.03	0	23.6	1.08	0.21	0	39.1	3.60		103	0.61	5.27	130	411	7.70	247	1.70

Desserts

Desserts	Calories (G)	Protein (G)	Carbs (G)	Fiber (G)	Fat (total) (G)	Fat (sat.) (G)	Fat (mono) (G)	Fat (poly) (G)	Cholesterol (G)	Vitamin A (RE)	Niacin (Mg)	Vitamin B6 (Mg)	Vit B12 (Mcg)	Folacin (Mcg)	Vitamin C (Mg)	Vitamin E (Mg)	Calcium (Mg)	Copper (Mg)	Iron (Mg)	Magnsm. (Mg)	Potassium (Mg)	Selenium (Mcg)	Sodium (Mg)	Zinc (Mg)
Plsing Pumpkin Pie,pc	214	5	26	4	11.2	1.38	6.29	2.88	0	72.1	1.35	0.11	0.15	20.9	3.11	2.86	100	0.41	2.12	53.7	336	17.4	331	1.10
Pumpkin Pie, slice	367	9	51	5	15.7	5.70	6.08	2.75	109	1805	1.22	0.11	0	20	1	1.23	212	0.22	2.63	40	400	9.62	338	0.99
Simply Slky Chsck, sl	261	11	33	3	11.8	2.03	3.75	5.18	0	10.8	0.44	0.10	0	24.7	1.07	4.96	131	0.32	6.86	139	252	5.10	63.3	1.37
Cream Pie, piece	455	3	59	1	23	15	4	1.10	8	0	1.10	0.17	0	18	0	0	46	0	1.10	19	133	0	369	0.79
Strawberry Pie, piece	305	5	43	4	14.8	1.90	5.02	6.95	0	6.95	0.62	0.11	0	23.2	43.8	3.87	56.4	0.20	2.94	63.8	248	5.21	60	0.80
Strwbry Chiff. Pie, pc	372	5	46	3	19.8	7.04	2.80		40.7	6.30	1.28	0.01	0.01	20.5	31	0.60	43.7	0.16	1.45	15	151	5.43	259	0.31
Tht's Ncel Spce Ck, sl	309	4	48	2	12.6	6.10	4.81	0		1.60	1.80	0.11	0	18.7	5.13	2.77	20.9	0.18	1.63	31.8	206	14.1	182	0.62
Yule Fruit Salad,1/2 C	152	3	9	2	8.50	1.99	3.57	2.37	0	7.46	0.05	0	0	13.6	29	2.19	36.7	0.10	1.75	36.9	174	1.69	4.77	0.32

Cheeses
Gravies
Sauces

	Calories	Protein (G)	Carbs (G)	Fiber (G)	Fat (total) (G)	Fat (sat.) (G)	Fat (mono) (G)	Fat (poly) (G)	Cholesterol (Mg)	Vitamin A (RE)	Niacin (Mg)	Vitamin B6 (Mg)	Vit B12 (Mcg)	Folacin (Mcg)	Vitamin C (Mg)	Vitamin E (Mg)	Calcium (Mg)	Copper (Mg)	Iron (Mg)	Magnsm. (Mg)	Potassium (Mg)	Selenium (Mcg)	Sodium (Mg)	Zinc (Mg)
All Str Amcn Chs, 1T	33	2	4	1	1.23	0.15	0.39	0.47	0	15.3	11.5	0.94	1.60	51.1	5.28	0.07	6.80	0.04	0.45	11.8	86.2	6.11	162	0.86
Chickee Cheese, 1T	40	2	4	2	1.86	0.30	0.85	0.53	0	9.82	3.66	0.65	0.50	35.7	3.67	0.29	9.71	0.11	0.58	15.7	76	2.71	102	0.59
Cracker Brl Chdr,1T	97	3	4	2	8.56	1.19	3.20	3.72	0	13.6	5.55	0.88	0.67	35.7	5.63	0.21	23.9	0.25	0.96	55.5	107	8.09	140	1.85
Cheddar Cheese, oz	114	7	0	0	9.38	5.97	2.66	0.27	29.9	5.69	0.02	0.02	0.23	4.99	0	0.18	204	0.01	0.20	7.69	28	4.02	176	0.80
Crmy Cheese Sce, 2T	84	3	2	2	6.27	1.09	3.14	1.62	25.5	9.73	1.69	1.33	51.2	9.21	15.2	0.70	15.2	0.27	0.99	40.7	143	7.32	228	1.44
Dream Crm Chse, 1T	39	1	1	1	3.47	0.33	2.25	0.73	0.01	0.21	0.01	0	2.60	0.21	1.34		17.4	0.07	0.24	19.2	50.3	0.28	98.3	0.21
Tangy Chse Sauce,2T	82	4	5	2	6.12	0.69	1.42	3.62	26	7.62	1.37	1	55.1	8.76	19.6		1.88	0.21	1.07	47.1	140	10.8	226	1.19
Gravies & Sauces																							
Bar-b-Que Sce, 2 T	6	0	1	0	0	0	0	0	0	14.5	1.46	0.25	0.19	7.89	1.84	0.01	3.33	0.12	0.14	3.08	55.5	9.09	25.6	0.10
Chickmm Gravy, 1C	181	7	14	3	12.2	2.36	7.01	2.01	0.39	203	35	2.66	111	0.11	60.3	1.03	3.82		5.86	145	276	13.4	475	2.86
Chicken Gravy, 1 C	326	7	13	0	27	6.72	12.2	7.16	0	4.16	0.05	0.24	4.44	0	1.06		11.5	1	5.86		224	3.68	776	0.44
Peanut Gravy, 1 C	219	11	16	3	14.3	2.68	6.49	4.15	0.42	217	36.7	2.54	109	0.13	1.76		160	0.64	3.16	125	333	11.5	529	2.04
Picnic Salsa, 2 T	16	0	4	1	0	0	0	0	32	0.38	0.07	0	10.7	12.7	0.34		8.51	0.06	0.30	8.23	149	1.92	140	0.11
Salsa Maravillosa, 2T	11	0	3	1	0	0	0	0	27	0.27	0.04	0	7.17	8.88	0.32		6.45	0.04	0.23	5.39	105	0.66	270	0.56
Sicilian Spg. Sce, 1C	93	4	15	4	3.48	1.19	1.74	0.26	160	10.2	1.67	0.16	56.2	34.2	0.92		63.9	0.38	2.11	38.3	659	4.04	58.4	0.98
Tasty Tofu Gravy, 1C	102	7	13	3	3.25	0.43	0.72	1.72	5.22	65.9	11.4	0	69.2	0.54	2.06		85.3	0.38	4.38	92.5	170	2.18	174	1.05
Terrific Trtan Grvy,1C	258	10	19	4	18.1	3.17	9.14	4.68	1.11	201	34.3	2.93	131	0.87	75			1.18	4.63	182	342	20.8	463	4.09

Miscellaneous

	Calories	Protein (G)	Carbs (G)	Fiber (G)	Fat (total) (G)	Fat (sat.) (G)	Fat (mono) (G)	Fat (poly) (G)	Cholesterol (G)	Vitamin A (RE)	Niacin (Mg)	Vitamin B6 (Mg)	Vit B12 (Mcg)	Folacin (Mcg)	Vitamin C (Mg)	Vitamin E (Mg)	Calcium (Mg)	Copper (Mg)	Iron (Mg)	Magnsm. (Mg)	Potassium (Mg)	Selenium (Mcg)	Sodium (Mg)	Zinc (Mg)
Banana Smoothie, 1	131	1	34	3	0	0	0	0	0	10.8	0.78	0.51	0	26	28.3	0.29	21.4	0.17	0.72	36.8	451	1.59	2.33	0.25
Berry Blst Smoothie,1	154	2	27	2	5.30	1.07	2.54	1.52	0	6.20	0.52	0.19	0.26	13.6	3.63	1.52	231	0.18	0.57	25.8	195	1.63	58.3	0.44
Chick-it Season, 1/4 t	1	0	0	0	0	0	0	0	0	41	7.03		0	2.86	0	0	8.52	0.09	0.45	15.4	4.36	0.03	103	0.04
Desert Date Smthie,1	179	2	25	2	9.19	1.09	5.10	2.59	0	5.76	0.57	0.32	0.26	15.8	4.73	0.43	233	0.21	0.49	31.7	332	1.75	58.3	0.69
M'M'Mxcn Ppcrn,1C	57	2	7	2	2.62	0.36	0.98	1.10	0	13.1	30.1	5.14	0.34	19	0.43	0.07	15	0.15	0.89	48.6	63.9	3.58	70.9	8.15
Prestol Popcorn, 1C	62	1	6	1	3.82	0.52	2.66	0.44	0	1.06	29.9	5.10	0.37	14.9	0.01	0.43	7.10	0.09	0.54	34.1	36.2	1.95	69.2	0.40
Seasoned Eatings,1/4t	1	0	0	0	0	0	0	0	0	0.44	1.30	0.22	0.19	5.67	0	0	0.47	0	0.20	0.54	8.20	0.51	4.71	0

Recipe Index

Breakfast

Entrees

Entrees *(continued)*

Soups & Beans

Cheeses (continued)

Breads & Muffins

Desserts

Desserts *(continued)*

Miscellaneous

Menus

Other Materials available

VitaMix

Highly recommended by Dr. Vicki Griffin for serious, time-conscious cooks! "I have used the VitaMix for years," Dr. Griffin says, "with tremendous results. It grinds grains, makes super 'total' juices, and whips up beatiful vegan cheeses, sauces, and spreads virtually in seconds. You'll save the cost of the machine in the first year alone by making your own breads and cracked-grain cereals. I've tried every machine out there—there's nothing like a VitaMix!"

Call for FREE information!

Videos

• Let's Eat! For Strength — Ten 1-hour cooking / health programs. Award-winning, fast-moving, information-packed programs on 10 different topics. Co-hosted by Dr. Vicki Griffin and Dane Griffin with many guests! Great recipes!
• Excitotoxins: Cradle to Grave — A 45-minute blockbuster video, with Dr. Russell Blaylock, that motivates you to read those labels and love your brain!

Audio Cassettes

• Stress, Science and the Scriptures — A 12-cassette series by Dr. Vicki and Dane Griffin covering excitotoxins, milk, mood & food, exercise, sleep, and much more. Practical tips on stress reduction anyone can do and afford.
• Wellth Watch, vol. I & II — Two, 12-cassette series consisting of radio interviews with todays leading experts on health on 24 different topics. This series is jammed with intriguing up-to-date information you need to know.

Books

• *Excitotoxins: The Taste That Kills* — A must read for every American concerned about mental and physical health. By Dr. Russell Blaylock.
• *MOOOve Over Milk* — Udderly fascinating book on the latest scientific findings showing the dangers of milk. 148 pages; more than 350 references. Easy to read. Filled with charts and graphs. By Dr. Vicki Griffin
• *Healing the Broken Brain* — You don't have to become senile. Learn how to rebuild your brain through lifestyle choices. By Dr. Elden Chalmers.
• *Health & Happiness* — A classic book on health and healing. This books has helped thousands discover the fountain of health! By E. G. White.
• *Living the Life of the Life Giver* — This set includes 4 books that give practical, easy-to-follow counsel for every area of life. A must-have!
• *Bible Study Companion Set* — If you're interested in discovering more practical tips on living from the Bible, you must have this set! By E. G. White.

For more information, or to place an order, call:

1-800-453-8732

LifeStyle Matters • PO Box 2001 • Leicester, NC 28748

www.lifestylematters.com